The Tragic Vision of African American Religion

Matthew V. Johnson

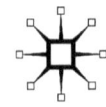

THE TRAGIC VISION OF AFRICAN AMERICAN RELIGION
Copyright © Matthew V. Johnson, 2010.
Softcover reprint of the hardcover 1st edition 2010 978-0-230-61889-3

All rights reserved.

First published in 2010 by
PALGRAVE MACMILLAN®
in the United States—a division of St. Martin's Press LLC,
175 Fifth Avenue, New York, NY 10010.

Where this book is distributed in the UK, Europe and the rest of the world, this is by Palgrave Macmillan, a division of Macmillan Publishers Limited, registered in England, company number 785998, of Houndmills, Basingstoke, Hampshire RG21 6XS.

Palgrave Macmillan is the global academic imprint of the above companies and has companies and representatives throughout the world.

Palgrave® and Macmillan® are registered trademarks in the United States, the United Kingdom, Europe and other countries.

ISBN 978-1-349-38163-0   ISBN 978-0-230-10911-7 (eBook)
DOI 10.1057/9780230109117

Library of Congress Cataloging-in-Publication Data is available from the Library of Congress.

A catalogue record of the book is available from the British Library.

Design by Newgen Imaging Systems (P) Ltd., Chennai, India.

First edition: May 2010

10 9 8 7 6 5 4 3 2 1

Black Religion / Womanist Thought / Social Justice
Series Editors Dwight N. Hopkins and Linda E. Thomas
Published by Palgrave Macmillan

"How Long this Road": Race, Religion, and the Legacy of C. Eric Lincoln
Edited by Alton B. Pollard, III and Love Henry Whelchel, Jr.

African American Humanist Principles: Living and Thinking Like the Children of Nimrod
By Anthony B. Pinn

White Theology: Outing Supremacy in Modernity
By James W. Perkinson

The Myth of Ham in Nineteenth-Century American Christianity: Race, Heathens, and the People of God
By Sylvester Johnson

Loving the Body: Black Religious Studies and the Erotic
Edited by Anthony B. Pinn and Dwight N. Hopkins

Transformative Pastoral Leadership in the Black Church
By Jeffery L. Tribble, Sr.

Shamanism, Racism, and Hip Hop Culture: Essays on White Supremacy and Black Subversion
By James W. Perkinson

Women, Ethics, and Inequality in U.S. Healthcare: "To Count Among the Living"
By Aana Marie Vigen

Black Theology in Transatlantic Dialogue: Inside Looking Out, Outside Looking In
By Anthony G. Reddie

Womanist Ethics and the Cultural Production of Evil
By Emilie M. Townes

Whiteness and Morality: Pursuing Racial Justice through Reparations and Sovereignty
By Jennifer Harvey

Black Theology and Pedagogy
By Noel Leo Erskine

The Theology of Martin Luther King, Jr. and Desmond Mpilo Tutu
By Johnny B. Hill

*Conceptions of God, Freedom, and Ethics in African
   American and Jewish Theology*
   By Kurt Buhring

*The Origins of Black Humanism in America: Reverend Ethelred
   Brown and the Unitarian Church*
   By Juan M. Floyd-Thomas

Black Religion and the Imagination of Matter in the Atlantic World
   By James A. Noel

Bible Witness in Black Churches
   By Garth Kasimu Baker-Fletcher

Enslaved Women and the Art of Resistance in Antebellum America
   By Renee K. Harrison

*Representations of Homosexuality: Black Liberation Theology
   and Cultural Criticism*
   By Roger A. Sneed

*Ethical Complications of Lynching: Ida B. Wells's Interrogation
   of American Terror*
   By Angela D. Sims

The Tragic Vision of African American Religion
   By Matthew V. Johnson

*Uncovering Womanism: Ethical Themes and Values in Alice
   Walker's Non-Fiction Work*
   By Melanie Harris (forthcoming)

Women's Spirituality and Education in the Black Church
   By Yolanda Y. Smith (forthcoming)

Racism and the Image of God
   By Karen Teel (forthcoming)

For Moriah and Nya

Loud he sang the Psalm of David!
He, a Negro and enslaved,
Sang of Israel's victory,
Sang of Zion bright and free.

In that hour, when night is calmest,
Sang he from the Hebrew Psalmist,
In a voice so sweet and clear
That I could not choose but hear,

Songs of triumph, and ascriptions,
Such as reached the swart Egyptians,
When upon the Red Sea coast
Perished Pharaoh and his host.

And the voice of his devotion
Filled my soul with strange emotion;
For its tones by turns were glad,
Sweetly solemn, and wildly sad.

Paul and Silas, in their prison,
Sang of Christ, the Lord arisen.
And an earthquake's arm of might
Broke their dungeon-gates at night.

But, alas! What holy angel
Brings the slave this glad evangel?
And what earthquake's arm of might
Breaks his dungeon-gates at night?

"The Slave Singing at Midnight," Henry Wadsworth Longfellow

Contents

Acknowledgments ix

Introduction: "Yet Do I Marvel!" 1
1 Seeing through the Dark: Elements of the Tragic Vision 13
2 Sparagmous, or "The Crucified" 41
3 A Look beneath the *Souls of Black Folk* 63
4 Deep Calls unto Deep:
 African American Christian Consciousness Pt. 1 85
5 Life within the Veil:
 African American Christian Consciousness Pt. 2 107
6 From Strength to Strength: Toward a
 Theology of African American Christian Consciousness 123

Epilogue: The Fate of Dionysius or Everything Is
Going to Be Alright 153

Notes 163
Bibliography 175
Index 179

Acknowledgments

Since this is my first major effort to articulate some of my ideas in book format, I would like to take the liberty of giving some long overdue expressions of gratitude. The ideas in this book began to take shape early in my graduate career at the University of Chicago. They were a serious deviation from the prevailing norm for reflecting on African American religious phenomena and experience at the time. Black theologians showed little interest in phenomenological or philosophical analysis of African American religious experience. Those few individuals doing phenomenological and philosophical analysis of African American religious experience showed little interest in the theological implications of their insights. My intellectual pursuits fell somewhere between the two, a virtual no-man's land in the established academy. Yet, I persisted. I did so only with the encouragement of multiple people, who in the words of Langdon Gilkey, thought I was "on to something." Although he is now deceased, I owe him an immeasurable debt of gratitude for a right word placed at the right time. The impact of his encouragement continues to resonate throughout my intellectual pursuits.

David Tracy, by far, occupies the most prominent place in my sense of gratitude for my formation. It was David who first recognized the emergent pattern in my intellectual pursuits and helped me give them what coherence I could at the time, given so little contemporary work of a similar nature in the field. He has continued to encourage me to put my ideas in print. While the present effort is rather schematic, the encouragement I received from him will serve me well as I continue to develop my ideas. There were no African Americans on the permanent faculty during the most of my career at the University of Chicago Divinity School, but he served me well as both adviser and friend. I don't know that I could have found a more sympathetic ear or model of intellectual courage and devotion to the life of the mind. Likewise,

Donald Browning has sustained a sympathetic interest in my intellectual development far beyond my graduate years. He strongly encouraged me to persist in seeking an avenue of publication.

Two other individuals stand out in this regard as well. The always kind and considerate Cornel West expressed an interest in this project from the beginning. He read an early draft of the text and recommended it for publication. Theophus Smith of Emory University read the same draft. He offered some very helpful suggestions, both formal and substantive, that were later incorporated into the text. He also recommended publication at that time. While it has been some time since they first offered support, their initial vote of confidence has remained an enduring source of inspiration and encouragement. I owe them both a debt of gratitude.

Others have been significant in helping me meet some unusual challenges. They are indeed too numerous to name, but I live continuously in a profound sense of gratitude for all the grace I've received along the way. Rory Johnson, my friend, brother, and colleague, is of course among the most significant of these. The students at various institutions—Wake Forest University, Livingstone, Morehouse, and Spelman colleges—have made contributions by raising questions and posing thoughtful challenges. A special thanks to my assistant Karen Young, who in the absence of a research assistant or the resources of the academy, performed invaluable service at key points in the development of this project. A special thanks goes to my good friend and conversation partner James Noel and his lovely wife Deanna; to James for his insightful criticisms and suggestions and to Deanna for tolerating us both.

Thanks to the superb editorial staff of Palgrave Macmillan, whose efforts have certainly made this a much better book. Their commitment to the spirit and substance of the project and sensitivity to the author's concerns made for a much more enjoyable process. Christopher Chappell, with whom this project began, and Burke Gerstenschlager, with whom it reached completion, along with the always prompt and exceptionally efficient Samantha Hasey, have been wonderful to work with. I owe a special debt of gratitude to the series editors Dwight N. Hopkins and Linda E. Thomas, for their confidence and continuing commitment to creativity, excellence, and insight in black religion, womanist thought, and social justice. Their efforts in this series, as well as their individual contributions to the field of African American religious thought, will leave an indelible imprint on our future.

Acknowledgments xi

To my wife of almost twenty-eight years, I owe more than a debt of gratitude. I owe twenty-eight years or more of life. I have lived between two worlds for most of my career, my body and soul lodged solidly in the church, but my mind firmly planted in the academy amid its questions and concerns. It was my wife, Arnetta, my children—Muriel, Nile, Selah, Matthew Jr., and Danube—and more recently, my son-in-law Jamil Drake, who kept me from being torn asunder. They listened to me wrestle endlessly with the challenges of the African American church, people, and culture. They've watched me agonize over the years and strained to understand my burden. It was Arnetta's voice, calm and soothing, that kept the floods at bay. Thank you.

Mama (Ethel Johnson), my paternal grandmother, and my mother (Muriel K. Johnson) are gone now. They did not live to see the publication of this book, which is the distillation of experiences pressed through their lives like a sieve until they ran over mine with the oil of strength, insight, and joy. Yet they are here in every hymn or gospel I hear sung at the hour of worship and each time I stand to preach or lecture. Papa (Eddie Johnson), my paternal grandfather, is gone too, but lives on in whatever native goodness or noble aspiration I posses, in the protective and loving care I extend to my offspring and my own grandchildren. Daddy is thankfully still with us. I thank him for his fierce courage, fearlessness, and strength, his unapologetic and uncompromised manhood, without which I may have surrendered. My sister Tracy, who I really believe thought me an oracle, was killed in a car accident. She thought everything I ever wrote was worthy of publication. I am so sorry she is not with me now. However I yet enjoy the love and support of my eldest sister Donna and for that, I am thankful. My brother, Travis "Shane" Johnson, will live on in me forever. Did he ever celebrate the pride and joy of life! Yet no one I know, or have known since his untimely death, ever knew more of its pain. He taught me more about the tragic than either Aristotle or Storm.

Having offered these expressions of gratitude, I must of course take full responsibility for whatever shortcomings this effort may prove to have in the eyes of others. May the ancestors forgive me for any errors I might have made.

Introduction

"Yet Do I Marvel!"

> Yet do I marvel at this curious thing;
> To make a poet black, and bid him sing!
>
> Countee Cullen

This book grew out of a long and sustained engagement with the African American journey through the Christian faith. While the insights garnered along this path far exceed what can be manageably shared in any one book, I think the present work shares some of the most basic. This engagement was, and continues to be, no less experiential than academic. I was born into and bred in the traditional faith of my African American mothers and fathers. I have been in the ministry since the ripe old age of seventeen, and the church has been the source of some of my greatest joys, deepest angst, and profoundest frustrations. Yet there is no aspect of my life—intellectual, social, political, or personal—that has not been processed through my faith and amid my ongoing struggle to come to terms with its strengths, deficits, continuities, failures, and fragmentation. This particular book, however, is a labor of love, driven and motivated by what may be the casual passing of one of the most glorious and disclosive testimonies to the power of the human spirit at life's limits, where, I believe, its relation to the divine is worked out amid the storms that rage at our extremities.

My pastoral journey, now in excess of twenty-five years, and my intellectual struggle and academic pilgrimage have run parallel through my entire adult life. To call the two trajectories simply parallel, however, is somewhat misleading. They indeed provide the warp and the woof, the very loom on which the fabric of my existence is spun, a life that has always been and shall remain essentially a spiritual journey. My intellectual explorations and the problems I brought to my research were, in part, generated by my experiences in the church, and my intellectual pursuits have nourished, challenged, and often taxed my experience of the Christian faith. Through it all, I have struggled to maintain a creative tension. Many of my intellectual concerns and curiosities may seem to exceed those traditionally accepted as relevant to contextual religious matters. However, for me, it all comes to bear. The hard-and-fast divisions that roughly correspond to "appropriate" academic disciplines drawn by many in the field of religion, particularly African American religion, have always struck me as artificially, narrowly, and, in the end, destructively ideological, even refractory.

Throughout my graduate and postgraduate experience I focused on philosophical theology. It offered the methodological space for my varied research interests and my interdisciplinary intellectual orientation. I was attracted to the kinds of questions raised and problems posed in the discipline and the methods employed in pursuit of answers and solutions. The problem of evil in its classical formulation was never far from my mind, nor was the question, What is the relation of God to human anguish? I focused on the genteel metaphysical tradition, particularly its personalist and process orientations. Both schools sought the philosophical version of the "theory of everything" and remained concerned with the challenges and opportunities presented by modern science as they sought a relatively adequate solution to the "riddle of the Universe."

My preoccupation with human suffering, on the other hand, fueled a deep and abiding interest in psychoanalysis and its various schools of thought. I think psychoanalysis has a lot to say about the nature of human experience, which remained very much at the center of personalist metaphysical preoccupations. The confluence of these interests suggested to me another formulation of the problem of evil as it is classically formulated, or the problem of excessive suffering and pain, as I prefer to call it. Consequently, I formulated the question with a different philosophical nuance. "What kind of God or vision of ultimate reality does the nature of human experience, suffering, and the religious response to it imply?"

Due to my immersion in process thought (Alfred North Whitehead/and Charles Hartshorne) and personalism (Edgar Shefield Brightman and Peter A. Bertocci), Langdon Gilkey, my

PhD co-advisor, suggested I drop one or the other side of the dyad, because in his words, if I did not, I "wasn't likely to learn a damn thing" from my dissertation research. By then my focus had clearly become the tragic themes in those philosophical systems' views of both penultimate and ultimate reality and their theological offshoots and implications. Gilkey suggested I pick up Nicolai Berdyaev, for whom the tragic was a central motif, and his use of literary sources for religiously inspired philosophical reflection. This contrasted nicely with the other thinkers' emphasis on the findings of science for the purposes of philosophical theological reflection and deepened and enriched the element of human experience. It was love at first read. It was suggested by David Tracy, my PhD co-advisor, that it was my own religious tradition that made these questions particularly poignant for me. I was struck by the immediate gravitas of the obvious that drew the full weight of the implicit into an explicit orbit. Suddenly, my intellectual/spiritual Du Boisian "two-ness" collapsed into a philosophical, theological, and existential "oneness" that I have been working to articulate ever since. My engagement with the philosophical questions and my struggle with various formulations, with notions of divinity, and with abstract discussions on human nature and subjectivity are a clear case of "thinking in the dark." Moreover, discomfort with the treatment of religious folk experience and the methodological orientation to African American religious experience in the various versions of black theology which, even in its more contemporary forms, consists more of a going back than a going deep, left me out at sea.[1]

My preoccupation with the tragic was due in part to the incitement of a particularly provocative footnote in Cornel West's *Prophesy Deliverance*[2] that referred to African American experience as a sort of tragic, Good Friday state of existence. This became something of an intellectual mantra for me because of its deep resonance with something profoundly intuitive about my experience of the Christian faith within the framework of my tradition. It resonated with the way I experienced worship in the African American tradition, evoked the modes of experiencing life and faith in my community, and reflected the descriptions I encountered in my research on the historical nature of African American religious experience and expression as codified in cultural forms. These cultural forms ranged from the spiritual and traditional gospel, through the blues to the folk preaching on which I was spiritually bred—the moaning, the shouting, the weeping, and the wailing and outbursts of paradoxical joy as men and women shrieked and smiled through tear-stained eyes—even on to modern R and B.

While working through this material I became interested in the concepts of mourning, loss, longing, and desire as articulated in psychoanalytic thought and psychologies of meaning as categories to help get at the substance of African American religious experience and its polyvalent significations. It wasn't long before I came to a particularly provocative intellectual and existential intersection. The hymns I heard raised throughout the church during worship and revivals with a particular poignancy in places such as Chicago and South Carolina, the "folk" preaching, which for me *was* preaching, the weekly negotiation and working out of our pained existence through the unique liturgical style of the African American Church, all seemed to indicate a spirituality profoundly at variance with the traditional theological categories and categorical abstractions imposed on the experience, often by its own practitioners. Even the partial emergence of Liberation theology in some churches with seminary-educated pastors still did not do justice to the rich, polyvalent signification of African American religious experience. This suggested the necessity of a phenomenological orientation grounded in a philosophical hermeneutical approach. This book, then, is an examination of African Americans' experience of the Christian faith as they struggled to manufacture meaning out of the raw material of their pain and what their experience may suggest about the nature of ultimate reality as conceived within the framework of a transfigured Christian faith.

It is my position that Africans and their biological, and no less spiritual and cultural, progeny in the New World, African Americans effectuated nothing less than a spiritual transvaluation of the Christian faith they were introduced to in the New World. This occurred as they availed themselves of the faith in the context of their marginalized existence. This "state of being" entailed, among other things, a distinctive mass experience of loss and longing, of marginalization, chronic mourning, and pain. All of this was constitutive of a traumatic field that provided the existential context for the emergence of African American religious experience. African Americans found a powerful tool of expression, as well as a tool of spiritual and cultural adaptation, in the resources of a biblical faith. Their version of biblical faith was shaped by a dialectical interaction between key biblical themes, paradigmatic figures, events and situations, and their circumstances. While the adoption of some of the themes and so forth were obviously, at the very least, partly conscious, they did not set out self-consciously to create an alternative version of the faith. I think it safe to say that they believed that the expression of the faith as they created and experienced it was the *legitimate* one. However, the transvaluation went a lot deeper than the theological position that the God of the Bible was the God of material or political liberation.

The transvaluation of the Gospel took place at other levels and calls for some subtle yet fundamental adjustments to be made at the level of self-conscious reflection on the meaning of the faith and its role in human spirituality, which is the domain of theology proper. It is my further conviction that any attempt to articulate a theology that purports to be grounded in African American religious experience in any meaningful sense must, of course, begin with reflection on the experience of the community of faith. Different communities, for different reasons, have expressed themselves religiously in various ways that correspond to their deepest needs and presuppositions about reality. Granted, when it comes to religion, these presuppositions are supplied by the faith itself; but given the broad birth of context and the nature of human interaction with reality, as well as the nature of the hermeneutical process, there will always be variations on key themes and a plethora of alternative visions that are grounded in the inherent polysemy of texts and contexts. While I do not believe in an absolute or essentialist interpretation of the faith, I do believe in more relatively adequate renderings or expressions of its meaning(s) and that the different renderings are open to examination and evaluation.

There are at least two levels at which this criterion of relative adequacy should operate in a project such as this. First, there is the issue of whether or not the explication of the faith of a group is accurate with relevance to its particularity. One must examine a particular expression with tools of inquiry appropriate to the subject matter to get at the experience itself. One must labor to uncover or lay bare the dynamics that constitute the experience in order to give it discursive articulation. Second, once one has uncovered the formative dynamics of the experience and given articulation to the living faith, then one may proceed to examine and evaluate the theological vision in light of normative concerns. There is, of course, a whole set of sticky methodological issues concerning normativity given the always already historical nature of the faith taken as a whole; but these difficulties must never be an excuse to shrink from the task of clarifying what it means to be *Christian,* what it is to be *Christian,* and more particularly in this case, what it means to be an African American Christian.

Although this text is by no means exhaustive (nor is it intended to be) and there is much more room for expansion and clarification, it aims at no less than providing a new foundation for practicing theology in an African American key, and given its link to the larger and ongoing tradition of Christianity, it is a challenge to reconsider some central issues of the faith taken as a whole. The condition of the modern world, or postmodern world if you choose, has opened up new windows of opportunity for viewing the faith. The challenge thus posed must be taken up by the Christian tradition if it is to preserve any sense of integrity or relevance and remain a viable option to future generations. The faith can no longer be held hostage to the imperialistic pretensions and chauvinism of the European and European American, whether these pretensions are militaristic, economic, or cultural. Either the Christian faith is a faith of, and open to, all peoples or it is a farce, an ideology, with no legitimate status in the academy or the church.

In chapter 1, I attempt to articulate the elements of the tragic experience. While defining the tragic in any exhaustive sense may be as difficult as defining religion, there are some fundamental dynamics that help us to more effectively identify it, particularly as it manifests itself in African American religious experience. Hopefully, the meaning of the tragic will continue to unfold and strengthen as the argument develops throughout the text in a mutually correlative mingling of other sources with the substance of the experience itself. These elements combine in such a way as to yield a distinctly tragic view and experience of the universe. I want to make the argument that the tragic is ontological. It is fundamental to human experience. It may not always be recognized as such, for this painful and deeply disturbing view of human existence and ultimately reality can be and is often evaded through foreclosure, that is, the imposition of artificial closure on the fundamental uncertainty of reality through closed belief systems.

The ontological claim also indicates that the tragic vision is logically prior to tragedy as a genre, with its earliest manifestations perhaps in religion. The tragic vision is a consequence of the encounter with nonbeing, which always carries with it the threat of meaninglessness for the human subject. I argue that the tragic vision is not the encounter with the threat of meaninglessness or the perception of the "horror" of existence per se, but rather the always already aesthetic representation of the encounter, which preserves its terrible truth in a transfigured vision of existence. Hence the tragic vision is life affirming while at the same time the facilitator of the recognition and embrace of the darker, more fundamental truths of life.

The vision entails the fragmented nature of our historical existence and a concomitant affective response. The apprehension of the tragic vision is transformative and has the effect of predisposing the subject or subject community to be receptive of ambiguity, encouraging resistance to the foreclosure so characteristic of the fundamentalisms of our age. The tragic vision is a different mode of knowing. It provides a different epistemological posture. In this sense, a tragic Christianity encourages a healthier, tolerant, and more creative spiritual life, and the tragic vision is almost a necessary presupposition of an authentically democratic culture and society.

One of the most characteristic features of the tragic experience as articulated in chapter 1 is the *sparagmous,* or the rending to which humans are subject when the tragic is encountered. In chapter 2, entitled "Sparagmous, or The Crucified," I detail the tragic rending to which African Americans were subjected on multiple levels. In a word, I try to give articulation to the structured instantiation of the tragic world of the African American, thereby grounding the emergence of her uniquely tragic vision and response firmly in historical experience.

In chapter 2, the significance of trauma for understanding the emergence of African American religious experience takes on a particular poignancy. The nature, profundity, and ubiquity of the trauma and the persistence of the tragic-traumatic field would have sustained the sparagmous and the fragmentation and disturbed anything like subjective or intersubjective coherence. Once you factor in the nature and impact of trauma and the emergence of this field, especially one as thoroughgoing as that undergone by the Africans and African Americans, both during and after slavery, the equation changes dramatically. Mechal Sobel makes the most systematic and coherent case for the emergence of a coherent religious worldview based on the Western philosophical assumption that interlocking beliefs or sets of assumptions provide existential coherence, that is, (implicitly) *ideas,* in this case, in the form of beliefs, can provide the antidote for trauma-induced toxins. However, I take issue with Sobel's case for the emergence of a coherent African American Baptist or any other worldview based on African retentions, not because there weren't significant retentions[3] but because they could not and would not bring about the kind of existential wholeness or coherence implied. In addition, her thesis runs the risk of, perhaps inadvertently, numbing the comprehension and appreciation of the dark, titanic forces tearing away at the African American subject and subjectivity, and consequently actually serves to provide a perception that mitigates the depth and uniqueness of African American anguish as they underwent their sparagmous or protracted crucifixion as a race. Yet her work is very insightful and remains exemplary partly because its systematic presentation and clarity of argument helps to bear out the difficulties and dangers of these approaches.

In chapter 3, "A Look beneath the *Souls of Black Folk*," I interrogate this classic text as disclosive of the "mood structure" of African American tragic experience. The articulation of the mood structure is disclosive of a key element in the tragic consciousness of African American religious experience. My intention is not to give an exhaustive account of Du Bois's views of religion, which of course developed over time. My intention is rather to articulate the vision of African American religion as it emerges in his efforts to frame African American life in lived experience. Clearly, *Souls* was written to reveal the inner dynamic of African American life in the midst of the struggle to come to terms with the harsh realities of their existence against the backdrop of their striving to preserve the viability of their humanity. I connect both the content and form to the dialectic of hope and resignation identified in chapter 2 as constitutive of the tragic vision and laud Du Bois's singular achievement in the melding of content and form to capture just that. It was an amazing literary achievement, which, in its peculiar form, preserved the sense of the experience in potentia, rendering the "movement" and feel of this singular lifeworld available with each new read and reader.

Souls, however, is not the only source of this mood structure, nor is it a theoretical articulation. I employ other sources and methods for the purposes of explanation and theoretical articulation, but it remains supremely illustrative as a literary and historical document. Sigmund Freud's classic phenomenological description of "Mourning and Melancholia" in his metapsychological papers, as well as other psychoanalytically informed modes of analysis, provide rich resources for looking at how the impulses of affirmation and resignation are essential parts and primary indices of the mourning process. Chronic mourning and irretrievable loss are key elements to understanding the emergent subjectivity and intersubjective universe shared by African Americans that provided an essential contextual component for the formation of African American religious experience as, in, and through the tragic. It provides significant theoretical grounding for the palpable pain attested to throughout the literature on the texture of African American religious life. Moreover, it provides a theoretical grid beyond the Christian faith for an experience that is smore fundamental and at least logically prior to its articulation through the available Christian categories. In chapter 4, "Deep Calls unto Deep: African American Christian Consciousness Pt. 1," I make several challenging claims about African American religion. I argue that it was a mode of adaptation to prevailing conditions that helped to facilitate psychic survival. That may not appear to be as challenging initially. That argument is not new. Yet it is where I situate the claim in the overall assessment of the nature of African American Christian consciousness as it took shape under the exigencies of the situation. It was the need for adaptation in an inherently ambiguous atmosphere fraught with uncertainty and pain that led to a unique fusion of European and African elements into the creation of the "bittersweet" tragic soul life of the African American. As such, it was both a response to and a reflection of their reality. The Christian Gospel, as it became available, provided a resource for its expression and in turn was transfigured into something uniquely beautiful and powerful and supremely expressive of the tragic nature of existence. The "existential genius" of the formation was that it facilitated life amid ambiguity, fragmentation, and pain, while embracing its terrible truths and without the lapse into denial. This tension created space for both sanity and hope.

Here I put the experience in conversation with Nietzsche's classic text on the tragic vision, *The Birth of Tragedy*, not incidentally initially subtitled *From the Birth of Music*. Nietzsche's text reads like a running commentary of the titanic struggle of African Americans expressed through their rich soul life in spite of it being a classic "European" text aimed at glorifying the achievements of the Greeks through their "creation" of the tragic vision. It is an inadvertent affirmation of the magisterial achievement of African Americans in their embrace and spiritual articulation of the tragic in the formation of African American Christian consciousness.

In chapter 5, "Life within the Veil: African American Christian Consciousness Pt. 2," I continue my analysis of the African American Christian consciousness and case for the tragic as it crystallizes in music and religious expression. I thicken the analysis by attempting to show how the mood structure was given concrete expression more particularly through the resources of the Christian faith—its symbols, paradigmatic stories, and images. I explore the effectual work of the

African American aesthetic in the emergence of the expression of the tragic and argue for its authenticity as a rich and unique contribution to the family of Christian faith expressions despite its tragic nature. With a deeper understanding of the tragic, I strain to show that its contribution transcends the confines of African American culture to speak meaningfully to a Christian faith struggling to remain viable in a meaningful way in what some call the postmodern era. I, however, see postmodernity as the emergence of the underside of modernity and the maturation of its implicit themes.

I use Du Bois's categories of the "essential" characteristics of the African American Church—the preacher, the music, and the frenzy— because they provide very basic and useful phenomenological categories for exploring the depth dimension of the "worship" experience. Du Bois has a lot more to say about the African American Church and American Christianity,[4] but this particular tripartite division of what he identified in *Souls* as the essential components are particularly useful for my purposes of getting at the manifestation of the tragic, its expression in the liminal space of worship, and the work of worship in transfiguring both the African American experience of suffering and the Christian faith. In a word, the choice was phenomenologically pragmatic. I place the explication of the experience in a deeper conversation with Nietzsche's *Birth of Tragedy* because I think Du Bois's position in *Souls* bears perhaps a little more than a family resemblance to the spirit of Nietzsche's work. Although I cannot say with anything like scholarly certainty that Du Bois was directly influenced by a reading and subsequent application of the text, I think the time he spent in Germany as well as the subject matter, language, and poetic allusions he employed in the text suggest a strong connection.

Finally, in chapter 6, "From Strength to Strength: Toward a Theology of African American Christian Consciousness," I explore what the tragic vision of African American religious experience might have to say to us about a theology grounded in a deeper understanding of it. I am to some extent in agreement with Schleiermacher that theology should be the articulation of the church's consciousness, although I obviously get at that consciousness in a different way. One key difference would be the positing of a theological unconscious. I pointed out earlier my perception of a certain incommensurability of the theological abstractions imposed on African American religious experience and what the experience itself suggests. I don't think that the theological consciousness is transparent to itself any more than consciousness in general is. Asking what early church thinkers thought about specific issues or identifying particular preoccupations in their writings is not enough to qualify a theology as true to the consciousness or experience of the church. In the case of African Americans the same holds true. Moreover there may be some real differences between a discursive self presentation of a community's theology and their operational theology. I try to get at this distinction in chapter 6.

I take on a few basic but very significant Christian symbols and assumptions and reimagine them through a more "experience near"[5] theological examination and explication based on my exploration of the tragic vision of African American religious experience. A more thoroughgoing systematic articulation exceeds both the aims and scope of the present work and will have to wait for a later effort, an effort already in progress.

In the epilogue, "The Fate of Dionysus or Everything Is Going to Be Alright," I give a brief estimate of where I think the tradition has gone. I affirm the ongoing reality of the sparagmous and how it articulates itself at some levels in contemporary American culture. Yet my sense is that under some pernicious influences we are moving away from the health-yielding dynamics of the tragic vision and its emergent liturgical forms of expression, as the church and its perception of itself is drawn into a swirl of ideological balkanization and rampant commercialism.

Yet there are indications that the deep structures I believe I have identified remain very much embedded in the African American psyche and intersubjective universe. I indicate this by a reference to the manifestation of indications in some sectors of hip-hop musical culture, that is, Rap music. There, in a place many would think has moved farthest away, the dialectic of hope and resignation betrays itself in some powerful pieces. I point out a few pieces where it is particularly apparent. I am most fascinated by some of Tupac's work, among others, and here again a more systematic analysis must await a later treatment. I did, however, review those aspects limited and related to the illumination of the tragic vision of African American religious experience in conversation with Mahalia Jackson as exemplar.

By implication, I clearly affirm these cultural artifacts as legitimate sources for theological reflection in the African American key. I think that ultimately the tragic mood permeates and is generative of African American culture in a variety of ways. Religion provides a rich and useful foil for the deepest human aspirations. Perhaps wherever these aspirations manifest themselves they may be referred to as deeply and authentically religious. The religious need not and often is not expressed in creedal formulations. Belief systems are employed to the extent they are available and useful in expressing the deepest spiritual yearnings of the human soul. But no particular religion can contain, nor should it strive to restrict, the impulse of the human soul to transcend circumstances of oppression. When a religion or faith of any kind becomes restrictive to the end of human health and liberation or constrains the innate human impulse for meaningful transcendence and hope, it has outlived its usefulness, betrayed its value, and forfeited any claims to truth.

Chapter 1

Seeing through the Dark: Elements of the Tragic Vision

The drive to comprehend, to grasp, to explain is one of humankind's strongest instincts. It is one of the human being's innate responses to his or her reality. Like the drive for food and water, the need for meaning is fundamental. Victor Frankl has identified this drive as the "will toward meaning."[1] It animates human beings, calling from the very void of the need itself the cultural worlds that both organize a person's reality and define his or her place within it. Cultures differ at this level. This is true; but then, so do diets. The need to eat in spite of the differences, however, remains universal.

With the acquisition of language, we observe the child's first benighted efforts to lift herself from the muddle of ill-defined experiences and beat back the frontiers of mystery by naming and explaining. Human beings need to fit life and reality into categories that render experience existentially manageable, or, to put it simply, meaningful. When life is experienced as meaningful, we feel relatively secure. We feel at home in our world. The world is experienced as a familiar and less threatening place. This innate response to reality, this fundamental drive or need implies that there is a basic feeling of alienation or isolation that forms part of the core of what it is to be human, a constitutive yet generative tension that fuels our always already anxious, creative striving.

The appeal of the biblical myth of the Fall seems to rest primarily on its effective expression of this basic sense of alienation. It is one of the most effective expressions of this sense in both modern and premodern literature and one of the most effective attempts to place it in a meaningful framework. The myth of the Fall does not, interestingly enough, do away with this sense. In fact, if anything, it makes us aware of this reality in something of a controlled environment. The mythological framework objectifies this fundamental sense of alienation and isolation for us and in so doing universalizes (thereby normalizing) it and distances us from it at a personal level. Thus, it reduces the sense of isolation by rendering us fellow sufferers with the rest of humanity and allows us to transfer our anxiety (at the root of which is a generalized sense of guilt) to the world of the myth. The meaningful framework of the Fall provides those who engage it with something of a mythological containment for existential anxiety. It names the experience and explains it, making it less threatening and more bearable. The explanation reduces the anxiety component of the experience of alienation and therefore makes it existentially tolerable, although at root, of course, the tension remains.

Although this sense of being at home in the world is never absolute and human beings always experience angst to varying degrees, there are elements in our experience that function to provide a meaningful framework and reduce anxiety.

> The word is the first and basic cultural agency; this poses the question: How does the word reduce anxiety? The answer is that the word has power, psychic as well as intellectual. It has power, and all anxiety springs from lack of power. The word bans chaos, the threat of nonbeing, inside and outside of oneself.... [T]he creative word can keep it in limits and make life possible.[2]

These elements are the weapons with which we fend off the persistent press of disorder or, to use a familiar existentialist term, nonbeing. Albert Camus writes,

> A world that can be explained with even bad reasons is a familiar world. But, on the other hand, in a universe suddenly divested of illusions and lights, man feels alien and a stranger. His exile is without remedy since he is deprived of the memory of a lost time or the hope of a promised land. This divorce between man and his life is properly the feeling of absurdity.[3]

The common course of our daily experience, our routinized practices, familiar patterns of interaction, accepted standards of justice and morality, commonly held social mores, familiar frames of reference and meaning such as those provided by religion and myth, our interpersonal relationships with significant others, and so forth, to the extent that they are imbued with a pervasive sense of stability, all work together to provide us with a sense of rootedness in our world, a kind of ontological security.[4] They form a web of interconnected meanings in which we live, move, and have our being; a gravitational field that keeps our world in place while at the same time facilitating our movement about within it. These various dimensions of our experience provide the parameters of human being. They define for us who and what we are. They function at several different but overlapping levels as barriers against chaos (the dissolution and disintegration of the abiding sense of stability and order that provides the meaningful context and structure of life), the fragmentation of the self, and the concomitant feelings of emptiness, meaninglessness, and precipitous devaluation. The different dimensions of our experience function best when they function in unquestioned presuppositions.

> A general assumption that life should be meaningful does not ordinarily require that we be specific about what meaningfulness entails. Ordinary meaningfulness probably includes a sense that life has a structure that is both comprehensible and satisfying; that we understand the world, our lives, and our roles, and that we feel sufficiently able to negotiate its demands and achieve our goals. This ordinary meaning *rests* on *unexamined assumptions* [italics mine] about such things as safety, control, and justice, and subsumes our basic needs for cognitive clarity, order, nonrandomness, and self-efficacy.[5]

To state it differently, they function effectively to the extent that they are taken for granted or are acted upon *without a second thought,* so to speak. Writing from a sociological perspective, Peter Berger points out the existential significance of these meaningful dimensions of human experience in his discussion of "institutional order":

> On the level of meaning, the institutional order represents a shield against terror. To be in a state of anomie, therefore, means to be deprived of this shield and to be exposed, alone, to the onslaught of Nightmare. While the horror of aloneness is probably already given in the constitutional sociality of man, it manifests itself on the level of meaning in man's incapacity to sustain a meaningful existence in isolation from the nomic constructions of society. The symbolic universe shelters the individual from ultimate terror bestowing ultimate legitimation upon the protective structures of the institutional order [6]

Not every dimension indicated in the discussion above nor any you might think to add is always operative at the same level of intensity. At times they are present primarily in potential. They are more or less activated by circumstances or existential exigency. Any one area or our individual or collective experience can become activated or hypercathected (to use an outmoded but helpful term from classical psychoanalysis) depending on the circumstance. For instance, during a time of national crisis, the categories of religion, resplendent with symbolic resonance, may be called upon to help facilitate an acceptance of loss and sacrifice or summon the necessary resolve. During a personal crisis such as a painful divorce a man or woman may focus on and intensify the significance of other relationships, perhaps those with parents, siblings, children, friends, or faith community to help negotiate the loss and reestablish faith in the stability of their world and reaffirm their place, or rather that they have a place in it. In fact, it would not be overstating the case that this is done to affirm that their world is still there in a meaningful sense. Common phrases such as "I have lost my whole world!" or "Will you be *there* for me?" are indications of how fundamental this need is and yet how pervasively fragile and tenuous this sense of stability has become in late or post modernity.

When, however, our experience of reality exceeds our capacity to make sense of it through our common beliefs and presuppositions, we encounter the absurd.

> It is important, however, to understand that the institutional order, like the order of individual biography, is continually threatened by the presence of realities that are meaningless in its terms. The legitimation of the institutional order is also faced with the ongoing necessity of keeping chaos at bay. All social reality is precarious. All societies are constructions in the face of chaos. The constant possibility of anomic terror is actualized whenever the legitimations that obscure the precariousness are threatened or collapse.[7]

A breakdown in order or a crisis of meaning can be generated at any one or combination of the different levels. The existential consequences, however, are always the same: a disturbance of our ontological security, the fragile-ization and potential fragmentation of the self, the ensuing experience of meaninglessness to varying degrees, and anomie. In a word, the breakdown in order is always traumatic. On the other hand a breakdown is often precipitated by trauma. The crisis of meaning may occasion a glimpse of the abyss, the world outside of the matrix—the web of meanings that sustain our sense of meaningful reality, our sense of place. The abyss is like a black hole, an antiworld made up of antimatter. It may precipitate a flight from *reality*, a turning away in horror, to an alternative reality of a world of privately communal participation, such as the delusional world of the insane.

The crisis may even be generated at the intellectual level, where one, through careful and sustained thought and concentration, reaches the limits of one's basic categories in the consideration of some fundamental issue or issues perceived as having ultimate implications. The followers of Pythagoras are said to have had such an experience when, while operating under the assumptions that reality was fundamentally rational and that its secrets could be uncovered through mathematical analysis, they discovered an irrational and chaotic depth. The very contradiction of all their ultimate assumptions crisscrossed the heart of their sacred symbol. A number of the followers in the Pythagorean cult are said to have committed suicide. What is particularly illuminating in this story is that it indicates the close connection of trauma and the loss of meaningful explanation of ultimate reality. What was lost here was the *possibility* of a casual or ultimately meaningful explanation of any kind from within their assumptive world. The deep sense of suicidal despair is attributable to the *unmitigated* experience of the absurd, the abyss, in which meaning is not simply destroyed but swallowed up in the void, lost.

The greatest and most frequent challenge to our ontological security comes through an encounter with intense, multilevel suffering, pain, or catastrophe. When our ontological security is disturbed in this way, it often happens to an entire group or collectively. Suffering tends to be tolerable so long as it can be explained. If a reason can be found for suffering, if it can be placed in a larger frame of meaning or meanings that invest it with some value or purpose, no matter how intense that suffering is, in most instances, it can and will be endured (herein lies much of the attractiveness and power of heroic witness). Considering this issue in relation to nonmodern humanity, Mircea Eliade writes:

> In the frame of such an existence, what could suffering and pain signify? Certainly not a meaningless experience that man can only "tolerate" insofar as it is the inevitable, as, for example he tolerates the rigors

of climate. Whatever its nature and whatever its apparent cause, his suffering had a meaning: it corresponded, if not always to a prototype, at least to an order *whose value was not contested* [italics mine]. . . . If it was possible to tolerate such sufferings, it is precisely because they seemed neither gratuitous nor arbitrary. . . . In each case, the suffering becomes intelligible and hence tolerable. Against this suffering, the primitive struggles with all the magico-religious means available to him—but he tolerates it morally because it is not absurd. The critical moment of the suffering is perturbing only in so far as its cause remains undiscovered.[8]

I am using rationality and related terms to imply something broader than the narrow perspective commonly assumed and associated with "scientific" rationality. The typical Western understanding of rationality may incline one to see the entire mythopoetic consciousness as an essentially irrational way of looking at the world. In actuality, as a presumed frame of meaning, a particular mythological "explanation" of the world and human experience has an internal logic that yields its own unique coherence for orienting a person to the world and facilitating the assimilation of experience. I am, of course, alluding to discursive rationality, which is always tied to issues of meaning/meaningfulness. The traditionally assumed brand of rationality tends to skew one's orientation to linguistic fields, as their interpretation and value are often refracted through the influences of the exact sciences.

It may be helpful to point out here that the notions of meaning/meaningfulness and coherence add to our appreciation of why it is that "scientific" disciplines such as psychoanalysis, Marxism, or a particular theory in any of the scientific fields, even doctrinaire versions of atheism, often reflect a profoundly "religious" hold on its adherents. There is a level of the human psyche at which its explanatory power operates much in the same way as a mythopoetic view functions. Psychoanalysis, for instance, gives meaning to our experiences, even to the most confusing, poignant, and painful. The explanations provide orientation in the confused morass of our experiences, past and present. They introduce light into darkness and order experiential chaos. This is achieved by identifying causes, thereby grounding our experiences in tangible reality and placing them within a field of meaning or a system of meanings that deprives these experiences of their threatening, alienating power. Hence, the psychoanalytic system of interlocking concepts facilitates the assimilation of difficult experiences for the patient.

The discipline performs the same function for psychoanalysts, enhancing their sense of control and proportionately reducing their sense of vulnerability. Other sciences and theoretical systems have the same existential impact. The rearticulation or narration of the most painful aspects of a person's story within the framework of an explanatory system in which they've invested functions to impart meaning and meaningfulness at a rudimentary level.

The significant point is not so much that life, within a particular frame of meaning, gains some ultimate or transcendent meaning (although it may) that renders it worthwhile from an intellectual standpoint, but rather that life is less threatening, alienating, and unfamiliar. Lived experience takes on the character of meaningfulness. Where there was darkness with all its concomitant terrors of the unknown and the horror of not knowing, light appears. To paraphrase Freud, where id was ego is, and ever more shall be.

Frames of meaning, in their explanatory, orienting, and unifying function, enable human beings to affirm life as worthwhile in spite of the anguish occasioned by loss, pain, or catastrophe. Of course, the depth of suffering and its nature has an impact on the ability of certain frames of meaning to facilitate the integration of the experience. Under certain conditions, even if there is no logical contradiction or conflict at issue (that is, between a particular occurrence and what a system of meanings might imply about reality), an experience of suffering can be so overwhelming that the system is just "blown out," as if short-circuited by a power surge. There are moments in human experience when the strength of our feelings and perceptions so exceed the capacity of language to adequately express them that any articulation at all seems superficial and trite. In these moments one encounters the absurd and glimpses the abyss. These experiences are commonly and appropriately referred to as *traumatic*.

From Trauma to the Tragic

The human vulnerability to trauma, particularly the trauma of glimpsing the abyss, is inherent in the structure of reality and the nature of human experience. As humans we sense this vulnerability and erect meaningful structures to reinforce the always-threatened sense of self to which we are heir. However certain one might feel of the meaning, purpose, or security of one's life, existence, or world, like a swelling current beneath the placid surface of a tranquil sea there is an ontological undertow taxing the strength of our repose and the life of all that we hold dear. William Storm has argued that this condition is ontological and fundamentally tragic.

> Values, after all, are held by men and women, and it is human consciousness that perceives the dissonance between such values and external circumstances. What is manifested here, I believe, is a conflict that is based not only upon value and causality but also on the dialectic of interior and exterior conditions that are innately irreconcilable. The rending process that attends a tragic character arises not merely from internal clashes of held values but from an essential separation of the mind that holds such values from the outward conditions that deny them—a tearing of character apart from the world.[9]

It is rooted and grounded in the human being's vulnerability to schism and division. For Storm, the tragic, bearing the marks of its Dionysian expression, essentially involves the sparagmous, or the rending of the self or character (in tragedy as a genre), both internally and in relation to the cosmos. For him, this condition is endemic: "The tragic, as a Dionysian latency or passive condition, is indicative of an identifiable range of situations where division and separation are inevitable in existence."[10] He refers approvingly to August Wilhelm von Schlegel's position.

> The writer's use of the "we" construct draws all of humanity into a shared plight. More important, the writing is descriptive of a condition that is unchanging, one finally not open to qualitative variation, if only because no one is exempt from its terms. The condition that is described is one in which loss and separation attend every endeavor, every aspiration, every relationship.[11]

I wholeheartedly agree with the notion that sparagmous or the rending of the self is at the heart of the tragic. I am equally enthusiastic about the idea that the tragic is grounded in ontological structure. But at the risk of sounding too Kantian, I am less impressed with Storm'sattempt to argue that the term *tragic* can be applied to the ontological structure "in-itself," that is, outside of the human experience or recognition of the structure within a framework that is in some sense aesthetic.

> Far from affording the "metaphysical solace" that Nietzsche promises as a statutory effect of tragedy, what the tragic itself brings—and I

am speaking of its *unmediated, a priori condition* [italics mine]—is metaphysical terror. The extent to which the tragic forbids such ideals as union, wholeness, or "Oneness," plus the range of rifts and bifurcations that ensure the divisions within being and between being and world, and the utter solitude that invariably results, must finally be productive of a profound separation trauma in the beholder of such extremities. The tragic, in its pure and unrelieved state, implies a level of being that is so broken as to be untenable, and indeed unlivable.[12]

It is precisely the mediation of the experience that justifies the designation tragic. In fact once the experience is referred to as tragic, a meaning with profound aesthetic resonance has already been attached. Moreover, there are a variety of responses and a range of reactions human beings can have to such an experience. Some of these responses are healthier than others. The tragic vision, for want of a better term at this point, is one of the healthiest responses, if not the only one. The tragic vision is the creative response to the human encounter with the abyss.

Murray Krieger, in his text *The Tragic Vision*, draws an interesting distinction between the tragic vision and tragedy. While I want to distance myself from some of the nuances and conclusions he reaches in his general position, I think a discussion of his views will help to sharpen our appreciation of and focus our attention on some of the issues central to understanding the tragic structure of African American Christian consciousness.

Krieger draws a crucial distinction between tragedy and the tragic vision.

> The most obvious difference I would mark between the two is also a crucial one: "tragedy" refers to an object's literary form, "the tragic vision" to a subject's psychology, his view and version of reality.[13]

Krieger sharpens this point by arguing that the tragic vision is born within tragedy. It is the "possession of the tragic hero." Despite the obvious psychologism implied in his statement and his imputation of the qualities of consciousness to a fictional character, the distinction is a valid one. There is something we can identify as the tragic vision. It is the moving power of tragedy. Out of it individual tragedies are crafted, like incarnations of a larger spiritual phenomenon, each one approaching what can perhaps be called, for want of a better term, the essence of the tragic vision, but none exhausting its meaning or depth—some stronger, more thorough, instantiations, others weaker.

Different tragedies may be stronger in different dimensions of the tragic, and so on. In fact, the genre of tragedy itself is neither the origin of the tragic vision nor its only instantiation, perhaps not even the most meaningful. The tragic vision is both ontologically prior to and generative of tragedy as a genre. The oldest manifestation of the tragic vision is of course the mythopoetic, out of which tragedy as a genre emerges, if at no other level than the subject matter and the substance of Greek tragedy itself. But I do think it is more substantive than that.

The ontological condition that William Storm identifies as the tragic, "a condition mankind must inevitably live with," is the generative reality for all mythopoetic, particularly religious, formations. "The tragic, in short, is not simply that which is mournful, lamentable, or even catastrophic; it is that which is unmendable. As such, its core meaning is not grievous but rather divisive."[14] This reality and presence of that which cannot be ultimately domesticated is at the root of all longing for wholeness, coherence, "cohesion over the whole of one's existence,' order, redemption, and reconciliation that is the driving force behind religion and myth as phenomena in human history.[15] The tragic vision is at the very least implicit in virtually all religious phenomena. The mythopoetic in the religious context is also primary in the sense that it is the first-order response to the tragic predicament. It is the self-conscious effort to relate to ultimate reality through ritual and truth. In an aesthetic phenomenon, when the subject is aware of it as such (as in the case of tragedy as a genre or as a theatrical presentation), there is a structural limit on the subject's engagement. In the religiously contextualized mythopoetic, the intent is different. The subject's intent is to *approach* ultimate reality, to connect with it. In tragedy, the subject is always aware, in a mode analogous to Kant's transcendental apperception, that it is fiction, a work of art, a *play*; whereas in the religiously contextualized mythopoetic, the subject understands him or herself to be approaching reality—ultimate reality or the really real. Tragedy as a genre or experienced in theater would be in my view a second-order response in which the element of play becomes more prominent, affording the audience and the participants a certain "aesthetic distance"[16] from the tragic disclosure. In the first order response the aesthetic dimension remains thoroughly integrated into a larger whole with a self-conscious attempt at reconciliation, or if that is too theological, communion, connection, or engagement with reality. In the second-order response, any such connection or effect is at best a by-product. Having drawn this distinction, however, it must be born in mind that the distinction in classical Greek theater may not have been drawn quite this sharply at all levels by its audience.

More to the point, there is arguably a direct line from the mythopoetic expression of the tragic vision to tragedy as a genre, finding its first and perhaps clearest articulation in the Osiris myth of African origin. Osiris may perhaps bear a direct historical connection to the Greek god Dionysus, who in turn bears a direct connection to the rise of tragedy as a genre in classical Greek culture.[17] There can be no question of either the antiquity of, or the preeminence of, the themes of rending and divisiveness—in a word, crucifixion—in the myth of Osiris and the deeper, simultaneous "yes" and "no" to life that lies at the heart of the tragic effect and affect. Nor should it be greeted with surprise that something so fundamentally human as to be identified by Storm and others as ontological should make its first appearance and find its clearest, most elaborate mythopoetic expression in the birthplace of the human race—Africa. In the land of the most arresting spectacle of life in its fullness, and in the interplay of its extremes, of Eros and Thanatos, the great "yes" and "no" are played out on the sometimes bitter, but always beautiful, bacchanalian stage of survival.

Krieger attempts to separate the tragic vision from tragedy proper, arguing that tragedy proper is the aesthetic totality that renders the *tragic* vision bearable.

> Perhaps it would be more accurate to say that the tragic vision was born inside tragedy, as part of it: as a possession of a tragic hero, the vision was a reflection in the realm of thematics of the fully fashioned aesthetic totality which was tragedy. But fearful and even demoniac in its revelations, the vision needed the ultimate soothing power of the aesthetic form which contained it—of tragedy itself—in order to preserve for the world a sanity which contained it—of tragedy itself—in order to preserve for the world a sanity which the vision itself denied.[18]

By implication Krieger is arguing here that the tragic vision can be separated from the aesthetic element in tragedy. Yet the aesthetic element is part and parcel of tragedy, an essential element in its constitution. If what he is calling the *tragic* vision can be separated from the aesthetic element, and therefore tragedy proper, then the designation of this vision as *tragic* must be, so it seems clear to me, purely arbitrary, adding very little to our understanding.

The tragic vision is always already an aesthetic vision. From the moment human beings employ the element of creativity to meet the exigencies precipitated by the recognition, or existential apprehension of the condition of being, the aesthetic is implicated, though not necessarily the tragic. For in most cases what is sought, particularly in religious formations, is some form of closure or more accurately foreclosure, which we shall see a little later, is contrary to the tragic vision. In fact I would go so far as to argue that it is the tragic vision that problematizes, indeed foils, any attempt in tragedy as a genre to impose any kind of closure. It is the tragic vision that destabilizes tragic narration and problematizes all tragic denouement—in spite of what may or may not be the specific author's intent. Nietzsche tried to get at what is distinct in the tragic response while at the same time indicating its inseparability from the aesthetic in his assertion that tragedy emerges from a *musical* mood.[19]

> This truth is to be interpreted in light of my principle that art does not derive from a single impulse (i.e. the Apolline impulse towards beauty) but from two: the Dionysiac as well as the Apolline. From these starting points we can come to understand the dual effect of Dionysiac music on our Apolline capability. Music stimulates us to realize the Dionysiac metaphysical world in Apolline symbolism, which then, under the influence of music, acquires its highest significance. Hence the capacity of music to engender myth, especially the tragic myth that symbolizes Dionysiac wisdom.[20]

There is an experience that corresponds to what Krieger calls the tragic vision. It is better understood as the encounter or experience of the abyss, absurd, or nonbeing. It is the apprehension of the abyss in the interstices of fragmented reality. It is the recognition of the incommensurability of being and the concomitant shock to the self that brings the sparagmous in its wake—the rending of the subject, the shattering of the worlds. As if a heavy fog has lifted, the human being suddenly discovers that the ship he or she thought safely moored in a friendly and familiar harbor is in fact merely anchored on a lonesome rock in the middle of *anywhere,* surrounded by a watery waste. It is a destabilizing challenge to the meaningful frames of reference through which we assimilate and domesticate our experiences. It is such a shock, in greater part, because of the ontologically presumptive closure of most frames of meaning and the underlying trust invested in them by the human subject or community, an abiding trust these systems, consequently, mediate between the subject and reality at both the penultimate and ultimate levels. This encounter becomes tragic precisely at the point where and if the aesthetic element works its transfiguring magic. Elaborating on the tragic character of Herman Melville's classic Moby Dick, Richard B. Sewall writes:

> The book does not pronounce him [Ahab] good or evil, any more than the *Scarlett Letter* calls Hester Prynne good or evil. But by carrying him through his fatal action in all its tensions, paradoxes, and ambiguities, the book, like a true tragedy, goes deeply into the mysteries of all moral judgments. All categories are put to the sharpest test, not only Ishmael's, Starbuck's, Stubb's, and Flask's but Ahab's own. We see the nature of each, how far toward good-and-evil each can go. The book leaves us, again true to its tradition, somewhere between pity and terror, faith and doubt, heaven and hell; it leaves us in what Ishmael-Melville calls (in "The Gilder") "manhood's pondering repose of it." But we have seen the conditions of pity and terror, good and evil, heaven and hell, more clearly. "Doubt of *all* [italics mine] things earthly, and intuitions of some things heavenly; this combination makes neither believer or infidel, but makes a man who regards them both with equal eye.[21]

Sewall clearly indicates that the tragic mode of being disclosed in the text is one driven beyond familiar meaningful frames of reference and indicates a mode of being clearly beyond the possibility of ontological presumption or closure. The tragic (human) subject can never go back home or find one for that matter; but the tragic vision perhaps makes one at home in their homelessness.

The encounter of the abyss is a fundamental challenge precisely because the abyss, as such, cannot be assimilated. It is the encounter with the brute facticity of the inassimilable. This experience says to us that existence, in the final analysis, or in the ultimate sense, is strange, unpredictable, and entropic. It is the encounter with otherness at the heart of reality much like the Pythagorean encounter with the diagonal of the square.[22] This experience throws a person back on himself or herself and drives home the terrible truth of the human being's utter aloneness and vulnerability with a terrible sense of having been abandoned by an "I know not what." This encounter is not merely an intellectual crisis or breakdown, although it may be precipitated by one, but a far more thoroughgoing experience. It is a threshing and winnowing of the human soul that leaves the seed though separate from the hull, laying in the same composite heap.

Krieger argues that this terrible vision, which for him is already the tragic vision, is *overcome* through aesthetic form. Aesthetic form in the end defangs the experience and renders the vision innocuous. The threatening elements of the vision are "bound" by the order imposed by form.

> The purging of dangerously aroused emotions following as it does upon satisfaction, the soothing grace, bestowed upon wayward materials by aesthetic completeness, uses form to overcome the threat of materials and, consequently, these emotions.[23]

Krieger believes that the tragic genre is a higher unity into which the disturbing qualities of the vision are absorbed. The fact that the disturbing qualities are *incorporated* into a unity (of some kind) does not mean, however, that they are thereby done away with. The abyss does not vanish. It does not dissolve. The void is not filled. The vision persists and serves as a necessary pole in the tension that produces the unusual tragic effect (and affect).

The term *absorbed,* as it seems to function in Krieger's argument, suggests something like a chemical reaction in which the natures of the distinct elements are transformed into a new whole through a process. The presence of the individual elements are no longer discernible, having dissolved themselves in the creation of this new substance. This is a fundamental flaw in his reading of the tragic. That the tragic vision, as he calls it, is rendered bearable does not necessarily imply that it is absorbed in a higher Hegelian sublation. The value and power as well as the ethical and spiritual payout of both tragedy *and* the tragic vision lies in their facilitation of an *authentic* encounter with the abyss—life at its root or perhaps rootlessness—precisely because it allows us to experience it without falsifying it. It facilitates an authentic encounter with life at those points where human beings tend to move into denial or disavowal to stave off profound spiritual dissonance, psychic pain, painful alienation, or complete mental breakdown. The power of the tragic and perhaps its empowerment resides in its capacity to sustain sanity and the meaningfulness or value of experience while at the same time preserving a kind of radical objectivity or morally courageous realism. Tragedy and the tragic vision, as I understand them, grasp the integrity of human existence *as well as* its negation along with the facticity of their incongruity and hold them in a delicate and dynamic tension. Lucien Goldmann is particularly illustrative on this dimension of the tragic.

> Thus in every possible aspect of human life, however, minute, the reply of both "Yes" and "No" remains the only valid attitude for the man who has become aware of tragedy.[24]

Again he writes,

> It is, however, precisely this "Yes" and "No," both equally complete and equally absolute (the "Yes" insofar as tragic man remains in the world to demand that values be achieved, the "No" insofar as he refuses this world because it is entirely inadequate and offers no scope for the achievement of real values) which allow the tragic mind to achieve, on the plain of knowledge, a degree of accuracy and objectivity of a type never before attained. The man who lives solely in the world, but who remains constantly detached from it, finds that his mind ins freed from all current illusions and limitations which beset his fellows, with the result that the art and ideas which are born of the tragic vision become one of the most advanced forms of realism.[25]

Finally Goldmann writes,

> This is why tragic man, *torn* [italics mine] between "Yes" and "No," will always scorn those who choose an intermediary position, and will remain instead on the only level whose value he recognizes to be adequate: that of saying both "Yes" and "No," of *attempting* [italics mine] to realize a synthesis.[26]

The fact that life somehow coexists with and in the presence of its ultimate negation must be, at root, the source of tragedy's consolation and an essential dynamic in the pleasure it yields. What we get in tragedy and the tragic vision as I conceive them is more like an *effective* chemical mixture, where the elements preserve their distinct qualities, than a chemical compound, where all distinctions are lost. This is clearly what Thee Smith and others have recognized in the wisdom tradition of African American folk. It is the wisdom that rises from the ruins of woe. It is the tragic wisdom that comes to live with the creative but always titanic tension of life's polarities.

> The Wisdom Tradition of Black North American folk culture dissents from the predominant Western form of disjunctive thinking—that

conventional "either/or" in which rationalism insists on unambiguous, univocal meanings for things. Instead this tradition prefers the conjunctive "both/and" of archaic cultures, in which ambiguity and multivocity are taken for granted (even promoted).[27]

If one considers, for instance, the character Kurtz in Joseph Conrad's *Heart of Darkness,* one sees what can happen to a human being when he engages the abyss without the facilitation of the tragic vision. Having gone beyond the restraints of civilization, the frameworks of meaning erected like bulwarks around the soul to keep "the thing contained," he comes to see clearly. He sees the vision of the abyss and its terrible truth which is the *untruth* of those very frames of meaning, nay, even more, the untruth of framing itself. It was "a moral victory paid for by innumerable defeats, by abominable terrors, by abominable satisfactions."[28] Yet the payout of this victory was grim. The stark reality of the vision left him with an "intelligence [that] was perfectly clear"[29] but a "soul [that] was mad."[30] Looking upon the countenance of Kurtz rapt in the antirapture of abysmal apprehension, Marlow, the narrator, reports,

> It was as though a veil had been rent. I saw on that ivory face the expression of somber pride, of ruthless power, of craven terror—of an intense and hopeless despair. Did he live his life again in every detail of desire, temptation, and surrender during that supreme moment of complete knowledge? He cried in a whisper at some image, at some vision—he cried out twice, a cry that was no more than breath—"The horror! The horror!"[31]

Richard Sewell detects a similar insight in the experience of Melville's Ishmael in the classic *Moby Dick.*

> Ishmael, having learned the "wisdom that is woe," now learns the "woe that is madness"; and he learns it this time on his own pulses. He learns that he is not the "Catskill eagle," nor is Ahab, who can dive down into the "blackest gorges" and rise again into the sun. 'Give not thyself up, then, to fire [says Melville-Ishmael] lest it invert thee, deaden thee; as for the time it did me.[32]

This dialectic of knowledge, of the abyss/horror, and of madness plays itself out in *Moby Dick,* much along the same lines as it does *Heart of Darkness.* As the dark truth of the Pequod's mission, and the even darker truth of the maddened soul of the captain who masters it settles in on the chief mate, Starbuck, he ruminates leaning against the mainmast.

> Oh, life! 'tis in an hour like this, with soul beat down and held to knowledge—as wild, untutored things are forced to feed—Oh, life! 'tis now that I feel the latent horror in thee! but 'tis not me! That horror's out of me![33]

Captain Ahab's monomaniacal pursuit of the white whale, the mask behind which either some "unknown but still reasoning thing" or yet the great "naught beyond" has drawn near to him, lead Melville/Ishmael to the following observations:

> But in his narrow flowing monomania, not one jot of Ahab's broad madness had been left behind; so in that broad madness, not one jot of his great natural intellect had presided.... Now, in his heart, Ahab had some glimpse of this namely: all my means are sane, my motive and my object mad.[34]

Let us return to our examination of some of the more relevant an fundamental of Kriegers claims. A further difficulty I have with Krieger's provocative and insightful, if not always convincing, discussion of the tragic vision is that I am not sure that tragedy as a genre is a unity or whole in the sense that Krieger's argument presupposes it is, or rather needs it to be, in order for his overall thesis to work. There is something of an equivocation in the way the ideas of form, unity, and order function in his argument. He seems to have collapsed the very basic notion of sense or ordered discourse into the idea of a meaningful, universal moral order. I do not think that one can conflate these two notions, which operate at different levels of analysis, without creating some very complex confusion in the argument. When one begins to discuss aesthetic form, one is at a different level of analysis than when one is arguing for or against the notion of a universal moral order. Krieger collapses the two when he writes,

> Perhaps it was not for the Greek theoretical consciousness—even in as late a representative as Aristotle—to be as self-consciously aware of the disturbing implications of the tragic mentality as it was of the formal requirements which transcended, or rather absorbed, this mentality and restored order to a universe threatened by it.[35]

In his argument, Krieger seems to rely on the rather vague notion of reconciliation, as it was developed by Hegel, mingled with a somewhat embellished Aristotelian notion of catharsis. The *reconciliation* experienced is brought about by the catharsis achieved by the restoration of order through *aesthetic form*. His argument, then, rests on the unquestioned philosophical presuppositions at the basis of both the Hegelian and Aristotelian notions, not to mention the anthropological and psychological assumptions. The main assumption is that a universal order is restored in and through tragedy. This is predicated of course upon the assumption that there is a universal order that is harmonious, when our experience testifies to the contrary. There is difference and conflict everywhere. While it might be that value is natural in human experience, there is no natural value structure and no preestablished harmony or hierarchy. I am more in agreement with Max Scheler on this issue.

> It is an essential characteristic of our world—and thus of every world—that the course of casual events disregards completely the value of things. The exigencies of values as they develop toward a unity or as they unfold themselves toward their ideal fulfillment is not taken into account by the casual series.
>
> *There would be no tragedy* [italics mine] in a world which operated on an established system of laws whereby each thing had the powers and capabilities commensurate with its values, and whereby its activity was directed only towards the exigencies of developing or unifying these values.[36]

The disjunction of human experience and the casual reality of our world are ontological. We are at odds with it and ourselves. The sparagmous is ontologically grounded.

> These and many other experiences of the common injustices in the child's world provide sufficient evidence, along with the lessons of chemistry, auto mechanics, and arithmetic, that we all live in a world where things happen because of natural "forces" for reasons that have nothing to do with who has been good or bad.[37]

Krieger's position rests on the notion that there is, in the end, a rational resolution to the existential contradictions experienced in the dramatic process, and that the experience of reconciliation and catharsis is brought on by the closure in the tragic denouement.

True enough, the narrative has an end. There is an outcome. The play reaches its terminus. However, this in no way means that the issues raised or the contradiction(s) disclosed have themselves been resolved.

> Although many implications of this conception will prove valuable, none is more important than the idea that we expect literary works to be wholes; we expect a *feeling of completeness* [italics mine] in our concretion of a work. One of the features of a literary work that makes it seem whole is closure. At some point at or shortly after the end of the text, we expect to see all the prominent features of the work forming a harmony that can recede in memory as we turn to other objects in the world.
>
> As long as the idea this novel conveys is complete, *we can do without other forms of closure* [italics mine]. In fact, given the idea of *The Castle,* a lack of conventional closure may be a positive benefit. For K.'s life to take shape and gain meaning would work against the novel's insistently unkept promise of such a meaning.[38]

As Vernant has persuasively argued, "The questions are posed but the tragic consciousness can find no fully satisfactory answers to them."[39] Perhaps the sense of reconciliation or catharsis that comes at the end of a tragedy is merely the after effect of the dying identification of the audience with the imperiled principle players, in a way peculiar to the form of tragedy, hence the distinct form of the effect. Having gone through the gauntlet with the characters and having empathized with them through the terrible ordeal, when the identification terminates and the tension of the aesthetic distance[40] dies, the person is relieved to return to their comfortable world of regularities. Even then, however, it is a return to a world now not quite the same, tenuous, not as trustworthy, and morally ambiguous, with conventional life forms and value systems at best seriously problematized, and at worst deeply devalued. Think of Marlow upon his return home after following Kurtz to "the edge," indeed after he, Marlow, "seemed to have lived through *his* [Kurtz's: italics mine] extremity."[41]

> I found myself back in the sepulchral city resenting the sight of people hurrying through the streets to filch a little money from each other, to devour their infamous cookery, to gulp their unwholesome beer, to dream their insignificant and silly dreams. They trespassed upon my thoughts. They were intruders whose knowledge of life was to me an

irritating pretense, because I felt so sure they could not possibly know the things I knew. Their bearing, which was simply the bearing of commonplace individuals going about their business in the assurance of perfect safety, was offensive to me like the outrageous flaunting of folly in the face of danger it is unable to comprehend.[42]

Michelle Gellrich has argued convincingly that the theories of both Hegel and Aristotle were themselves attempts to nullify the disturbing implications of tragedy and the tragic vision.

> Hegel's theory produces interpretations of strife in tragedy that may be reassuring in their conformity to a dialectical scheme of conflict and resolution, but these interpretations are less the expression of the tragic dramatists than of the critics' need to find intelligibility in the experience of disorder.[43]

Others have argued persuasively that moral ambiguity is the hallmark of tragic experience.[44] This raises the whole problem of tragic guilt. To anticipate, consider the ways in which participation at any level in the system of slavery by African Americans, while resisting its ravages at various levels still, implicates them in the system's structuration. They participated in a tragic sense in their own systematized degradation, incurring a *tragic guilt,* a guilt that cannot be localized or attributed to the human subjects involved in any but a uniquely tragic way. African Americans were not unaware of their participation at various and intricate levels, experiences ranging from the deceptive acceptance of the imposition of stereotypical images to the production process that made their owners richer and even more powerful. This of course added to and intensified the torn or rendered state and the psychic pain entailed in the sparagmous that characterized the African American condition both during and after slavery.[45]

Decisions, actions, and their consequences play a key role in the structure of all classic tragedies. Then there are the underlying issues entailed in many tragedies and literature that aspire toward the tragic, that is, the ineffective nature of choice in situations where events were on a collision course no matter what the option acted upon, or where the character could not be reasonably expected to make any other choice but the one leading to dire consequences. The assignment of guilt in such cases becomes deeply problematized.

> The tragic consists—at least in human tragedies—not simply in the absence of "guilt" but rather in the fact that the guiltiness cannot be

localized. Whatever we can substitute, in place of a man who plays a role in the unfolding of a catastrophe, another man who is like the first but morally better—that is one who has a finer sympathy for moral opportunities as well as greater energy of moral will—to the extent that we can perform such substitution the growth of a feeling of tragedy is stunted by the amount of blame we can pin on the responsible person.[46]

There is no set formula for the particular moral dilemmas that complicate tragic plots. Efforts to reduce tragedy and the moral issues involved to any particular formula of conflict are at best misguided. The point is to grasp the moral ambiguity of human existence, an ambiguity that is grounded in its nature, or is, in a word, ontological. These decisions are made in the throes of great moral dilemmas with no clear or unambiguous options.

> Every essential confusion of the bounds of right and wrong, of good and evil, in the unity of action; every maze of threads, of motives, of views of duties, so presented as to seem to lead equally well to a judgment of "right" or "wrong"; every complication which is not based on necessary moral and legal wisdom but which instead produces from the circumstances alone an absolute confusion of our moral and legal powers of judgment—every such complication pertains to the subjective side of tragic feeling and thereby transposes us completely from the realm of possible "right" and "wrong," from possible "accusation" and "indignation." "Tragic guilt" is of a kind for which no one can be blamed and for which no conceivable "judge" can be found.[47]

The experience is so deeply disturbing because it discloses the fundamental ambiguity and instability of human existence, the fact that our moral schemes and value systems are not calibrated to fit neatly into reality, though prior to the conflict we may have comfortably believed them to be. This raises the disheartening specter that the reality with which we believed our schemes commensurate is not indeed what we thought it was, hence we do not know it. Our world is unfamiliar, disturbingly strange and threatening, perhaps—certainly—in some instances, menacing. The moral ambiguity then opens us up to the push and pull of competing claims of great consequence with respect to life and death, pain, and suffering, all in a context where the great consequence may, indeed, have no more meaning than the withering of an errant apple on a tree. The ensuing sparagmous or rending of the self is instantiated in psychic pain, rendering the conflict intimately tangible and palpably real.

Moral ambiguity becomes a window through which we gaze into the whole. It serves as a gateway that swings out into life's larger form and the reality of human existence taken as a whole. Moral convictions are the last line of defense. They are in the end the perimeters of our being. They define our existence. The historically close tie of religion and morality attest to the fact of how near the ultimate foundations of our stability our moral convictions lay. Hence a disturbance there is more than capable of "shaking the foundations." I am arguing, however, that it is not simply moral ambiguity, but the inherent ambiguity of life in general, which pervades moral experience, that is the hallmark of tragedy. "In tragedy, truth is not revealed as one harmonious whole; it is many-faceted, ambiguous, a sum of irreconcilables—and that is one source of its terror."[48]

The ambiguity reveals its terrible and tragic issue when it is disclosed or encountered amid great suffering. Together, the ambiguity *suffered*, the psychic, sometimes compounded by physical, pain, the profound anxiety, the embeddedness of agency in the tragic field[49] all converging on the site of the self (precipitating its sparagmous or rending) conspire to bring the human being to his or her limits. The interrogative state (whether implicit or explicit) *instantiated* by this inherent, albeit not always apparent, ambiguity (which is always already aesthetically tinged), is what deepens, intensifies and sharpens the experience of suffering until it crystallizes into the tragic vision.

Being in Question:
Longing and the Interrogative State

The interrogative state is the state of *being* in question. Martin Heidegger argues that the *dasein* is the being who can raise the question of being, but in the tragic vision, the human being is disclosed as the being for whom *to be* is to be in question. By implication, it is the judgment on all previously accepted answers. It is the indictment of human being in the tragic sense. It is the existential embodiment of uncertainty. It is the shadow over all value systems, convictions, and beliefs that shape our existence while at the same time an affirmation of existence itself in the face of *everything* denied—life against life, hope against itself. "Tragedy, to [Eugene] O'Neill ennobled in art what he called man's hopeless hopes."[50] This is why tragic longing inspires what at first sight appears to be paradoxical: action. "Longing leads men to actions and events, and no action or event is worthy of becoming the fulfillment of longing."[51] This kicking against the pricks, this flailing away at the whale, this cry against the elements, this complaint upon the ash heap, this "I feel like going on," "this keep on keeping on," all express that affirmative thrust in conscious recognition of denial—the greatest of all refusals, the elemental refusal of the refusal posed by the elements themselves.

Longing is the self-conscious expression of the interrogative state. The interrogative state, the experienced sparagmous, takes the shape of the "great longing," the desire for "cohesiveness over the whole of one's existence," that may be given concrete expression in a variety of symbolic forms, although none in which it can finally rest. The longing is generative, although no symbol can satisfy the great longing. All symbolic expressions of its fulfillment merely testify in *their* promise to *its* persistence. They symbolized fulfillment while they, at the same time, *mirror*[52] the longing itself. They are only penultimate or provisional satisfactions that function in a way analogous to Freud's description of a neurotic symptom or compromise formation. In the end they disclose the possibility of wholeness but conceal the reality of satisfaction or the reality sought after, that which would satisfy.

> Great longing is always taciturn and it always disguises itself behind many different masks. Perhaps it would not be a paradox to say that the mask is its form. But the mask also represents the great, two-fold struggle of life: the struggle to be recognized and the struggle to remain disguised.[53]

The great longing is the ultimate expression of human desire, at once in its most abstract and most concrete forms. Abstract because it is the ground of the tragic vision,[54] concrete because it is the expression of the historical subject at its core. Pure longing, says Lukács, is "the inherent center of the soul." We, however, seldom experience pure longing—like the god we dare not look upon lest we die. The unmirrored longing is like, or more accurately perhaps the product of, the bare recognition of the abyss. Unmirrored, the great longing becomes but mere emptiness. Like the eclipse that can be observed, indeed for what it is, but only in its reflection and never by the naked eye.

This state of being is characterized by a kind of omnitemporality. It is open to the past and for the future. It is open but oriented. The dialectical tension of the past and the future instantiate the living, open field of the present at the sight of the self. At the risk of oversimplification, the self makes meaning out of the past in the present for the future, without which there would be no future. The future would be vacuous, rendering the present meaningless. What the self makes of the past (in the present) in terms of meaning it projects into the future, illuminating or constituting futurity, giving it a mold or shape into which we pour the continual flow of successive presents. By so doing we restrict the feeling of vulnerability and shape future desires.

> "They are," said Schiller of the objects of human Longing, "what we once were; they are what we are not become once more." But the past—that which has been lost to us—has become a value because we create what has been lost to us, a way and a goal, out of its never-having exited; that is how longing rises above the goal which it has set itself, and this is how it ceases to be bound to its own goal.[55]

The form is driven and structured by desire, which always, as ground, surpasses the form which gives it articulation.[56] It resists closure. In all authentic, or I should say tragic, longing there is an implicit moment of despair that expresses the ontological absence of closure. It is the acknowledgment of the ongoing apperception of nonbeing. The great longing is the measure of the hole in the soul of being. Longing, while an expression of desire, even a species of hope, has always within it the sense of what is not, what may never be, the unreachable etc.... It also expresses the stubborn resistance of the desire. Longing and despair are integrally related; perhaps even flip sides of the same coin so to speak. The despair of longing is worked over by the aesthetic, even in the mythopoetic meaning-making orientation, as desire is given shape or rather aesthetic rearticulation in the mirroring. Nietzsche brings these elements together wonderfully.

> Now no comfort avails anymore; longing transcends a world after death, even the gods; existence is negated along with its glittering reflection in the gods or in an immortal beyond. Conscious of the truth he has once seen, man now sees everywhere only the horror or absurdity of existence; now he understands the wisdom of the sylvan god, Silenus: he is nauseated.
>
> Here, when the danger to his will is greatest, art approaches as a saving sorceress, expert at healing. She alone knows how to turn these nauseous thoughts about the horror or absurdity of existence into

notions with which one can live: these are the *sublime* as the artistic taming of the horrible....[57]

Naked despair is shapeless desire or desire that resists (for whatever reason) the imposition of substance-bearing-form or the imputation of form-bearing-substance. Longing is the voice of human being moving through the abyss that, even in the expression of its hope(s), takes on a mournful tone. With all the pain of grief implied, weeping Rachel refuses to be comforted in exile. The prophet Jeremiah expresses this longing in anticipation of the exile in the present perfect, the tense of all visionary prophecy, especially that which marks the end or terminus of an ordeal.[58]

> A voice was heard in Ramah, lamentation and bitter weeping: Rachel weeping for her children refused to be comforted for her children, because they were not.[59]

Longing without aesthetic sustenance shades over into despair which, in its extreme form is suicidal, but even then, in the final *act,* it betrays the indestructible affirmative moment. The symbols must approach ultimacy in order to have the gravitas capable of absorbing enough of the desire to render being bearable.

Let us now turn our attention once again to the issue of the relationship between the tragic, the absurd, and the characteristic affect of the tragic vision. The affective state that characterizes the tragic vision, as I understand it, goes through some modifications in the experience of tragedy as a genre. I consider what is experienced as the tragic effect in tragedy as a genre to be a species of the affect associated with the tragic vision. This affective state and its relationship to the tragic and the absurd/abyss or what I have broadened out into the concept of the inassimilable is given relatively clear expression in Albert Camus' *Myth of Sisyphus*. Camus' reflections are not only helpful in elucidating the relationship between the concepts, but will also serve us well as a transition to a consideration of the tragic nature of African American Christian consciousness.

Sisyphus is condemned to roll a giant rock up a hill throughout eternity, only to have it roll back down each time in Kafkaesque futility. It is his punishment for breaking an oath to return to the underworld. Having known life and the gloom of death he is allowed to know life once more, and though constrained by an oath to give it up he is unable to let it go. His passionate attachment to life restrains him from returning of his own accord. So he is seized by Mercury and forcibly returned to the underworld to face his fate.

> You have already grasped that Sisyphus is the absurd hero. He is, as much through his passions as through his torture. His scorn of the gods, his hatred of death, and his passion for life won him that unspeakable penalty in which the whole being is exerted toward accomplishing nothing.[60]

He later adds cautiously, "If this myth is tragic, that is because his hero is conscious."[61]

> The workman of today works everyday of his life at the same tasks, and this fate is no less absurd. But it is tragic only at those rare moments when it becomes conscious.[62]

Joseph Conrad writes in a similar vein.

> "What makes mankind tragic," wrote Conrad, "is not that they are victims of nature, it is that they are conscious of it.... As soon as you know of your slavery, pain, the anger, the strife—the tragedy begins...."[63]

The tragic vision is conscious and semi-self-conscious and cannot, therefore, be separated from the affective dimension of human experience. Here again, we observe that the tragic vision resists foreclosure. We have learned from psychoanalysis that denial *or* disavowal can occur not only with respect to ideational content, but also with respect to its concomitant affect. A human being may recognize or perceive a disturbing reality or truth intellectually, particularly when forced upon them, but in the end shields their psychological integrity from the threat of disintegration by repressing the affect. The resultant impact of this repression is a serious disturbance of the person's relation to reality, loss of perspective, and, depending upon the strength of the affect involved, some form of mental illness. In this chapter I have argued that the tragic vision facilitates an authentic encounter of the abyss, but it does so not only in recognition of, but by facilitating the appropriate expression of, affect, as it, too, is transfigured in and through the aesthetic moment as something palatable yet true. Here again this is accomplished by the preservation of a dialectical tension within the affective field itself.

This experience of the absurd/tragic articulated by Camus contains elements of both sorrow and joy. The tragic affect, like the tragic vision itself, grows out of a structural ambiguity. Camus first suggests a dualism or something like the coexistence of two possibilities. But as he clarifies his position, it becomes apparent that he is arguing more for a sorrow and joy that are dynamically related—two identifiable poles of one living and unique experience. Such a sorrow (i.e., one organically related to joy) and such a joy (i.e., one organically related to sorrow) is a unique and powerful experience, the integrity of which will not survive separation into its component parts or the disintegration of the dynamic tension that marks out the field of its affective resonance. Both the sorrow (later associated with resignation) and joy (later associated with affirmation) are transformed by the presence of the other as they coexist in a living tension. *It is the conscious content, feeling tone, or as I shall emphasize later, mood structure of the tragic experience.* This is what gives the tragic experience is unique poignancy.[64]

> If the descent is thus sometimes performed in sorrow, it can also take place in joy. This word is not too much. Again I fancy Sisyphus returning toward his rock, and the sorrow was in the beginning. When the images of earth cling too tightly to memory, when the call of happiness becomes too insistent, it happens that melancholy rises in man's heart: this is the rock's victory, this is the rock itself. The boundless grief is too heavy to bear. These are our nights of Gethsemane. But crushing truths perish from being acknowledged. Thus Oedipus at the outset obeys fate without knowing it. But from the moment he knows, his tragedy begins. Yet at the same moment, blind and desperate, he realizes that the only bond linking him to the world is the cool hand of a girl. Then a tremendous remark rings out: "Despite so many ordeals, my advanced age and the nobility of my soul make me conclude that all is well."[65]

Arthur and Barbara Gelb, writing of Eugene O'Neill, groped toward the same insight.

> To O'Neill tragedy had the meaning the Greeks gave it, and it was their classic example that he tried to follow. He believed with the Greeks that tragedy always brought exultation, "an urge [he once said] toward life and ever more life."[66]

The tragic vision is at the core of African American Christian consciousness. Although most people misunderstand the tragic vision, assuming it to be an essentially pessimistic view of life, and might recoil at the suggestion that it permeates a religious tradition so long credited with sustaining the hopes of an oppressed people, I hope that the forgoing discussion has helped to dispel this simplistic assumption. To appreciate the significance of an exploration of the tragic vision and African American Christian Consciousness one need but consider the profound resonance of the forgoing considerations and W. E. B. Du Bois's stirring description of the heart and soul of the African American faith.

> The Music of Negro religion is that plaintive rhythmic melody, with its touching minor cadences, which, despite caricature and defilement, still remains the most original and beautiful expression of human life and longing yet born on American soil. Sprung from African forests, where its counterpart can still be heard, it was adapted, changed, and intensified by the tragic soul-life of the slave, until, under the stress of law and whip, it became the one true expression of a people's sorrow, despair, and hope.[67]

Chapter 2

Sparagmous, or "The Crucified"

Drawn into the maelstrom of Western expansion, the Africans were torn from their homeland and swallowed up in the ever-increasing need for cheap labor in the pursuit of profit. With their participation in the process of Western expansion, objectified as chattel, the Africans and their descendants were doomed from the beginning to an existence characterized by social and cultural alienation; in a word, marginalization. This status would be codified by law, although it would extend much further into an evolving American culture and the African American soul.

> In 1705, almost exactly a century after the first colonists had set foot on Jamestown, the House of Burgesses codified and systematized Virginia's laws of slavery. These laws would be modified and added to over the next century and a half, but the essential legal framework within which the institution of slavery would subsequently operate had been put in place. It had taken the English in Virginia the best part of one hundred years to finalize their construction of a legal status quite unknown in the Common Law of England, to declare unequivocally that Africans were a form of property: that they were, and henceforth would remain, "Strangers" and "outsiders" who would be required to live out their lives according to an entirely different set of laws from those that governed people of European birth and ancestry.[1]

Their "old world" beliefs, practices, cultural taxonomies, and such would not easily translate into the semantic grid they were introduced to in the Americas. In fact their integration into Western culture was so limited that even if it had been possible to translate the better part of their beliefs, given the cultural and linguistic resources of the West they would not have succeeded.

The othering of the African American was so profound that it tended toward, and in some cases achieved, a kind of ontologization. The othering was a question of her nature, her very being.

> Indeed, when describing the physical characteristics of West Africans, some English commentators made direct comparisons between them and animals. It was to be no coincidence that such comparisons often involved the anthropoid ape, the animal that most closely resembled man and that sixteenth-century English visitors to West Africa were being introduced to for the first time. One fairly typical example of the comments that were made by the English was the observation that West African "men that have low and flat nostrils are libidinous as apes that attempt women." Another author, one of several who were appalled by the nakedness of many West Africans, especially the women, remarked that "the men and women go so alike, that one cannot know a man from a woman but by their breasts, which in the most part be very foule and long, hanging downe low like the udder of a goat." Such accounts called into serious question the very humanity of West Africans.[2]

Hence, from the earliest encounters with the English and other Europeans, the Africans' way to social integration or meaningful, healthy acculturation was being effectively barred. Culture and civilization were fairly equated at the time and identified with what it means to be human. The African's and the subsequent African American's cultural artifacts, including her religion, would be considered as errant and degraded shadows of human expression and hardly tolerated. This overall picture is not intended to imply that there was not significant retention of some aspects of African culture in the slave communities of the Americas. The literature bears out that there was.[3] But the term "significant" is, I think, relative.

The fact that there was some retention is significant. It is a marvelous testimony to the resilience of the human spirit in general and the tenacity of the African spirit in particular. It is eloquent testimony to the value that the Africans placed on themselves as reflected in their own way of life. The retentions also provided common points of contact between the slaves, which in turn, helped them preserve some residual sense of community among themselves independent of that defined by their oppressors. They also provided limited but somewhat effective components of the overall stock of resources accumulated and employed over time against the ever-present, impending sense of meaninglessness. Yet there is a difference between arguing that the fact that there were retentions is significant and establishing just what that significance is. The significance of the retentions must be measured or determined by the subject under discussion and the point being made at the time. For one, to suggest that the retentions of African culture among the slave communities in what was to become the United States of America was not significant enough to ward off the devastating consequences of chattel slavery as I am clearly arguing is not to say that the fact that there were retentions is insignificant. This seems to me to be an implied dimension of the ongoing debate in studies of the Americas devoted to the issue of the African Americans and their unique experience in the New World.

In order for the African to fulfill the function for which he was brought to America, he had to be broken. The process of slave breaking was designed to make the African as manageable as possible and easily employed for the purpose of production. The parameters of his being were established based on the purpose he was to serve. In a sense he ceased to be primarily or "legitimately" a person and became hardly more than a component in the burgeoning capitalist machinery that was later to reach monstrous proportions.

> The calculation of slave existence was determined by base conditions necessary for functioning as an effective laborer, and the extent of protection to life and limb vas decided by diminutions in the value of capital. Within these boundaries, degrees of injury and magnitudes of labor decided the meaning of the slave person. It is difficult to acknowledge this savage quantification of life and person as a recognition of black humanity, for as argued earlier, this restricted stipulation of humanity intensified the pained existence of the enslaved. This scale of subjective value was a complement rather than a corrective to the decriminalization of white violence that was the foundation of slave law.[4]

In terms of the history of capitalist labor, the Africans were some of its first victims and on the whole probably its most devastated. The fact that they were reduced to merely a means to the enhancement of the life of European Americans through an excessively cruel and traumatic process of dehumanization is difficult enough for us to fathom, but to have an entire cultural apparatus constructed to define and maintain such a horrible affront to humanity is virtually unthinkable. Perhaps that is why Americans can live in disavowal of the depths of its horror. There seems to be a sense in which both the African American and European American continue until today to suffer from this initial trauma. African Americans suffer through the continuing legacy of cruel oppression and the failure to acknowledge its chronic legacy. Whites on the other hand cannot or will not process such a debilitating and fatal blow to the sense of moral and cultural superiority to which the apparatus of modern white identity seems so indebted.

Even when other victims of a rampant capitalism could take some solace in the values of the fledgling democracy that began to sprout in America the African could not. In point of fact he could not even be called an American because as a slave he was neither a citizen nor a man in reigning cultural taxonomy. The black person had no inherent human dignity that the whites were bound to acknowledge.

The process of slave breaking entailed stripping the Africans of as much of their native culture as possible, rendering them helpless and dependent. They were forbidden to use their own language, and even their native religious expressions were "outlawed." I do not believe that the motivation for human behavior is ever monolithic. Even when a primary motive can be identified, such as "production," there are other factors that color and season our experiences, giving them their character and taste or perhaps, I should say, their edge. The slave breaking process was undoubtedly influenced and colored by the chronic inability of whites, in this case, to deal reasonably or live peaceably with otherness, even the otherness of those on whom they were so dependent and to whom they were so indebted. The fact that the African was perceived to be fundamentally different, animalistic, ugly, libidinous, and morally inferior, spurred the transplanted Europeans on in the slave breaking or desocialization process and seemed to justify or excuse any level of cruelty and abuse—all the while strengthening the barriers and resistances to healthy acculturation. After determining that the enslavement of the Native American would be too problematic, whites simply hid what they did not kill by confining them to reservations and continuing to this day in a sort of pathological denial of this concomitant horror. The horrors of the twentieth century were indeed nurtured and cradled in those that came before.[5] For W. E. B Du Bois it was all of a piece and firmly rooted in the hypocrisy of the would-be Christian West, as Ed Blum illuminates beautifully in his well-crafted text, *W. E. B. Du Bois: American Prophet*.

> Religious hypocrisy, in fact, was the dominant theme of western society. "The white followers of the meek and lowly Jesus stole fifteen million men, women and children from Africa from A.D. 1400 to 1900 and

made them working cattle in America. There was no Nazi atrocity," claimed Du Bois "which the Christian civilization of Europe had not long been practicing against colored folk in all parts of the world."[6]

I chose to use the term *desocialization* because the slave masters were primarily concerned with depriving the slaves of any cultural resource that may inspire revolt or resistance. They were not concerned with providing an adequate replacement, certainly none that took the Africans seriously as full human beings. They weren't concerned with making the slave a full partner in the colonial enterprise with a nice new European identity or later inviting her to become a fellow American. They did not want the slave to ever get the idea that he could share such an identity because that would lead to the dangerous and unprofitable notion that he should be free, or that he was not created for the express purpose of servitude. The extent to which they were integrated into the new society or socialized was determined almost exclusively by the necessities of production or some other dimension of the peculiar institution. As socialization did take place, the Africans/African Americans were integrated into a set of roles, beliefs, assumptions, and cultural taxonomies that defined them in terms of chattel with all the concomitant racist and racialized discourse. What exactly this entailed is well documented in the extant historical literature on the subject. The fact that the African was so defined and his existence reduced primarily to a use value made any effective integration at the psychic level relatively impossible. I will say more about this later.

Even when slaves were finally allowed the opportunity to convert, slave masters were concerned first and foremost with the possible interference of this new status with the slave's perception of himself or herself as a bondsperson.

> While Jones, Capers and other spokesmen for the plantation mission consistently reiterated the distinction between temporal and spiritual equality, there remained among slaveholders, even those generally favorable to slave conversion, a lingering suspicion that the two could not be as clearly segregated as the missionaries claimed. In brief, they objected "that religious instruction tends to dissolution of the relations of society as now constituted: and...that it will really do the people no good, but to lead to insubordination." They felt that Christian fellowship between master and slave, unless very carefully regulated, would corrode the proper social hierarchy—the essential inferiority of blacks and superiority of whites—upon which the system rested.[7]

It wasn't until the master was convinced by the missionary organizations that the conversion of the slave would lead to more devoted and docile slaves did they allow the various organizations like the Society for the Propagation of the Gospel to have access to the slaves on their plantations. "Slave conversion had to be measured by the rule of slave control, and a plantation manager would be dangerously remiss if he allowed anyone but himself to do the measuring."[8]

> After vehemently denying that slaves should be "acquainted with the whole Bible," or every doctrine therein, Seabrook argued that it was "absolutely necessary" for them to become "intimately acquainted" with "the prominent portions of Scripture which shew the duties of servants and the rights of masters." Moreover, any attempt to make the religious knowledge of slaves "co-extensive with that of their owners" was sheer lunacy.[9]

Hence, in practical terms we can safely assert that besides being stripped of the coherence of their own culture, the Africans/African Americans were not allowed to participate in the culture of the new world in any but a deeply disturbed and profoundly conflicted sense. They were traumatically wrenched from their own cultural milieu, which fundamentally compromised the effective quality of residuals,[10] stripped of their structural trappings; then forced by the nature of the case to internalize deeply problematized fragments of American culture that could not fill the void. This cultural deprivation with its concomitant consequences did not take place haphazardly or at random. It was intentional and systematically carried out. As Vincent Harding points out, from very early on, Africans/African Americans were the target of a wide variety of legislative acts designed to effectively strip them of any status other than that of chattel in the New World.

> So in the course of the seventeenth century, the freedom-loving English colonies developed a series of laws and judicial rulings to define the black situation. Beginning in Virginia at the end of the 1630s, laws establishing lifelong African slavery were instituted. They were followed by laws prohibiting black-white intermarriage, laws against the ownership of property by Africans, laws denying blacks all basic political rights (limited as they were among whites at the time). In addition, there were laws against the education of Africans, laws against the assembling of Africans, laws against the ownership of weapons by Africans, laws perpetuating the slavery of their parents to their

children, laws forbidding Africans to raise their hands to whites even in self-defense.[11]

With the creation of these laws in the various colonies and later, of course states, the parameters of African/African American being were established. These laws, or slave codes as they came to be called, became a key source of legitimization for the cultural assumptions and assertions extant about the meaning, function, and value of black being in the New World. The African/African American was obviously shut out of the dominant society, and the way to significant participation in the predominant meaningful dimensions of American culture was effectively barred.

But there was an even more sinister and damaging dimension to this duly established and legally enforced marginalization.

> Then besides setting up legal barriers against the entry of black people as self-determining participants into the developing American society, the laws struck another cruel blow of a different kind: they outlawed many rituals connected with African religious practices, including dancing and the use of drums. In many places they also banned African languages. Thus they attempted to shut black people out from both cultures, to make them wholly dependent neuters.[12]

This dimension of their marginalization struck deep at the African/African American consciousness, with serious repercussions for the formation of their subjectivity and their sense of self. Not only were their basic sources of ontological security destroyed, but they were effectively prevented from freely establishing new ones. This chronically marginal state of being was seriously aggravated by the potential and actual disturbance of the more intimate and personal dimensions of life.

> The account Jones made of his later attachments was similarly interpolated with the dread of sale: "I had a constant dread that Mrs. Moore would be in want of money and sell my dear wife. We constantly dreaded a final separation. Our affection for each other was very strong and this made us always apprehensive of a cruel parting." Likewise Lewis Hayden: "Intelligent colored people of my circle of acquaintance as a general thing felt no security whatever for their family ties. Some, it is true, who belonged to rich families felt some security; but those of us who looked deeper and knew how many were not rich that seemed so, and saw how fast the money slipped away were always miserable. The

trader was all around, the slave pens at hand, and we did not know what time any of us might be in it." Under the chattel principle, every advance into enslaved society—every reliance on another, every child, friend, or lover, every social relation—held within it the threat of its own dissolution.[13]

They were dependent on what was, for the most part, the whim of the slave masters, which left all intimate relationships in a precarious state. In a chapter entitled "The Chattel Principle," Walter Johnson points out how common it was for slave relationships to be dissolved.

> They lived as parents and children, as cotton Pickers, card players, and preachers, as adversaries, friends, and lovers. But though they were seldom priced, slaves' values always hung over their heads. J.W.C. Pennington, another fugitive, called this the "chattel principle": any slave's identity might be disrupted as easily as a price could be set and a piece of paper passed from one hand to another. Of the two thirds of a million interstate sales made by the traders in the decades before the civil war: twenty-five percent involved the destruction of a first marriage [misleading because they were not routinely recognized] and fifty percent destroyed a nuclear family—many of these separating children under the age of thirteen from their parents. Nearly all of them involved dissolution of a previously existing community. And those are only the interstate sales.[14]

The emotional trauma of these dissolutions and their reverberations throughout the African/African American population was immense and contributed to the creation of a traumatic field wherein the sparagmous characteristic of the tragic in and of human existence was an inherent dimension. If one of the main sources of our rootedness in this world is the strength and comfort we find in meaningful, intimate relationships, then the African could never be at home—never at rest.

> In the wake of traumatization the familiar has become unfamiliar. The unfamiliar familiar is, Otto Rank pointed out, the uncanny. Loss of the familiarity of the self and the world is the loss of a basic assumption that organizes identity. The uncanny shattering of identity in traumatic loss is the loss of the assumption that one exists, and a collapse of valuations that sustain the self, meaningfulness, and the world. Related to this is a sense in which shared familiarity and a feeling of being at home are subverted in the unfamiliarity, foreignness, strangeness, and undiscloseable nature of traumatic experience.[15]

The other dynamics, such as loss of bodily integrity, abandonment, subjection to arbitrary violence, alienation from one's self, and denial or disavowal of one's true affect for the sake of survival and adaptation, all created constituent lines of force within this field; experienced within a framework characterized by sparse and fragmented, always problematic cultural resources for existential containment. African American subjectivity was constituted as always already threatened with fragmentation and existentially at risk. African American subjectivity constituted within this field and filtered though their profoundly aesthetic sensibility emerged as a tragic subjectivity.

In the first chapter, I pointed out some of the elemental features of our ontological security system. One main feature was the taken-for-granted nature of those dimensions of existence that serve as generative resources in the creation of our ontological security system. But it was precisely this foundational reality that was lacking or at least severely disturbed in the life of the African captives and their offspring. In the world of the slave, continuity could never be taken for granted. The world of the slave was subject to arbitrary disruptions. Their primary relationships were subject to interruptions at any time according to the whim of the slave master, and there was little to nothing the slave could do about it. This state of affairs, along with some other factors, encouraged the development of a certain quality of resignation at deep levels of the African/African American psyche or being, as you might have it, functioning both as a coping device and defense mechanism.

> To begin to understand the sadness and pessimism of victims involves not simply recognizing that they may now see the world and themselves differently and more negatively but also that, underlying these new views, is the experience of loss. Psychologically, the shattering of fundamental assumptions produces a state of both loss and disintegration: the known, comforting old assumptive world is gone, and a new one must be constructed.[16]

The sense of resignation is permeated with something that may once have been referred to as melancholia and today would be diagnosed as depression, but I prefer the less pathologizing terms *deep sorrow* and *mourning*. The acceptance of fate does not necessarily imply that African Americans in slavery had given up, offering no internal or external resistance. While it may sound somewhat paradoxical, it could also mean precisely the opposite. This sense of resignation was a survival mode, protecting the African/African American in slavery from the onslaught of hopelessness and despair that would naturally result from ruined expectations. It allowed the slave the psychic space in which to dream, hope, and visualize a brighter tomorrow, a space that fear of failure and the unbearable pain of impossible possibility would have "normally" prevented. The existential retirement that I refer to as *resignation* rendered hopes remote, and in so doing vouchsafed their safety from the immediacy of a crushing daily reality. Though rendered remote in resignation, they remained available for retrieval when psychic and social space, however fleeting, opened for their expression.[17] Not all dreams deferred fester or explode. There where the cracking whip echoed but its sting failed to reach, longing took shape in fragments, shards of hope from the broken vessel of what *may* never be.

It is here in this remote location that eschatological longing resides, taking shape in symbolic form and often fused with earthly aspirations and invested with their affective resources. They are activated in the liminal space of worship through symbolic mirroring and mediation preserving both the depth and power of the eschatological while at the same time giving vent to the aspirations of the here and now. "I got shoes you got shoes, All of God's children got shoes. And When I get to Heaven I am going to put on my shoes and walk all over God's Heaven." Unleashed in the power of their affirmation, they breathe the fresh air of expression and revitalized, return to the place where whip, racism, and oppression could not reach. I will have more to say about this in later chapters; but here I would like to point out that this is the resource that Pastor Martin Luther King Jr. drew upon to spiritually empower African Americans during the Montgomery Bus Boycott. The boycott in turn helped to set off a national movement in and beyond the immediate African American community. The national African American community, by and large, became galvanized, and even those not directly involved in organized agitation—through the activation of these shared aspirations symbolically codified and ensconced in an intersubjective field—became a part of the spiritual reservoir that those who were directly involved drew upon to sustain struggle. This is the power that ideology or theological systems may draw upon but cannot of themselves engender or provide. Theological systems such as Liberation or Black theology, for instance, may become the foil for expression of this power and the aspirations it entails but cannot on their own provide the energy or mass motivation.

The stress and strain of being cruelly subject and subjected to arbitrary cruelty and unable to reach something so powerful and so fundamental to human being in these conditions as freedom would have overburdened the psyche, as it was threatened constantly with dissolution and existential exhaustion; that is to say, psychic death. Baumeister et al. have pointed out that "the operations of the self involve the consumption of a limited resource." They argue that any human being has only a finite amount of energy to devote to adaptation and coping. The condition of chronic stress taxes that resource to the limit. "Stress makes severe demands on this resource, because people must engage in active responding and must regulate themselves so as to adapt to difficult circumstances. One major consequence of stress is that the resource becomes depleted."[18] As a result of their research in animal studies they are able to specify the conditions under which people undergo exhaustive stress.

> Extrapolating from these animal studies to human beings, one may suggest that people experience considerable stress when many responses under uncertain, ambiguous conditions are required in order to deal with threat, or when there is no clear positive, desirable option available. Such situations may be regarded as the operational definition of hard choices, and such choices are presumably especially draining of the individual's psychological, volitional resource. Thus, even when the threat can be objectively defeated, active coping responses may take a severe toll on the individual.[19]

Resignation is more of a passive coping technique. "Passive coping refers to subjective adaptation when one cannot alter the outcome itself." It serves as the "ego cast," which operates in an analogous way to a cast on a broken bone.

> When a muscle is pulled or a bone is broken, it is often necessary for the person to immobilize it for a period of time in order for it to recover. If this analogy is indeed applicable to the self that has been severely drained from coping, then something akin to an "ego cast" would be desirable. Just as a cast immobilizes an injured limb to allow for complete, uninterrupted rest, an "ego cast" would allow the self to remain substantially inert, in order for it to replenish the volitional resources that have been consumed.
> Hence, recovery from stress (and from coping) may require the person to find a way to live without making serious demands on the self for a period of time.[20]

This deep and abiding sense of tragic resignation, however, provided the existential refuge necessary for the African/African American "to keep on keeping on" or, to borrow a phrase from Anthony Giddens, to "get on" in life.

In evaluating the impact of the disturbance of primary relationships, separation, and the lingering threat of the same, there is another layer that we should consider, given the difference between the way many in the Western world conceptualize reality and the way it is conceptualized in traditional African cultures. Moreover any issues of separation were going to be particularly crucial for Africans/African Americans because of the already aggravated conditions under which they were brought here, the residual and transgenerational impact of the dislocation, and the marginalization they experienced once they "settled." The unresolved issues of being stolen from their homeland and transplanted to a strange land governed by different customs and core beliefs, by virtue of the fact they were never allowed to fully integrate into American society, would loom large in the formation of the African American psyche.

In traditional African cultures great emphasis was placed on the interpersonal dimension of human existence. It served as the primary matrix in which those notions of order and experiences of regularity were generated on which human societies depend to cordon off the boundaries of meaningful existence. Robin Horton helps us to appreciate the comparative significance of interpersonal relationships in traditional African cultures and the burgeoning modern cultures of the West in his article, "African Traditional Thought and Western Science."

> In complex, rapidly changing industrial societies the human scene is in flux. Order, regularity, predictability, simplicity, all these seem lamentably absent. It is in the world of inanimate things that such qualities are most readily seen...In the traditional societies of Africa, we find the situation reversed. The human scene is the locus par excellence of order, predictability and regularity. In the world of the inanimate, these qualities are far less evident. Here being far less at home with people than with things is unimaginable. And here, the mind in quest of explanatory analogies turns naturally to people and their relations.[21]

When these relations are broken, fragmented, rendered tenuous, or overshadowed by threat of dissolution, reality cracks, "things fall apart," so to speak, and the abyss is glimpsed, nay, encountered, in the fissures. It becomes not simply a question of the meaning of reality; its very meaningfulness is threatened. In view of the radical differences between the cultures in terms of how personal and communal relations figured in their value systems and experience of reality, it requires real mental effort and dexterity for persons in the Western hemisphere, particularly whites, to appreciate the depth and disorientation of the trauma of Africans of the middle passage and their African American descendants.

The assumption that all residuals of African culture necessarily lead to unambiguously positive results is also called into question here. The fact that people of African descent maintained this way of valuing personal relationships may have had—and I believe did have—the unintended consequence of sustaining a traumatic depth that further exacerbated the pain of their oppression. This is not a matter of whether or not it was good or bad that any particular value was preserved. Beyond good or bad, it demonstrates the utter ambiguity, often ambivalence, of values and an inherent tragic dimension of the experience. In addition, given the value reversal implied in the quotation above, imagine the utter senselessness and incredulity of the African and her progeny when they were demanded, under the imposition of force, to conceptualize their being and forced to behave as though they were no more than white people's property or things.

We must also consider the impact on the self and the danger posed to its coherence and its internal integrity as a result of being violently torn from those larger frames of meaning that render existence less strange and threatening and not being effectively integrated into new ones. There is a shock and shattering of the self in the wake of such initial and prolonged trauma, a kind of rending, shredding, and desperate attempt at mending all going on at once in the face of enduring forces of tension and fragmentation.

The presence of these frames of meaning, which, especially in the case of people of primal cultures, are closely related to the land are important factors in the constitution and the preservation of both individual and group identity and cohesion. A sense of identity is also of the utmost importance in maintaining a centered self. These frames of meaning contextualize life. They domesticate reality. As a result of the function of these frames of meaning in the stabilization of the human psyche the level of tension and anxiety of the individual is lowered. The relation of the group moves forward with less tension. Good relations are facilitated, and things like general good will are enhanced. When deprived of these realities or when at least they become dysfunctional, the individual experiences heightened tension and anxiety, and the overall quality of experience depreciates significantly.

The following quotation taken from an article on the psychological complications involved in the relocation of the Navajo Indians can be transferred almost without remainder to the situation of the African. The African was stolen from his own land and violently and traumatically "relocated" across the waters, far away from the gods and ancestors who were at once intimately tied to the land and served as important factors in the constitution of tribal and hence individual identity.

> Virtually all learning in traditional Dineh culture is experiential; it occurs in the process of raising livestock and making prayers in a particular ancestral place. It involves becoming a part of that place. And that place serves as a point of reference for all else: memory, knowledge of the past, prayer, relationships, home, self, a vision of life. Closeness to the land and their place on the land is their way of being grounded in tradition, in the traditional ground of their tribal ancestors. Their sense of history and even their sense of time itself are dependent on this closeness to their land. It is through their experiences of the land that they stay in touch with their ancestors and with the gods of the place. Leaving the land means abandoning their ancestors and their gods. It means loss of orientation, and ultimately, loss of group identity, loss of self.[22]

The repercussions of such an involuntary "relocation" for any people are of course devastating. The existential consequences of this kind of traumatic relocation are given clear articulation as Lassiter waxes prophetic toward the close of the article.

> The fate of the Indian people removed from their ancestral lands has far reaching implications for the future society we are preparing. We, too, are now finding ourselves increasingly vulnerable to the kind of "psycho pathology" experienced by the Dineh relocates: hopelessness, disorientation, rootlessness, alienation, loneliness, depression, and despair.[23]

Although I think that terms such as "pathological" ought to be used guardedly when characterizing large groups of people in situations such as these, I do insist that there was and is to this day a great deal of fragmentation in the experience of Africans and their descendants brought to the New World. This state of fragmentation, alienation, and often despair did not simply disappear over time. In fact it became institutionalized and perpetuated through legal, social, and cultural barriers. It became, in a word, *chronic* through historically specifiable conditions. Granted that the kaleidoscopic shifts of history's ever-changing surface provided for different manifestations of or reactions to the situation, nonetheless, fundamental aspects of the condition remained constant. These constants generated, under changing historical circumstances, some expressions that lend themselves more readily to the designation of "pathological" but some also that inclined toward genius and strained toward the divine.

Before moving any further, however, let us return to the issue of "retentions" and worldview for just a moment. There have been notable efforts to demonstrate that some effectual vestiges of African culture survived the tortured trip to the New World and the dark passage into plantation life. There can be no doubt that the thought patterns, beliefs, and practices of traditional African culture were embedded too deeply in the soul of the African to be totally obliterated by the legal decrees of the early Americans and the diabolical practice of slave breaking. Culture is not simply a phenomenon that we hold but rather a phenomenon that holds us and, perhaps even more significantly, hold us together. It makes us what we are. The self is historically constituted and fundamentally shaped by the culture into which the human subject is born. Yet when considering African Americans in relation to African cultural heritage certain claims are made in a way that tends to underestimate the countervailing influence of traumatic relocation and its historical aftermath. Distinctions must be made as to the different levels these influences operated on and their relative strengths vis-à-vis each other given the prevailing historical conditions.

One of the most notable attempts to demonstrate the effectual presence of retentions, particularly their impact on the African American religious imagination and the part they played in the formation of a coherent worldview is Mechal Sobel's *Trabelin' On: The Slave Journey to an Afro-Baptist Faith*. I learned a great deal from the book. The book was stimulating, enlightening and intellectually provocative but, in the end, I found the overall argument overstated. Sobel's work, like some others, makes certain claims that tend to lessen or mitigate the horrifying dimensions of the slave journey, although, admittedly, this may not have been the intention. In an attempt to show how resourceful the Africans/African Americans were in the reconstruction of their life world, thereby enhancing the quality of psychic survival, and to emphasize the uniqueness of African American culture that survivedin significant portions of the African worldview, Sobel and others advertently or inadvertently downplay the level of disintegration and fragmentation experienced. Hence, in the attempt to demonstrate the resourcefulness and the ingenuity of the African American slave, they actually obscure these aspects, render an the depth of their suffering and the dimensions of their epic struggle opaque.

A closer look at *Trabelin' On* may help to demonstrate what I am trying to get at and also help to enrich our analysis. In the text, Sobel argues that the slaves built a *coherent* worldview through an amalgamation of European Christianity and traditional African modes of thought.

> In-depth reintegration of the Black soul took place in the creation of the black or Afro-Baptist faith, which began as early as the 1750's but which was at different stages of development in different black communities.... It is suggested that this process involved the creation of a new Sacred Cosmos, one which integrated African and Baptist elements into a unified whole, so that the black was at one and the same *at home again and whole with himself in America*.[24] (Italics mine)

She claims elsewhere that the coherence of this worldview was responsible for blacks being able to "overcome" certain restrictions. "The ability of Virginia blacks to overcome the harsh restrictions born of white fears is further evidence of the coherence of their worldview and the strength it provided in adversity."[25] The notion that African Americans had at any point overcome the cruel daily realities and degradation of American slavery or subsequent manifestations of American racism is a gross distortion and at best dangerously misleading. It is belied by the testimony of African Americans themselves in the spiritual "We Shall Over Come...Someday." Obviously they hadn't. A significant dimension of the tragic, as I understand it, in the experience is that it involves the experience of always already overcoming, yet never having overcome, i.e. enduring. Lerone Bennett Jr. captures this lyrically in *The Black Mood*.

> It was from out of the unknown that the Negro came, bringing with him the gift of the sun. Billowing out of the slave ships and the embryonic Harlems of the plantations was the sun of a fierce and irresistible will to life. And the sun within the Negro sustained him and made him the white man's greatest collaborator in the taking of the land. *The*

Negro endured: let us begin with that contribution. By the simple act of survival, the Negro made an inestimable contribution to his posterity and to his native land. When Europeans settled in the West Indies, whole groups of people disappeared from the face of the earth, leaving nothing behind but a few bones and artifacts. In other places and in other climes, brown and red men drank the white man's whiskey, read his Bible, became demoralized and wasted away into nothingness. The Negro drank the white man's whiskey, read his Bible, did his work-and his tribe increased. He descended into the hell of slavery, was denied books, pencil and paper, was denied the sanctity of marriage—*was crucified* [Italics mine], in fact, and rose again some three hundred years later in Chicago and Harlem and Atlanta and Washington. *The Negro endured.*[26]

Alex Bontemps, while discussing the complex and ambiguous status of Creole African Americans, make this point well.

Creole status, that is, promised an alternative identity—the possibility of being other-than-Negro in a world where Negro symbolized a wretchedness that could only be survived. Creole status therefore offered an escape from the stigma of wretchedness, in the same sense that acculturation promised, if not freedom, then acceptance and a life less wretched than that of Negro slaves. The limit of each promise was the realization that neither could ever be realized. Being Negro was an indelible stigma because it symbolized an innate characteristic, thereby keeping alive for each survivor the possibility that the creolized African was the slave, not the "outlandish" captive, that to survive was to endure, *not to overcome.*[27] (Italics mine)

I do not doubt that there were resources from which the slaves drew to combat the persistent threat of meaninglessness. A significant measure of those resources may have and in some cases clearly were drawn in spirit and content from the rich reservoir of African origin. But there appears to be a rationalism at work in Sobel's thesis that tends to refract the true nature of the experience. This rationalism tends to divert attention from some more fundamental aspects of the experience that functioned to preserve something of a tense and fragile psychic equilibrium for the slave. These more fundamental aspects of the experience may very well have notable implications for any general theory of how religion functions to promote health under severely stressed and strained circumstances, as well as theological implications for any serious consideration of the historically immanent dimension of the divine reality.

Sobel's use of the phrase "coherent worldview" suggests a well-integrated, well thought out system of interlocking concepts that not only render life meaningful but seem to imply a return to a pretraumatic stability, a sense of invulnerability, and the restoration of fundamental or basic trust. This, in the nature of the case, is simply absurd. If a coherent worldview that she claims enables the subject to "overcome" their predicament does not include these dimensions then I am not sure what making the claim could possibly mean. I am afraid that the level of coherence that she argues was reached at an intellectual level by the African slaves and their later descendants suggests a stability that I simply do not believe could be reached under the conditions of that most peculiar of peculiar institutions. She puts more weight on the ideas and their organization then they can stand. The Herculean task of holding the fragments of the self together amid the stress and strain of slavery and subsequent oppression was not accomplished through the creation of a worldview intellectually conceived and constructed and implicitly static. This task was achieved, at least within the purview of those exposed to some of the more notable biblical narratives and basic Christian conceptions, through the genius of a peculiar kind of experience that involved the employment of the ideas she has correctly identified but in a much looser and more intuitive manner then she seems to suggest. There was no cosmos, so to speak of, but an ongoing process of "cosmosing." A sense of meaning, elements of identity, and meaningfulness were drawn from the ongoing flux of available and renewable fragments, so that they were actuated and emphasized as needed.

In the form of a written text, the information gathered and placed in a narrative form could give the impression of the kind of coherence Sobel seems to be arguing for. In a word then, it is an illusion of narrative prose that this intellectual construction or coherent worldview, as she calls it, ever actually existed and certainly not at the level of rational coherence she argues for. When placed in the context of the lives of individual slaves and relatively isolated groups on plantations scattered throughout the American South, the suggestion of this level of coherence diminishes significantly in persuasive force.

I have been arguing thus far that the African experienced a devastating loss by being violently torn from his land and ripped out of the frames of meaning and the living context that rendered his life meaningful. The Africans' ontological security was at best radically interrupted and at worse totally destroyed. This is attested to by the countless suicides and the severe melancholy documented in much of the literature. This profound sense of loss could have been mitigated, especially in succeeding generations, if they were adequately and effectively integrated into the new mythology governing the evolving "American mind." This, however, did not happen. It did not take place because of the purpose for which the Africans were acquired—to serve as a cheap and enduring source of labor for the "legitimate" settlers of the New World. Hence the sense of loss became a chronic and constitutive element in the formation of African/African American subjectivity.

Now some socialization did of course take place. The African was socialized into the system at a specific level. Within the context of the evolving American system he was to serve as a slave. Various definitions, roles, cultural taxonomies, and so on grew up around this category as the system began to take shape. The slaves were expected to internalize these definitions of their selfhood and function within the confines of the established parameters of their being. To the extent that the slave was a part of the new culture, he internalized these definitions. If they were to have some psychic comfort and reestablish their ontological security to any degree, they would have to negotiate at least a partial settlement with the new categories that defined their being. Given the presence of an awareness of their own humanity and selfhood as previously defined by their own culture and intimated by what retentions there were, the Africans were left with an inevitable conflict that became deeply embedded in their psyche. They underwent a kind of inner crucifixion where division, tension, fragmentation, and disassociation ravaged and tore at the African American soul and subjectivity, which was always already constituted in a shared intersubjective field. This predicament evolved over time and in one manifestation crystallized somewhat later into what Du Bois identified as the "double consciousness."

> After the Egyptian and Indian, the Greek and Roman, the Teuton and Mongolian, the Negro is a sort of seventh son, born with a veil, and gifted with second-sight in this American world, a world which yields him no true self-consciousness, but only lets him see himself through the revelation of the other world. It is a peculiar sensation, this double-consciousness, this sense of always looking at one's self through the eyes of others, of measuring one's soul by the tape of a world that looks on in amused contempt and pity. One ever feels his two-ness, an American, a Negro; two souls, two thoughts, two unreconciled strivings; two warring ideals in one dark body, whose dogged strength alone keeps it from being torn asunder.

The history of the American Negro is the history of this strife,—this longing to attain self-conscious manhood, to merge his double self into a better truer self.[28]

The internalization and the enforced capitulation to the definitions of his being embodied in the cultural taxonomies that grew up around the institution established images of the self and points of contact with the world around him that severed his consciousness and divided his being. Like the crucified Dionysus, the consciousness/self-consciousness of the Africans both as group and individuals became partitioned. Herein lay the threat and indeed the reality of the fragmentation so frequently referred to throughout this chapter. Their struggling sense of their humanity was caught between the two poles of awareness of their past and personhood and the definitions the white world enforced. The pressing realities of day-to-day life as a slave forced them to live out the reality of the roles defined for them in the system by way of an emergent cultural taxonomy regarding their being and warred against any reestablishment of identity based on retentions of any kind.

Due to the nature of the system, then, the mourning process could not be completed in any meaningful sense. The sense of loss became transgenerational and chronic. This matrix of historical circumstance, psychic structure, and feeling generated deep within the African American psyche a two-dimensional sense of longing, a longing for home (with its pluravocity of meaning) and wholeness. So then longing became a constituent element of the African/African American consciousness or frame of mind.

The nature of this experience, the anguished spawn of the peculiar forms of oppression experienced by the enslaved and their descendants is given classic expression in Du Bois's *The Souls of Black Folk*. Here he discloses the mood structure that was at once the product of severe oppression and the force by which some of its more devastating effects were more or less warded off. In this work he also discloses (implicitly at least) the significance of the aesthetic transformation of the experience of their suffering that rendered it bearable. He achieves this task, remarkably, at two levels; first, in the substance of the text, in his explicit discussion of the "Sorrow Songs" and the ritual of African American religious experience; and second, and most remarkably, in his own style of presentation.

The Souls of Black Folk reads with the weight of a tragic text. It discloses a tragic experience and a people's experience of the tragic.

The historical situation of the African/African American engendered a certain kind of suffering that had been raised to the level of art in order to be endured. Our discussion of the Du Bois text will serve as the transition to and a conduit for a more direct discussion of the nature and structure of African American Christian consciousness and religious experience.

> Why did God make me an outcast and a stranger in mine own house? The shades of the stubborn prison-house closed round about us all: walls strait and stubborn to the whitest, but relentlessly narrow, tall, and unscalable to sons of night who must plod darkly on in resignation, or beat unavailing palms against the stone, or steadily, half hopelessly, watch the streak of blue above.[29]

Chapter 3
A Look beneath the *Souls of Black Folk*

> Literature can be called revolutionary in a meaningful sense only with reference to itself, as content having become form. The political potential of art lies only in its own aesthetic dimension.[1]

In the *Souls of Black Folk*, Du Bois strove to present, in a quasi-detached manner, a picture of the African American experience. Du Bois well understood that in order for us to understand and appreciate the existential texture of the "kingdom of color," we would have to have more than the dead statistics, historical descriptions of the condition of slavery and its poignant aftermath. To appreciate the impact and power of the strange dynamics operative in the "kingdom of color" on the person we had to follow them into the actual lives of the people and therein witness their strange and terrible issue. Like following some half-familiar river snaking its way through an unexplored jungle, Du Bois followed its labyrinthine course into the back eddies, beneath the low overhangs, the occasional rapids and along the shadowy banks of black folks' souls and spoke to us of the things he saw. The text was not an outright history, but no one should attempt to write one of his people without first consulting it. It was not an outright sociology of black life, but he who would write one must first pause before the awesome images Du Bois gives us until they are firmly stamped on his statistics and they take on the souls of living beings. This text was not a theoretical evaluation or examination of the religion of the African American, but he who would understand the dark and Dionysian dance that is the African American church ought first to tarry before this altar until seized by its mood. In the end *The Souls of Black Folk* is a testament, written by a modern-day Moses, gifted in the arts of Egyptian learning and culture to the end and for a group of human beings recently released from slavery and groping toward some sense of peoplehood. The lack of any clear or generic discipline to which the text can be summarily ascribed is a testimony to the nobility of its aspiration. It aspires to capture life, a life, and lives. We do not live in areas carved out of life's bewildering morass that neatly correspond to academic disciplines. They are abstractions. To capture life and to grasp the broad birth of its movements, its shifts and tides, its terrible hopes and noble disasters, the disciplines must come together, incarnate only in the insights that disclose for us the meaning of the whole and perhaps then only after being carefully strained through the sieve of artistic imagination.

Du Bois succeeded in conveying to the world something of the depth mood of African American experience, of what Cornell West called "a kind of Good Friday state of existence." This mood has deep psychological, sociological, and cultural roots and defies moral categorization. It is, in a sense, "beyond good and evil" and is the ground of African American culture and spirituality. This mood may in fact shape the way African Americans approach good and evil, but the mood itself is existentially prior. The African American experience in religion as well as other aspects of African American culture emanate out of this mood. In a word it is the common source of the spirituals and the blues. Lerone Bennett Jr. wrote of this mood in an often-overlooked but powerful and unusually insightful little book entitled *The Negro Mood*: "The essence of the black tradition is the extraordinary tension between the poles of pain and joy, agony and ecstasy, good and bad, Sunday [morning] and Saturday [night]."[2]

The dominant characteristic of this mood is the perpetual dialectic of affirmation (hope) and resignation (muted despair). By the use of the phrase "perpetual dialectic," I wish to indicate and emphasize the dynamic and interactive nature of these constitutive elements. It is like the stormy surge and the listless retreat that are at once present in the jostled swells of a sea in the grip of a tempest. This dialectic creates a tension or an affective field out of which the tragic mood arises in African American experience taken as a whole. I think that this mood is, in the end, characteristic of all authentic tragedy or tragic experience wherever it may be found, whether in classic theater, poetry, novels, or common human experience. It is the telos of the efforts of every novelist, playwright, or poet that would dare plumb the chthonic depths of the demystified struggle of the human being to come to terms with what it means to be.

The essence (if I may be allowed to use this term) of tragedy, the signature of its nature, lies in its effect. In an essay titled "Emotion and Meaning in Greek Tragedy," Oliver Taplin argues precisely this point.

> That is to say, the intellectual burden of the tragedy and its value as teaching has to do with the quality of the audience's experience.... it seems to me, then, that Gorgias is right that tragedy is essentially the emotional experience of its audience. Whatever it tells us about the world is conveyed by means of these emotions."[3]

The specific psychic qualities involved in producing the full emotional effect in the experience of tragedy are affirmation and resignation in a dialectical, yet creative tension. In his discussion of Sophoclean tragedy, Bernard M. Knox writes,

> Between these two views of the human situation, the Aeschylean and the Euripidean, these poles of hope and despair, Sophocles creates a tragic universe in which man's heroic action, free and responsible, brings him sometimes through suffering to victory but more often to a fall which is both defeat and victory at once; the suffering and the glory fused in an indissoluble unity."[4]

In the chapters ahead I will have occasion to explore the impact that this experience has on persons in a particular context. For in the end, the influence that the experience of the tragic exercises on particular lives or a life, depends on the context in which it is experienced.

In *The Souls of Black Folk,* Du Bois blends matter and form in such a way that the text itself becomes a disclosive moment in and of African American experience, revealing the effectual, even central, presence of this dialectic. The two constitutive poles of the African American experience and the mood they generate, which permeate and color the entire fabric of the experience shines through the pages and in fact draws you into the dialectic itself. Herein lies not only the text's artistic value but its potentially subversive character as well. In these pages, the experiences of the people live on even long after the individuals themselves have perished. Du Bois selects experiences that are themselves representative or better yet paradigmatic of the experiences of African Americans. He effectively speaks of the lives and longings of an entire race of people through the experiences of a few. The text captures the mood of the African American experience in such a way that it preserves the memory of suffering.

Because of the aesthetic form of this "preservation," it invites the participation—in fact compels the participation of the reader—in a way that mere historical narrative does not. This form of presentation facilitates not simply sympathy but a level of empathy on the part of those who truly engage with the text. And this "true engagement" with the text is itself facilitated by the aesthetic instantiation of the experience because it moves more easily across the defensive barriers and passes other potentially refractory psychic dynamics. The memory is preserved in a sort of congealed potential, a dynamic so to speak. With the merger of content and form at critical points in the text, what is preserved is not simply the memory as recorded fact, but something of the experience itself. With each human encounter (with the text), the memory, in its depth, breathes a sustaining breath through the reader and potentially comes alive.

There is something that gropes toward the eternal in the nature of artistic truth or perhaps I should say truth captured artistically. The experience does not die and seldom fades. As memory it serves as a dialectical negation to all those perspectives that would gloss over, in macrocosmic historical approaches, the suffering of the individual subject and the victimized peoples of history in their particularity. Du Bois's approach, which combines art and history, argues for the value and the integrity of the experience of the individual and summons us, again and again, to the real world of sorrow and joy, aspiration and disappointment, hope and despair, affirmation and resignation. It places us in contact with what is real in life and does so by placing the experience he wishes to record and convey in the living movement of life itself, in the midst of its "*Sturm und Drang.*"

There is also a prophetic dimension to this artistic presentation of the African American experience that must not be overlooked. There is a tendency to accept the dominant ideology and the explanations of reality as they are given by the oppressors or at least those who benefit from the prevailing conditions disproportionately. There is a tendency for those who are not even "directly" responsible for the suffering of African Americans to readily participate in the denial that lies at the heart of the Anglo-American state of mind because of the psychological benefits that accrue.

> When people and groups are locked in conflict, they are—beyond their immediate interests in securing sovereignty over another land or people—*already* experiencing intangible gains. This argument appraises both conventional perspectives on war and prevailing

assumptions about what it means to be "at peace." For instance, a group's "gain" might consist of the pleasure received in depleting another's freedom.[5]

But this representation indicts that prevailing reality and challenges it in a way that shakes its foundation in the accepted presuppositions that constitute the very soil in which the oppressive apparatus is rooted, that is to say in the affective structure that orients the apperceptive field through which the morass of data concerning different experiences is filtered.

Du Bois achieves this in his work by inviting and facilitating empathy with the sufferers. He thereby encourages contempt for the conditions that engender and sustain the suffering and pain, and by doing it artistically he defies recrimination. Art, by avoiding the antinomies and endless modes of ratiocination to which conceptual and ordinary argumentative discourse is subject, strikes the participant/reader with a prophetically disorienting "word." In this instance, art functions to issue a challenge and a call to conversion. It is a call to see life through the eyes of the suffering, those who pain and pine away under the yoke of oppression. Herein lies the subversive power of memory when its truth is artistically preserved. There can be no doubt that Du Bois intended this work to perform precisely this prophetic function. Indeed, as Ed Blum has clearly shown, spiritually motivated prophetic intent permeates the entire Du Bois opus.[6]

It is in the chapter "On the Meaning of Progress" that the artistic representation of the dialectic reaches a crescendo. Here one gains an acute sense of the tragic effect of the presentation and the tragic reality it preserves. It must be borne in mind that I am not arguing simply for the effectiveness of presenting an experience in a certain way to facilitate empathy. I am arguing that it is an accurate reflection on the experience at an existential level. This is "their" life. The sense of life communicated through the narrative is the sense that one "understands" life or "knows" life (almost in the sense of a personal acquaintance of some kind). Writing of Oedipus, Sewall notes, "He is in no sense 'born again.' But he has enlarged his domain as a human being. He has a new sense of the powers that shape human destiny. Even, like Job, he has a new sense of kinship with them...."[7]

This deeper acquaintance with life is one of the effectual dynamics in producing the feeling of an uneasy kinship or strained comfort associated with the tragic effect by many theorists. Suddenly life is not so strange because one has experienced the range of its reality, even in the depths and horror of its wrath. Life is encountered and accepted at this level and, in fact, can only be authentically accepted at this level, that is to say, only once one has experienced it is its fullness. It is this "acceptance" that translates into a sense of "resignation."

This chapter has a distinctly melancholic mood. It is a "remembrance of things past." In this chapter Du Bois reminisces on his first teaching experience and his return to his same area later. At the opening of the chapter one can sense an atmosphere of excitement and hope. In the spring of his youth and career, armed with the inherent idealism and hope so characteristic of this phase of life, he moves across the hills of Tennessee to launch his career. He tells us how he found out about the job and his first encounter with the commissioner and the first intimations of the stubborn facticity of the shadow that would eventually steal across his swelling hopes. Those who would suggest that Du Bois's insights, depth, and acumen were somehow circumscribed by his "Victorian elitism" would do well to pay heed to his profoundly personal pathos and participation in the pain of the veil. Aside from the other considerations such as serving in African American institutions of higher education, administering the actual struggle for civil rights though years of hard labor with the NAACP, dying in exile, and so on, those who suggest he suffered from a shortsighted circumscription from their lofty positions in cushy white—might I say, elitist—universities would do well to consider his profound existential immersion in Jim Crow reality. Du Bois writes,

> Come in, said the commissioner—come in. Have a seat. Yes, that certificate will do. Stay to dinner. What do you want a month? "Oh, I thought, this is lucky": but even then fell the awful shadow of the veil for they ate first, then I alone.[8]

Again, he writes of a conversation he had upon his return ten years later.

> Uncle Bird was grayer and his eyes did not see so well, but he was still jovial. We talked of acres bought—one hundred and twenty-five—of the new guest chambers added, of Martha's remarrying. Then we talked of death; Fanny and Fred were gone; a shadow hung over the other daughter and when it lifted she was to go to Nashville to school. At last we spoke of the neighbors as night fell, Uncle Bird told me how on a night like that, Thenie came wandering back to her home over yonder, to escape the blows of her husband. And the next morning she

died in the home that her little bow-legged brothers, working and saving, had bought for their widowed mother.[9]

It is not difficult to see the dialectic of hope/affirmation and resignation played out in the context of a tragic view or sense of life in the passages quoted at some length above. The tragic sense of life emerges out of the play of the polarities in the living context of life provided here by the narrative form. It is a mood more-or-less that does not simply inhere in the literary structure of the text but rather one that is engendered by the encounter of the text with a living being capable of empathy and identification.

We must resist the temptation to see in Du Bois's representation of African American life nothing more than the implicit notion that "life is a mixture of the good and the bad." For to see what he has accomplished in this work in such simplistic terms would be a gross trivialization of a very profound insight. The categories of good and evil are mental constructions that are the result of the efforts of the human being to order and process experiences in accord with his prevailing value system. It is reflective and somewhat fictional. They are reflectively constructed and imposed on experience. (Even here, however, I am guilty of reification because the process by which these categories themselves are developed remains dialectical and interactional but still the fictional quality, once these categories are formulated, remains.) The tragic sense of life, however, occurs at a more primordial level. The experience at this level lies beyond good and evil. Berdyaev writes, "It is impossible to moralize about tragedy for it lies beyond good and evil." It is existentially prior to any sharp formulation of these categories. While humans may think in these terms and use these categories to try to make sense out of their experience and answer the question, "How ought I to live under any given circumstances?" they may yet feel and live in a tragic universe, though their reflective evaluations may seem to contradict it. Here, I will resist the temptation to elaborate the level and nature of the alienation this bifurcation implies. I will, however, return to this issue in a later chapter.

The two passages above can also be used to demonstrate how this genre or mode of presentation, its form, becomes one with the content. They operate dialectically, complementing each other and cohering in a powerful manifestation of the tragic moment. Let us now turn our attention to a more direct examination of the tragic as it manifests itself in the content.

The two passages quoted above are a part of the larger dialectic at work in this chapter as it plays itself out in a distinctly tragic and for our purposes paradigmatic fashion in the life of Jose. When we first encounter her, Jose is a paragon of virtue. She is a sterling example of everything virtuous, good and noble. In spite of the always already implied circumstance of oppression with all its concomitant burdens, she is nevertheless eager and full of hope. Before the close of the chapter, we see that "the slings and arrows of outrageous fortune" that in the nature of the case are structural conditions, pierce her gentle soul event by event until she is bled free of life. She does not die as a result of some fatal injustice, of some particular event. He suggests that what is even more tragic is that she is destroyed by life—by life against life. Endowed with a spirit of life that wells up in her powerful soul until it overflows, she is borne along by its terrible current, teeming with the elements that make life most worthwhile and set on a collision course with its equally terrible tide of historical circumstance. Her exuberant joy is transformed to utter terror. Life, like the Janus-faced Dionysus in Euripides' *Bacchae*, exalts and destroys in the same cruel stroke. For in the end, it is her nobility, her love, and her aspiration that set her up for demise. She soars so high on the wings of aspiration that the fall to the hard earth of circumstance knocks from her ennobled lung the precious breath of life.

Jose is of such a stature that she can best be understood and appreciated from the perspective of tragic heroine. She refuses to accept the limitations imposed on her by virtue of historical accident. At one level it is her own choice but then she is of such a spirit, which by the way is also a result of historical accident that it is meaningful to claim that she could not have "chosen" otherwise. In the end it is her refusal to accept that limitation that brings on the despair. Had she resigned herself to her circumstances or even at the end, her fate, had she not dreamed so deeply or held on so tenaciously, had she not cared so much, she would not have died. It was this hold that could not be broken that broke her. Her death suggests that she never let go. She was a member of the ghostly aristocracy of the spirit that haunts the deep places in the kingdom of the soul and indeed "of the manner born." Like Antigone, she preferred death to surrender. Had she lived it would have been at the cost of life but in dying the life in her transcended death. On the obvious question of whether Jose's suffering was merely pathetic or authentically tragic, we are instructed by Kaufman's reflections on the subject.

> Many writers distinguish sharply between what is merely pathetic and what is truly tragic. Not all of them invoke precisely the same criteria, but there is widespread agreement. The major point is that not all suffering is held to be truly tragic. The suffering hero must be great or noble; he must fail but be more admirable in catastrophe than ever before; the unhappy end must be inevitable and issue from the hero's own decision in a moral conflict in which disaster was inescapable whatever choice he made.[10]

There are serious challenges to some of the assumptions upon which this whole discussion rests, as Kaufman points out. Whatever position one assumes in these matters, however, it still remains true that there is a distinctly tragic brand of suffering that this discussion helped, somewhat, to clarify. Jose's suffering qualifies or at least argues for inclusion in that category even when narrowly construed.

There is something in her death that is purifying, disturbingly encouraging and, in the last instance, affirmative. Life and circumstance are deprived of complete victory for they are never able to destroy in her the values upon which her spirit rests. Life won out over life in death. "O death, where is thy sting? O grave, where is thy victory!" The human being, forced to contend in the realm of the gods holds her own, ennobling by her efforts the entire race. Her story was the story of the *believing "negro"* who against all hope, hopes anyhow. She never descends from the cross. Her aspirations, her dreams, which lived on even if only in her own imagination, and her moral sensitivity became, as it were, a thorny crown—but a crown nevertheless. In describing the Sophoclean conception of the tragic hero, Bernard M. W. Knox writes,

> Between these two views of the human situation, the Aeschylean and the Euripidean, these poles of hope and despair, Sophocles creates a tragic universe in which man's heroic action, free and responsible, brings him sometimes through suffering to victory at once; the suffering and the glory are fused in an indissoluble unity. Sophocles pits against the limitations on human stature great individuals who refuse to accept those limitations, and in their failure achieve a strange success.[11]

At the opening of the chapter entitled "Of the Meaning of Progress," Du Bois pictures Jose with an amazing zeal for life that catches the reader somewhat off guard. Her spirit is basically the opposite of everything her condition suggests that it should be. Her mood is upbeat, full of hope and overflowing.

> She seemed to be the center of the family; always busy at service.... She had about her a certain finesse, the shadow of an unconscious moral heroism that would willingly give all of life to make life broader, deeper and fuller for her and hers.[12]

After Du Bois describes the fateful eclipse of Jose's brother's potential as a result of being jailed due to a racially motivated entrapment and the toll it took on her when both brothers are forced to steal away becoming permanent fugitives; after describing how they were displaced, having to sell the old farm and move nearer to town and how Jose toiled to furnish it (her education no longer a possibility although something she still no doubt longed for), he writes,

> When spring came and the birds twittered and the stream ran proud and full, little sister Lizzie, bold, thoughtless, flush with the passion of youth, bestowed herself on the tempter and brought home a nameless child. Jose shivered and worked on, with the vision of school days fled, with a face wan and tired—worked until, on a summer's day, someone married another; then Jose crept to her mother, like a hurt child, and slept—and sleeps.[13]

In 1903, W. E. B. Du Bois, trained in German sociology and aware of the progressivist notion of history, no doubt well acquainted with the theories of the inevitability of human progress extant at the time, decades before Reinhold Niebuhr's classic critique of these ideas in *Faith and History*, prior to World War I or II, Hiroshima and Vietnam, by looking sensitively at the experiences of a few otherwise nameless black folk, raises this disturbing question, "How shall man measure progress there where dark Jose lies? How many heartfuls of sorrow shall balance a bushel of wheat?"[14] And then, in a characteristic shift that typifies the movement of the work as a whole, he keeps the dialectic meaningfully alive as he muses. "How hard a thing is life for the lowly and yet how human and real! And all this life and love and strife and failure—is it the twilight of the nightfall or the flush of some faint-dawning day?"[15]

Before moving on to a direct discussion of African American Christian consciousness, commonly referred to throughout this text as religious experience, I would like to further the analysis of some of the insights garnered thus far by locating them in a different semantic grid. My intention is to facilitate a deeper understanding and a broadened appreciation of the quality or psychic tone of the experience, as well as its complexity. One of the most consistent and egregious trends in the study of African American religious experience is oversimplification. Most treatments of African American religious experience tend toward the historical, theological, and the social ethical with the notable exceptions of C. Eric Lincoln, E. Franklin Frazier, Charles Long, James Noel, and in addition, Howard Thurman, Dwight Hopkins, and Anthony Pinn at points and the deeper existentialist strains in the opus of James Cone. Moreover the abiding racist assumption that African Americans are child-like, easy to understand, constitutionally devoid of complexity, and so on, have become divorced, perhaps, from the original racist intent but are for that matter no less demeaning. I think the situation is the opposite. The nuance and extreme complexity of the African American engagement of religion in the Americas calls for the broadest application of available disciplines and commands serious academic research and attention. In fact I think the entire African American trajectory in religious experience must be rethought and reconfigured in light of the wealth of information now available in studies of loss, trauma, traumatic loss, coping, and chronic stress. I believe any attempt to think through the implicit and explicit theological meaning and implications of the experience must take place within an expanded phenomenological field of understanding with an explanatory moment. I hope that in some small way this text will serve as a contribution to that end.

I plan to use dynamic categories in this portion of our examination stemming from the psychoanalysis of Sigmund Freud and the derivative self psychology of Heinz Kohut. I will employ something roughly approaching "clinical license" in the use of these insights, avoiding for the moment, the rather thorny methodological issues implied in applied psychoanalysis, not to mention the more-than-formidable epistemological questions. I admit at the outset the experimental and speculative flavor of this venture but insist on its usefulness and the value of its insights.

The "dynamic" semantic grid has at least scientific aspirations and possesses a universalizing intentionality that facilitates the linking of the unique experience under examination to our common human experience. It helps to provide points of contact at a disciplinary level, inviting and encouraging a wider conversation, whereby others may gain a healthier appreciation and perhaps some level of empathy for the experience though they may not have shared in its particularity.

African American culture has, to say the least, wide appeal in America and throughout the world. It has exerted unparalleled influence on popular culture in America and the world over. Its powerful strain and familiar cords, its rhythms, cadences and tonality are readily identifiable. There is a resistance in some quarters of the larger society to recognize the uniqueness of *anything* African American because of a strange combination of their attraction to it, which implies value, while at the same time feeling the need to deny the capability of African Americans to contribute anything of worth to the wider world community that can be called uniquely their own. This problem becomes particularly prominent when the contribution is linked to or identified as a product of African American pain. The implicit indictment and the suggestion of the ongoing nature of African American oppression grate against the white American cultural apparatus of *denial* and the apparatus of cultural *disavowal* in some quarters of the African American community. One consequence of this strange and contradictory stance has been the tendency of many whites to mimic African American forms of expression effectively dispossessing African Americans and feeding a perverted hunger to portray themselves to themselves as the originator or cause of all things of worth.

African American cultural expression is the moving force behind so much of popular American culture and its appeal around the world. The appeal of our oratory and music in American culture goes far beyond the simple and trite notion that it sounds good or that it makes folk feel good. The larger question is, "Why does it sound good to us?" Again, "Why does it make us feel better?" Questions such as these get little to no serious attention partly or perhaps primarily, due to the tendency in the West to devalue everything associated with emotions or feelings. Everything in the West that has been too closely associated with feelings or the emotions experiences a distinct devaluation due to the deeply and firmly entrenched prevailing white patriarchal mind-set. There is something inherent in the cultural strains of the African American that awakens, or at least stirs, something basic in almost all who encounter it openly and authentically, particularly in this age of the "tragic man." It is "the deep calling unto deep." Henry Wadsworth Longfellow, in his deeply moving poem "The Slave Singing at Midnight," captures this at multiple levels, including the power of the slave's expression, its tragic ambiguity, the dialectic of hope and resignation, joy and sorrow, and its powerful appeal across race and culture to something profoundly human. It is peculiarly disclosive.

> Loud he sang the Psalm of David!
> He, a Negro and enslaved,
> Sang of Israel's victory,
> Sang of Zion bright and free.
>
> In that hour, when night is calmest,
> Sang he from the Hebrew Psalmist,
> In a voice so sweet and clear
> That I could not choose but hear,
>
> Songs of triumph, and ascriptions,
> Such as reached the swart Egyptians,
> When upon the Red Sea coast
> Perished Pharaoh and his host.
>
> And the voice of his devotion
> Filled my soul with strange emotion;
> For its tones by turns were glad,
> Sweetly solemn, and wildly sad.
>
> Paul and Silas, in their prison,
> Sang of Christ, the Lord arisen.
> And an earthquake's arm of might
> Broke their dungeon-gates at night.
>
> But, alas! What holy angel
> Brings the slave this glad evangel?
> And what earthquake's arm of might
> Breaks his dungeon-gates at night?

In the text *The Restoration of the Self,* as he accounts for some of the differences of emphases as well as theoretical formulations in his approach versus those of Sigmund Freud and classical psychoanalysis, Heinz Kohut argues that this epoch is less characterized by "guilty man" than it is by "tragic man."[16] He argues that the problem of our time is how to overcome the wholesale tendencies toward the fragmentation of the self, emptiness, meaninglessness, and despair rather than how to deliver the self shackled by neurotic guilt engendered by anxiety over sexuality. Kohut argues for a qualitative difference between the type of anxiety that characterizes tragic man than that characterizing guilty man.

> The second [that of tragic man] comprises the anxieties experienced by a person who is becoming aware that his self is beginning to disintegrate; whatever the trigger that ushered in or reinforced the progressive dissolution of the self, the emphasis of the experience lies in essence on the precarious state of the self and not on the factors that may have set the process of disintegration into motion.[17]

While considering the gradual process of enlightenment experienced by the subject in therapy, he gives us another clear description of the state of being that characterizes the tragic man.

> And the expression of the ill defined yet intense and pervasive anxiety that accompanies a patient's dawning awareness that his self is disintegrating (severe fragmentation, serious loss of initiative, profound drop in self esteem, sense of utter meaninglessness) also may initially be veiled; the analysand may attempt to express his awareness of the frightening alterations in the state of his self through the medium of verbalizations about circumscribed fears—and it is only gradually and against resistances that his associations will begin to communicate the central content of his anxiety which, indeed, he can only describe with the aid of analogies and metaphors.[18]

African American religious experience and its expression, in particular, as well as various, more general cultural forms of expression have developed in response to, among other things, the kind of fragmentation anxiety that broadly characterizes this epoch. According to Gary Greif this is the function of culture as opposed to civilization in Kohut's view.

> A culture provides a selfobject atmosphere in ways similar to those in which an individual habitually relives self experiences as structures of the self. Just as self structures depend on past selfobject experiences to keep selfobject support alive within an individual, so a culture relies on shared memories of self object experiences throughout society. And just as self structures are activated through images associated with common selfobject experiences, so cultures depend on shared images which are associated with common selfobject experiences and which therefore serve to activate and sustain them. Images associated with past selfobject experiences promote renewal of self structures and therefore function as a means for sustaining self vitality. If such

experiences have been associated with images and activities shared by a large number of individuals, the images and practices are the means for sustaining a culture.¹⁹

Fragmentation anxiety in all essentials was certainly a constituent element in the fabric of intersubjectivity and subjective experience of African Americans during and after slavery continuing right up to the present and likely to go on. The individualistic presuppositions inherent in both classical psychoanalysis and self psychology are fundamental, theoretical weaknesses due primarily to the sociocultural and intellectual matrix by which these thinkers were conditioned. Therefore, I think that any theoretical application of the dynamic categories arising out of these schools of thought must be augmented to include in the etiology of "fragmentation anxiety" or "melancholia" (Freud) other crucial social and cultural factors. This move is even more crucial when exploring those societies, or peoples for whom these other dimensions are crucial in significant psychological processes and when, particularly for our purposes, determining the quality of subjectivity and identify formation. Finally, I will be employing these concepts at a phenomenological level, which means that the metapsychological considerations that ground the insights we will be employing are not as theoretically significant for our purposes as the insights themselves.

There are some illuminating insights and some provocative parallels in Freud's discussion of melancholia and its relation to mania and the African American experience of what I have identified as the dialectic of hope and resignation, particularly its manifestation in religious expression. The pervasive presence of the experience of melancholia is referred to by most serious observers of African Americans and their cultural forms of expression. It was present in the "sorrow songs" and the mournful chants of the slaves of yesterday, as well as in the blues, traditional gospel, and the lyrical preaching extant in the African American churches of today. It was apparently present from the very beginning. It was observed during the earliest of contact with the captured and enslaved African. Vincent Harding writes,

> But like so much of our singing and dancing at white command ever since, the activity was not primarily for our benefit or entertainment, but for white profits, ordered because dancing was considered therapeutic, was supposed to ensure us against the "melancholy" that drove countless thousands of Africans to suicide in the course of the middle passage.²⁰

The relationship between this expression of melancholy and the experience of traumatic loss should be borne in mind throughout this discussion. It will serve as a fundamental link in our reasoning as our examination progresses. Again Harding writes,

> And what were the songs we sang? One doctor who served on the English ship "young Hero" spoke with great accuracy when he said, "They sang, but not for their amusement. The captain ordered them to sing and they sang songs of sorrow. Their sickness, fear of being beaten, their hunger, and their memory of their country...are the usual subjects." Then late at night after their songs were over, from the darkness of the lower decks of the "young Hero" and a thousand other ships, the sailors often would hear "an howling melancholy noise, expressive of extreme anguish."[21]

Freud is not, of course examining the expression of melancholy in his papers, but rather the psychological condition. We must however link the internal state to the external expression in cultural forms to appreciate (1) the expression as a symptom of and cipher to subjectivity; (2) understand how that cultural form aids or impedes healthy or unhealthy adaptation and (3) its possible religious and/or philosophical significance. Peter Homan's points this out in commenting on Jay Winter's *Sites of Mourning: The Great War in European Cultural History*.

> It then turns to cultural reflections on the war, represented by interwar artistic experimentations and movements in literature, the arts, and popular religiosity. The process of collective or mass mourning is the single thread linking these clusters. Winter's focus is how mourning and cultural symbols came together—how a people can create ceremonies, religious beliefs, monuments, and art in response to their shared loss, and how the workings of the culture they have created can represent and to some extent heal the wounds of loss and the sufferings it causes.[22]

The condition of melancholia was the appropriate response to the traumatic loss, chronic existential taxation, and marginalization endured by the Africans/African Americans. The condition of loss, as I have mentioned, became institutionalized and chronic. It is its chronicity that served as the ferment for the development of the cultural by-products as well as their assuaging, therapeutic, even adaptive, meaning-making qualities.

Indications of the presence of something bearing a distinct family resemblance to melancholia and its psychological complement, mania, by way of symptomatology (and, as I might add, in the context of the aforementioned dialectic), as well as its chronicity is evidenced in the following observation taken from Du Bois's classic.

> The mass of those to whom slavery was a dim recollection of childhood found the world a puzzling thing; it asked little of them, and they answered with little and yet it ridiculed their offering. Such a paradox they could not understand, and therefore sank into listless indifference or shiftlessness, or reckless bravado.[23]

The "listless indifference or shiftlessness" referred to in the passage above bears witness to a phenomenon fundamentally related to melancholia and the "reckless bravado," to something fundamentally related to mania, an aspect of the same psychological complex.

Of the symptomatology of melancholia, Freud writes,

> The distinguishing mental features of melancholia are a profoundly painful dejection, abrogation of interest in the outside world, loss of the capacity to love, inhibition of all activity and a lowering of the self-regarding feelings to a degree that finds utterance in self-reproaches and self-revilings, and culminates in a delusional expectation of punishment.[24]

Careful consideration of recurrent phenomena in the cultural expressions of African Americans in an interdisciplinary framework holds promising possibilities in helping to solve many riddles surrounding the mysterious mind-set and the concomitant complications of the African American. In my consideration of what I call the "theological unconscious of the African American Church" I will argue that there is an appreciable difference between what a group or an individual for that matter may believe in terms of intellectual assent or discursive rationalization and what they may believe in a functional sense at the level of emotional, existential or psychological reality. The tongue of psychic depths, that often indecipherable, unknown language of the soul that manifests itself in paradoxes such as mournful shouts of joy, often tells a story far different from that of the common tongue. Only through the great pains, a heroic hermeneutic of sorts, may we access the mysterious truth emergent from the chthonic depths of the human being in intense and intensely prolonged duress.

This point is particularly crucial in forming an informed view of African American Christian consciousness, its uniqueness and the significance of its theological contribution. For instance, the belief system of the evangelical brand of antebellum and post–Civil War American Christianity provided an available foil for feelings such as those Freud identifies as part and parcel of the melancholic frame of mind, such as self-deprecations, abrogation of interest in the outside world, lowering of the self-regarding feelings to the point of self-revilings, delusional expectation of punishment, and so on. Religious language legitimizes this state of being, in many cases encourages it, clothes it symbolically, and mystifies it, locking it away behind an impenetrable wall of piety. Considerations such as these will help us understand the different meanings these evangelical, linguistic (conceptual, doctrinal) expressions of the Christian faith held for African Americans versus whites, as well as the different levels of meaning they operated on. It will also help us to adjudicate the ways and the extent to which the African American's encounter of the Christian faith was and is a healthy or unhealthy experience. Let us now return, however, to the crux of our initial examination.

Freud also suggests that a further complication of the condition of melancholia may be that the individual is unable to adopt a new loved object, except in so much as it reminded the person of the lost object, since that would imply replacing the lost loved object.[25] (At the risk of an awkward complication and anticipation of later reflections, I might point out that this dimension of the experience, in the African American case, while in no wise serving as the primary explanation may represent a complicating factor in their inability to accept the new land as home.) I will speak more to this subject later. In the same paper, he points out that "the most remarkable peculiarity of melancholia, and one most in need of explanation, is the tendency it displays to turn into mania accompanied by a completely opposite symptomatology."[26]

Dealing with the manifestation of a group phenomenon is naturally more difficult than that of an individual easily placed under the careful scrutiny of a clinical context. Yet it is possible, once certain conclusions have been reached concerning the nature of certain experiences isolated in the clinical context, to hazard guarded generalizations when warranted by observation. Having said that, admitting that the characteristics of the "clinical manifestation" of melancholia are not present in an obvious form in all African Americans at all times, I do think that they do exist in most to differing degrees and subsist and manifest themselves at different levels in individuals and the group as a whole and certainly the appeal of collective cultural forms to the group indicates a reservoir of common experience. I can say with a significant degree of certainty that the loss of self-esteem or at least a severely damaged sense of selfhood and refracted self-image, as well as a lowering of regard for the group as a whole, permeates the African American experience. This experience is usually accounted for by indicating the internalization of the definitions of the African American housed in the cultural taxonomy and lexicon of modern America with its symbolic surplus of meaning. While this is a significant factor I do not believe that the common explanation accounts for or exhausts the explanation of the presence of this damaged sense of self or for its stubborn resistance to the rational argumentation leveled at the ideology of inferiority. We are, however, still working at the level of symptomatology. More to the point for our purposes is the generative conditions of this state of "chronic melancholia." I would like to make one final note at this point concerning our broadened application of Freud's explication of this concept. Freud himself does in fact hold out the possibility that there may be variations in the manifestation of this condition.

The melancholic mood and its "symptoms" are engendered, according to Freud, by the loss of a love object.[27]

> In one class of cases it is evident that melancholia too may be the reaction to a loved object; where this is not the exciting cause, one can perceive that there is a loss of a more ideal kind.[28]

In the African American experience the melancholic mood complex is not simply the result of the loss of family, friends, and so on, that took place at capture continuing through the lifetime for first generation slaves, family sales, and separations throughout slavery, but also the loss of land, culture, security, bodily integrity, and control. Moreover, there was the destabilization of all primary and other significant interpersonal relationships in the peculiar institution, through actual loss, or, at the very least, the ever-present threat of the same—due of course to the designation of the slave population as chattel. This state of affairs served to exacerbate the deep ontological insecurity endemic to the situation. The loss of the basic sense of security and control engendered what would be referred to in dynamic language as regressive responses and the disturbances or I should say the chronic destabilization of basic trust systems within a traumatic field created fragmentation and the threat of emptiness. The sparagmous was intersubjective, reflected in external and internal realities.

During periods of crisis persons in which the basic conditions of security and control are threatened or lost, by the very nature of the case attempt to return to that which is foundational in human experience, that which gives us a sense of rootedness and belonging, defining for us the who and the what we are, i.e., the transcendental conditions of "Dasein"—land and culture. This reclamation/reaffirmation of the "who" and what we are yields, or tends toward, an affirmation of the meaningfulness of life. Land and culture represent the fortress in which a beleaguered humanity takes refuge when overwhelmed by destructive and bewildering forces and events. Due to the nature of the peculiar institution, African Americans did not have an existentially available "land" of their own and only scattered retentions of their own culture which themselves remained available only in an existentially ambiguous sense. This resulted from the overarching cultural ambience, traumatic field, and geographical location that, in contextualizing the existential appropriation of retentions, effectively limited their existential availability.

Since the *absence* of land and culture as well as the concomitant stability that results from being firmly ensconced in a nexus of stable and secure relations were constituent elements of the institutional arrangement, they became constitutive dynamics in the formation of African American experience as such. This is crucial. Langdon Gilkey writes,

> Somehow each self needs a "place" in order to be a self, in order to feel on a deep level that it really exists. We are apparently rootless beings at bottom. Unless we can establish roots somewhere in a place where we are at home, which we possess to our selves where our things are, we feel that we float, that we are barely there at all. For, to exist with no place is to fail to exist altogether.[29]

As John W. Blassingame points out, the slave did create some space in the slave quarters. Nevertheless, this place as well as their own bodies and labor remained the master's property. No place was free from arbitrary intrusion, interruption, or disruption for that matter. Even after manumission the ownership of property still could not provide a ground for a firm sense of identity rooted in the available nexus of meanings implied in the label "American"; for they still lived *in* a "land" that was not their own. The way to claiming America as their own was effectively barred by the persistence of the cultural taxonomies and definitions that sustained the marginalization of the descendants of slaves. This marginalization or the fact that the African American's position on the sociocultural topography of America is still extremely ambiguous and this sense of still having no place "to be" continues. This fact is and has been from the beginning reinforced through a legal system that operates with a terrible and obvious double standard that serves as a constant reminder that the question of the color line has yet to be settled. African Americans are still unsettled and cannot comfortably rest where we are.

If one is without land, one can find root and grounding only in an identity provided by a strong cultural heritage, as with the Jews, for instance. Of course, in the case of the Jews there was a much more coherent attachment to a particular parcel of land than that found among the descendants of African slaves. Moreover, they did not have the same difficulty appropriating their land as African Americans did because of the way Africa was defined, evaluated, and represented. The symbolic internalization of Africa as their land was seriously disturbed by, among other things, the racist characterizations of life on the "dark" continent.

When one is without "a land" or a coherent culture, one has no place to stand. This fundamental disturbance of the ontological security of African slaves and their descendants was exacerbated by the unusually harsh and oppressive circumstances of daily life. Cruelty was rife, and the personal relations that could render life a bit more bearable were themselves fragile, threatened, and often destroyed. The situation made the need for the very things that the slave was forced to live without, the more pressing and urgent. There is no place of grace, no area of life left uncovered by the pall of nonbeing. Under these circumstances identity becomes diffuse; the situation becomes perplexing and potentially absurd as the forces of primordial chaos surge on every side, and the self becomes fragmented, depleted, and torn. This is the matrix out of which the unique religious experience of the African American emerged and the circumstances to which it was a response.

Chapter 4

Deep Calls unto Deep: African American Christian Consciousness Pt. I

In an attempt to articulate what I consider to be the salient features of African American Christian consciousness I will make extensive use of *The Souls of Black Folk* and "The Religion of the American Negro," both authored by Du Bois, and will also draw upon Friedrich Nietzsche's vision of the tragic, first articulated in his classic study *The Birth of Tragedy,* then further developed and fleshed out during the course of his lifetime.[1] It is my opinion that Du Bois's *Souls* is to date the classic work on identifying the distinctive elements and spirit of the African American religious (Christian) experience. Unlike many of his successors, Du Bois did not conflate the normative task of the theologian and the descriptive moment of analysis. He had no theological ax to grind and no latent or manifest theological agenda, just a profound appreciation of the depth and power of the experience itself.

On the other hand, he did not launch into any self-conscious attempt to analyze the deep structures of the experience, seemingly content with a rudimentary identification of the primary elements and their mode of manifestation. An analysis of the deep structure or structures of the experience is necessary, however, to fully appreciate the meaning of the experience to the individual and the collective community. An analysis of this experience will also facilitate a deeper appreciation of the creative responses of human beings under oppressive conditions and the part that religious and cultural resources play in the process of adaptation and psychic survival. Put another way, it shows how these resources are employed to stave off complete absorption in the social and psychic death that pervades and everywhere threatens to completely consume the living lost of the slaveocracy. In the instance of the African American, it will also help to appreciate the depth and multilayered nature of communal suffering, by unearthing and articulating a dimension of the experience that has heretofore been taken for granted as understood. This dimension is, while all but impossible to explicate using so-called empirical forms of analysis, pivotal to the understanding of black being in America, past, present, and future.

African American religious experience as a cultural product took shape in the crucible of stark and multilayered oppression. It did not develop in an historical vacuum. It evolved at a time when European colonialism was in full swing, bringing in its train the inevitable clash of cultures; a time when certain assumptions having to do with color, nationality, and the nature and destiny of "man" were becoming entrenched in the discursive consciousness of the West. Both the African and European experience played a part in the development of and evolution of this distinct experience in religion, but not at the same levels. Part of the difficulty with previous attempts to determine the distinctiveness of the African American experience of the Christian faith is that there was little nuance in the differentiation of levels of influences and a less-than-sophisticated appreciation of the historically constituted nature of subjectivity.

The evaluations have taken place in a flattened out, one-dimensional universe where different elements are identified, then teased out and compared ("side by side") to see whether or not there were enough identifiably distinct African elements to justify a claim of uniqueness. This has been a fundamental flaw in most previous analyses.

It is my position that the particular configuration of elements derived from the European and African heritages under the dynamos of prevailing circumstances with their inherent ambiguities and contradictions, complemented by the dire need for subjective adaptation and psychic survival, yielded the bittersweet fruit of the tragic soul life of the African American. We shall now move to a description of the psychic tone and texture of the experience, and from there to an articulation of the generative or deeper structure of African American Christian consciousness.

One root feature and the most identifiable element of the experience is the pervasive sense of suffering and a magisterial sorrow elegantly portrayed in poetry, sermon, and song. The suffering of the African American is woven deeply into the warp and woof of his religion. Traditional African American religious expression and spirituality in its most authentic mode approaches the character of a dirge or lament. It is commonly believed and argued that the characteristic element of our experience is joy or celebration. This is, however, a superficial view of the experience that has cheapened it considerably, refracting serious study and precluding a depth understanding of African American spirituality. There is a powerful strain of something approaching joy present in the mix, but it is wrapped in a foil of sorrow, anguish, and lament. It would be easy for those who have not been a part of the community, those who are viewing the experience from outside the total range of feelings and experiences constituting the daily life of African America, to characterize it as celebration or cheap emotional exuberance. Then, too, there are those who, perhaps under the pressure to belong, have succumbed to a psychic mechanism akin to identification with the aggressor and internalized the caricatures and misconstrue both the nature and the depth of the experience. Some misdirected others claiming an epistemological privilege that inheres in a presumed ontological blackness have set up as normative their own poorly understood, shallow sense of the experience firmly couched in caricature. The irony is that the same white institutions that often operate under the sway of the caricature serve to legitimize and validate these persons and portrayals in both communities. Consciousness however is not transparent to itself; no, not even in the oppressed or the educated among them. The joy of African American religious experience is a joy dogged by reality. It is the glow of an illuminated shadow; a veil sewn from the rich tapestry of an ambiguous cloth. Then again, this flight to cheap celebration may be motivated by the fear of the chthonic depths and the horrors they hold for those who dare draw near. Perhaps, too, the horrors of one's own depths, akin to the dark and strident tones of an African American spirituality that tells us that even in joy there is a heart of darkness, encourages flight into the flat surfaces of a two-dimensional faith.

Some African American religious thinkers and practitioners under the sway of certain unquestioned and inherited theological presuppositions (you see this a lot with those from the Pentecostal community and those under its influence) rush to deny any elements of pessimism or despair in African American religious expression. Such a thing you see would be considered, from a normative theological standpoint, unacceptable. So they cheapen the whole experience and trivialize the pain of African Americans by saying or implying they were celebratory (with that optimistic shading) in spite of their condition. According to these persons the fact that there was no despair makes African

Americans not just good Christians but faithful people of "the way." It is, of course ridiculous, simplistic, and not a little childish (another instance of the caricature). This is a knee-jerk defensive posture of so many who feel it incumbent upon them to justify the rightness of everything African American according to whatever values they happen to hold as normative. The cheap celebratory mode is more akin to optimism than hope. It is unable to speak meaningfully to the reality of having to hold the titanic tensions generated by deep aspiration and seemingly insurmountable obstacles together. The depth and value of African American religious experience, however, may lie in precisely the presence of a heroic pessimism.

> The union of Apollo and Dionysus expresses the essence of Nietzsche's tragic view which, as noted above, is also defined as "pessimism and its overcoming." However, in defining it thus, we have to bear in mind that the concepts of "tragedy," "pessimism," and "overcoming" are not used by Nietzsche in a familiar or traditional sense. The tragic view, although growing out of a pessimistic foundation, is nonetheless positive, leading to the affirmation of the totality of life and being, where even the negative and destructive aspects are seen as necessary and ultimately productive.[2]

The far deeper and more courageous faith, indeed the one most resonant with the traumatic depth of African American suffering, is the one that embraces the pessimism of strength, for it accepts reality, absorbs it, but is always "overcoming its darkness," even through creative affirmation of life's worth and value. Let me be clear. The "overcoming" is not rebuke or denial, but absorption and transvaluation. It is not a going against but rather a going through!

> This process does not aim at the total abolishment of the pessimistic foundation of life; rather, it is based on the awareness of its inevitability and its creative force, and on the recognition that annihilation and origination, good and evil, abyss and height, belong together and form an inseparable unity in the creative activity of nature and man.[3]

Again, there is a powerful affirmation of the life (i.e., joy) present, but it is meaningful and properly understood only when placed in the context of great existential strain, sorrow, and anguish. This joy has never been the shallow emotionalism African Americans have often been accused of by both those within the community and those outside it. It is, rather, a deep affirmation of something primal that asserts itself only after or in the midst of some great crucifixion. You may think here of blind Oedipus, Job on his ash heap, or Christ on his cross. The experience is not the escapist self-indulgence of a frenzied imagination, nor is it the delusional experience of those who are not in touch with the grave reality of their circumstances. The experience has within its *mood and structure* a profound acknowledgment of the contradictions and limits of life regardless of an individual subject's ability to express this discursively. It cannot be accurately characterized by stoic resignation, chthonic despair, or Olympian triumphalism. It is Dionysian. It is, in a word, tragic in its mood, matrix, and message.

The joy of the slave was, at one time and the same time, an affirmation and a longing. It was a longing given concrete expression through the symbolic medium of a deeply aestheticized religious expression. Levine has argued,

> The religious music of the slave is almost devoid of feelings of depravity or unworthiness, but is rather, as I have tried to show, pervaded by a sense of change, transcendence, ultimate justice, and personal worth. The spirituals have been referred to as "sorrow songs," and in some respects they were. The slaves sang of "rollin' thro' an unfriendly world," of being called "a-troubled in de mind," of living in a world which was a "howling wilderness," "a hell to me," of feeling like "a motherless child," "a po' little orphan chile in de worl'," a "home-less child," of fearing that "trouble will bury me down."
>
> But these feelings were rarely pervasive or permanent; almost always overshadowed by a triumphant note of affirmation.[4]

Levine's statement that the sorrow was not pervasive betrays a fundamental misunderstanding of the organic relationship between the sorrow and joy. However, they may play out diachronically in the process of expression, the fact of the matter is that the experience of sorrow and longing is a structural reality in African American Christian consciousness. They are a generative dynamic and, as such, they are constants. Therefore, to discuss them at the level of pervasiveness in terms of their "textual" expression is to make something of a category error. Had he argued that the religious music, that is, expression, of the slave was pervaded by a "longing" for change and ultimate justice rather than a "sense of change" and "ultimate justice," he would have been right on target.

There were few feelings of depravity expressed because of the sociocultural climate they were in. There was no need to dehumanize oneself with a theology of worthlessness when one considers that their worthlessness as human being was deeply embedded in the routinized modes of interaction with their "superiors" and the cultural taxonomies with which they lived daily. Unlike most white Christians, the slave needed no pious catechism on human depravity to be convinced of the vagaries of life afforded mankind by virtue of his wickedness. And with a more nuanced analysis of the experience, Levine would have realized that the affirmation of personal worth was really an affirmation of the worthwhileness of life in the face of the threat of meaninglessness and nonbeing and that this affirmation took place at another level of the experience than the one implied in his assessment.

Levine did not appreciate the tragic texture of the experience, in which the sorrow and the joy are always already intermingled, each presupposing in the quality of its psychological, emotional, and spiritual tone the presence of the other. One could draw the conclusion that there is something of a pathological bifurcation, schizophrenia of sorts, in the cultural consciousness of African Americans. This, however, is not the case. It is no indication of ignorance, confusion, lack of theoretical or theological coherence, or spiritual immaturity that the spirituals, and even the later development of traditional gospels, often demonstrated these seemingly conflicting tendencies in one and the same song. This dialectic actually extends clearly into the present in forms as unlikely, to the untrained eye, as some instances of so-called "gangsta' rap." In fact, anyone familiar with the living reality of the experience can attest to the fact that these tendencies are often expressed in one and the same sermon! Here the attempt is clearly to give discursive articulation to beliefs. But for religious expression to be effective in a traumatic environment, it must mirror the experience of the worshipper, thereby affirming his or her worth.

It is often the "mood" of the presentation that reflects the "dark" and melancholic side of the experience, whereas the ideological content reflects the profound aspirations, tensions, conflicts, and contradictions of the African American religious temperament. The linguistic level is, however, more often than not, shot through with references and allusions to the dark and somber side, but always is a (paradoxically) moment of or movement toward existential affirmation. While it is true that this affirmation (hope) is often couched in the traditional conceptual scheme of Christian triumphalism, it would be a mistake to make an exhaustive identification with the ideas of, say, Christ's all-powerful and perpetual presence with "the hope" that has characterized the African American experience of the faith.

In a very real sense, the depth affirmation of which the hope, couched in traditional Christian phraseology, is an expression is ontologically prior to any self-conscious linguistic formulation. When considered properly in the larger framework of African American historical experience, we are able to see then that the Christian gospel provides for a convenient but not unambiguous mode of expression for an experience that is fundamentally human and so fundamental that it is prior to and broader than the categories provided by any particular religion's conceptual scheme.

This hopefulness, which is always at once a longing, is not to be confused with the cheeriness of a blanket reassurance free of doubt and ambiguity. At root, the hopefulness that we encounter when we review the experience is a fundamental existential affirmation that manifests itself in an aspiration or longing born of lack, disparity, and the "Sturm und Drang" of the peculiar institution and its sociocultural, mutant offspring. It is a state of being, a very different experience from that which we commonly refer to as *hopeful*. It is an affirmation that lends to life the existential impact of hope. One presses on. This level is reached only after "hopes" have been challenged and the fundamental stabilities of a person's or a group's existence have been disturbed. This experience is the result of a decision about how to respond to the implied question inherent in the existentially ambiguous position of all human beings at the "limits," "To be or not to be?" It is the presence of the power to do so, that is, to say "to be," that is commonly referred to as *joy* or *celebration*. But here again I must press the point that this must be understood in the living context of what it is to be of African descent in America.

The African American lives under circumstances that facilitate frequent and intense encounters with the limits of life. The sociocultural context of the African American fostered and continues to foster profound and disturbing ambiguity. The African American community is a traumatized community in which the traumatizing forces are institutionalized and embedded in daily linguistic and social practices, making the experience an intersubjective field and, therefore, chronic. As a result of the initial trauma, wherein the common frames of meaning and interpersonal relations were permanently disrupted, destroyed, or subject to arbitrary destruction, the African in America had to live with and somehow cope with profound uncertainty and ambiguity. Life became Janus faced and threateningly disorienting for her, and she never knew what face it would reveal. Even the best of the experience amounted mostly to relief from its most menacing aspects.

The experience became as profound as it did, when it did, because there was no consistent, coherent, symbolic/conceptual system or frame of reference that could facilitate the domestication of these hostile experiences, if, in fact, such a thing could have existed, given the nature of the case. In the shadows of the slave experience the absurd, therefore, would always lurk with the full weight of its menacing presence.

The African did retain some of her worldview despite slave breaking, slave codes, cultural restrictions, and the Middle Passage, but it became more and more remote and the vestiges fainter as succeeding generations were born on American soil. While elements of their worldview became more and more remote, they were prohibited from fully assimilating into the larger culture. Hence, they were locked out of participation in those areas of American life by which meaningful existence was generated and defined, and left with only fragments and vestigial elements of their former culture. A lengthy quote from Levine sums up the matter well.

> Slave songs provide us with the beginnings of a very different kind of hypothesis: that the preliterate, pre-modern Africans, with their sacred worldview, were so imperfectly acculturated into secular American society into which they were thrust, were so completely denied access to the ideology and dreams which formed the core of the consciousness of other Americans, that they were forced to fall back upon the only cultural frames of reference that made any sense to them and gave them any feeling of security.... True acculturation was denied to most slaves. The alternatives were either to remain in a state of cultural limbo, divested of the old cultural patterns but not allowed to adopt those of their new homeland—which in the long run is no alternative at all—or to cling to as many as possible of the old ways of thinking and acting. The slaves' oral tradition, their music, and their religious outlook served this latter function and constituted a cultural refuge at least potentially capable of protecting their personalities from some of the worse ravages of the slave system.[5]

It should be pointed out that even in those minor instances and dimensions of existence where the slave was allowed to participate, it was always already in the sociocultural space constituted by the language and practice of domination. Hence, there was no affirmative experience of culture free from the inherent ambiguities fostered by the peculiar institution. Even his participation in the Christian experience was colored by his status. The Christian slave was aware that his religion was that of the oppressor, at the very least in a nominal sense. It is arguable, then, that even the acculturation that did take place served to exacerbate the ambiguity of slave existence, while at the same time providing some of the only, albeit limited, resources available for coming to terms with the existential disequilibrium spawned by the total matrix. This is quintessential tragic ambiguity and conflict.

One of the residuals of African culture was musical form. The music hidden in the soul of the African remained very much a part of his being. Because of the nature of music, the aesthetic expression of the soul of a people, it lingered just beyond the effect of the slave-breaking process, though not beyond its mournful spawn. It became one of the essential elements of the African American religious experience, although it was of course altered in the American context. This point should not be underestimated if one is to understand the experience. It was through the musical, or, more broadly, through the aesthetic dimension that the unique African American soul took shape, this aesthetic dimension through which every people express their core aspirations and affections.

When I speak of the fact that the music was altered, I do not wish to suggest that it was simply Europeanized, although some Europeanization did take place, particularly when theological categories provided the linguistic, symbolic, and conceptual foil for the expression. Moreover, when one is estimating the significance of Europeanization, one must take pains to identify the level on which it took place and what significance it might then have for the experience taken as a whole. The way in which the aesthetic soul of the African, and its musical expression, was transformed and the subsequent forms it took and developed into was determined by the specificity of African American historicity.

> The music of Negro religion is that plaintive rhythmic melody, with its touching minor cadences, which, despite caricature and defilement, still remains the most original and beautiful expression of human life and longing yet born on American soil. Sprung from the African forests, where its counterpart can still be heard, it was adapted, changed, and intensified by the tragic soul life of the slave, until, under the stress of law and whip, it became the one true expression of a people's sorrow, despair and hope.[6]

I have taken such pains to point up the intense existential ambiguity of the African American experience because it is essential for appreciating the tragic core and genius of the religiocultural expression. The power of the experience and its value as a mode of adjustment and adaption—in a word, its existential genius—is that it facilitates life amid intense ambiguity, extensive fragmentation, fragmentation anxiety, and personal as well as communal anguish and pain. It was the living expression and manifestation of the grace to "go on" amid unanswered questions, the magnitude of which always threatened and might at any time destroy the "will to live." This miracle of "spiritual" adaptation takes place precisely at the "limits" of life when ideology, thought, and belief systems have been stripped away, broken down, or otherwise rendered ineffective by overwhelming circumstances, in performing their normal function of facilitating the assimilation of experience in a way that preserves the meaningfulness of life. It facilitates life when the power of any and all frames of reference to answer the question of the "why's of life" (as experienced in and through one's particularity) is, in principle, successfully challenged. The experience is characterized by a deep "longing," the very nature of which implies the stubborn and even transcendent sense of the value of human existence. A rich and highly insightful quotation from Nietzsche's *Birth of Tragedy* will help us to appreciate the power of this aesthetic.

> Now no comfort avails anymore: longing transcends a world after death, even the gods; existence is negated along with its glittering reflection in the gods or in an immortal beyond. Conscious of the truth he has once seen, man now sees everywhere only the horror or the absurdity of existence; now he understands what is symbolic in Ophelia's fate; now he understands the wisdom of the sylvan god, Silenus: he is nauseated.
>
> Here, when the danger to his will is greatest, art approaches as a saving sorceress, expert at healing. She alone knows how to turn these nauseous thoughts about the horror or the absurdity of existence into notions with which one can live: these are the sublime as the artistic taming of the horrible....[7]

The nausea Nietzsche refers to can be compared to its counterpart, that of the African during the Middle Passage. In the belly of those floating whales, consumed by the cruel greed of an insatiable appetite for profit, the African captive groaned and regurgitated. He moaned and groaned until he found the melody that mirrored his wretchedness, and in expressing it thusly preserved and secured the value of his pain. In that magic moment of ghastly horror and naked heroism a new spirituality was born. Subsequent conceptual and symbolic formulations of transcendence trailed in merely as the afterbirth. The aesthetic experience enables the subject to experience authenticity at life's limits through its unique quality and power. This is a significant factor theologically because it is precisely at the limits when life in its fullest faces compromise through self-deception, flight into unreality, or qualitative collapse, as in the case of a severe mental breakdown. It has long been the conviction of some theological schools that the disintegration of sanity poses the greatest challenge to the traditional conception of the deity at the point of theodicy.[8] Ideology, belief, or thought systems would facilitate life by annulling ambiguity through closure, that is, by explanations provided by the general framework of the perspective system. Tragic experience, on the other hand, discloses and in a sense affirms the reality of the ambiguity that threatens meaning while at the same time empowering and enabling the subject(s) to live on. This is, I believe, the achievement and the genius of tragedy and authentic tragic experience.

Tragedy discloses the nonrational, often destructive side of reality, the mere existence of which threatens to upset those presuppositions on which the whole meaningful universe is founded, doing so in a way that allows, even encourages, us to "live on." (I realize here that the foregoing rationale seems to grant something of an ontological status to the nonrational. While I may hold that position, it is not necessary for the argument to work. I am reasoning from the data of human experience as I understand it.) We undergo an existential crucifixion and, to our amazement, we are not destroyed. We emerge feeling that we know life at its bottom, its root, and though it be a terrible thing, even its terribleness is no longer strange or able to undo us. We encounter the darkness, we pass through it, but the darkness consumes us not. The tragic vision consists of neither an escape into an illusion of Olympian bliss, nor the sheer terror of titanic monstrosity, nor even a lapse into chthonic despair. It consists in more of a Dionysian sublation of the three. The aesthetic element in tragedy or tragic experience is the Orphic lyre by which the Furies themselves are "tamed," perhaps, but hardly destroyed.[9] Nietzsche writes as follows of the tragic myth:

> The tragic myth, too, insofar as it belongs to art, participates fully in the metaphysical intention of art to transfigure. But what does it

transfigure when it presents the world of appearance in the image of the suffering hero? Least of all the "reality" of this world of appearance, for it says to us: "Look there! Look closely! This is your life, this is the hand on the clock of your existence."[10]

Because of my liberal employment of Nietzsche's tragic vision and insightful reflections on the nature of tragedy in *The Birth of Tragedy*, and the text's rather controversial status as an authority in the canon of Western classics, it is incumbent upon me to comment on my use of his ideas in relation to my own reflections before moving on to a more direct application. In spite of the difficulties surrounding the text and even Nietzsche's own qualifications of certain parts of it, it remains a classic statement on the subject. There are, of course the well-known, often reductionist readings of the text due to the passionate throes of Nietzsche's intimate relationship with Wagner or his intellectual dependence on Schopenhauer's philosophy. Nietzsche's infatuation with Wagner could well have been the primary motivation for many of his insights into tragedy and the tragic and their relation to the musical mood, but alas, the mere indication of the origin of an idea in psychological processes per se cannot serve in and of itself as an argument against its analytic value. Regardless of an idea's origin, its value must be determined by the merit of the idea itself; even in a case where the author himself retracts them. Who is to say whether or not it was the retraction that was overdetermined (as a result of his disenchantment) rather than the birth of the idea itself? With respect to his reliance on Arthur Schopenhauer's philosophy I can only say that Nietzsche's tragic vision continued to develop as his philosophy pushed past the sterile version of weak pessimism to the pessimism of strength; and Nietzsche's notion of the Dionysian, in which the tragic vision eventually came to rest, completely evolved past this initial formulation. My reading and employment of the ideas fleshed out in *The Birth of Tragedy* is colored and contextualized by these latter developments. They are articulated in a little-known but invaluable study conducted by Rose Pfeffer, *Nietzsche: Disciple of Dionysus*.

I will therefore employ Nietzsche's formulation without extensive commentary on the critical literature surrounding some of his more controversial formulations. I will employ the text pretty much as it stands, with some qualifications of the language he uses suggested by Silk and Stern and the metaqualification implied in his later works.[11] As I see it, the text carries with it a powerful resonance with experience, the weight of which seems to override the impact of some of the more academic and technical (primarily negative) evaluations of the work.

Nietzsche understands tragedy to be the by-product of the dialectical interaction of two distinct artistic trends, the Dionysian and the Apollonian.[12] These two concepts are best understood as paraliteral concepts. As such, they are neither fictitious nor literal, but something of a blend of the two.[13] While there is much in Nietzsche's formulation, I think that it is courting misunderstanding if we see these concepts as having an a priori status in relation to the creation and the reality of tragedy. They can be teased out of the subject matter because they are indeed there, but they cannot be properly appreciated, in the context of understanding tragedy, if they are assumed to have an ontological status divorced from one another. Stated another way, these concepts emerge from a meditation on the tragic vision as it manifests itself in Nietzsche's reading of Greek tragedy and in turn can be turned back on the tragic vision as heuristic devices to illuminate and help us better appreciate it. Both are trends that are constituted in relation to each other, held in a creative tension.[14] So far as tragedy goes, the Dionysian and the Apollonian are two distinguishable but interdependent dimensions. I do not think that we need to grant them any independent or a priori status for them to be used effectively as heuristic devices and as bridges to the appreciation of the experience of tragedy itself.

I should also caution that it would be a gross oversimplification and, in point of fact, downright wrong to view the interaction of the Apollonian and the Dionysian as that of the rational and the irrational, respectively. Nietzsche's philosophical and aesthetic position as it is reflected in the text is far more nuanced than such a reading would imply. Were one to read the text in this way, one would miss his profound critique of rationalism that returns like a Wagnerian leitmotif throughout the work. The ease with which this assumption can slip into a reading of the text that refracts the true spirit and sense of Nietzsche is demonstrated in the following passage taken from the otherwise extremely thoughtful and provocative work of Michelle Gellrich.

> The same phenomenon could be traced in an account such as Nietzsche's in *The Birth of Tragedy*. While exploring under the rubric of the "Dionysiac" various turbulent, agnostic, and unsystematic aspects of experiences in Greek tragic plays, Nietzsche nonetheless ultimately submits them to the mediating framework of "Apollonian"

form. In his emphasis on the synthesizing and reconciliation powers of dramatic structure, he carries on the tradition of Hegel, who has similar recourse to containing properties and formalistic closure in stabilizing the meaning of conflict in plays.[15]

This point would have been on target if Nietzsche had argued that the dialectic out of which tragedy emerged consisted of the interplay of the Dionysian impulse and the Socratic spirit (as he saw it). The form, however, with which Nietzsche was concerned, was aesthetic form. A much more nuanced analysis of Nietzsche would have been necessary before she could justify making the same claim that she persuasively argued for in relation to Hegel and Aristotle.[16] And then, I believe, it still would have failed.

The way in which Nietzsche uses the term *form* is tantamount to the most rudimentary sense that serves as the precondition for meaningful expression of any kind. In the case of tragedy, form at this level is always already an aesthetic one, which brings to it the uniqueness of the aesthetic form, which is most obviously not that of the strictly conceptual or linguistic "form" that so easily lends itself to the excesses of rationalism resulting in closure. I think that Gellrich (as her passing reference to the "reconciling powers of dramatic structure" might betray) is confusing Nietzsche's assessment and evaluation of the "tragic effect" with his assessment of the internal structure of the text.

It seems to me that she assumes that in order for there to be a feeling of "reconciliation," it must be communicated conceptually rather than "produced" (that is to say, in a more thoroughgoing dialectical fashion involving the distinctive properties of both the text of a tragedy and personal experience). The reconciliation that Nietzsche speaks of comes, precisely, in spite of the presence of the ambiguity and without producing the closure she speaks of, as I argued earlier.

The birth of tragedy can be seen from two different vantage points as it relates to Nietzsche's text. One dimension is, of course, the historical, and the other, the generative process of production—in Ricoeur's language, the synchronic and the diachronic. An analysis of the generative process will yield an appreciation of the deep structure at work in the "birth" of tragedy. It will reveal the constituent elements without which tragedy would not or could not be. It is the insights gleaned from this level of analysis that I hope to apply effectively in our efforts to elucidate the structure of traditional African American Christian consciousness and its tragic vision.

I should also note at the outset that while Nietzsche's use of and dependence on terms such as *mood, mythopoetic consciousness, mystical unity, oneness,* and so forth, as well as his references to oneiric phenomena, the experience of ecstasy, and intoxication may move us well out into a sphere of human experience that does not afford us the luxury of strict scientific verification, we should not dismiss the illuminative or epistemological value of his insights. One's evidence and method must be selected based on the nature of the subject under investigation. Therefore, any summary dismissal of his conclusions because of his implicit yet heavy reliance on introspection is arbitrary and doctrinaire, serving only to condemn certain essential areas of human experience to the shadowlands beyond our comprehension. Ronald Hyman has aptly observed in terms most appropriate for our primary subject of investigation,

> No one has pointed more insistently than Nietzsche has to the relationship between mood and insight, neurosis and statement, sickness and vision. The sick man, he contended, being more aware of what he lacks than the healthy man of what he possesses, is better qualified to write about health. In Nietzsche's mature philosophy, as in his school boy essays, his main weapon was self-observation. Malaise is conducive to introspection and it was Freud's opinion that Nietzsche achieved a degree of introspection never achieved by anyone else and never likely to be achieved by anyone again. Nor has anyone possessed a greater talent for working analogically outward from self-observation.... Nietzsche was ingenious at applying self-knowledge to social movements, cantilevering out into the remote past from analysis of his own needs for self assertion, reassurance, revenge, destruction, hero-worship. Writing about Socrates or Jesus, Schopenhauer or Wagner, he was always writing about himself, but to recognize this is not to depreciate his perceptions. On the contrary, it was his awareness of illogicality in his own consciousness that made him so knowing about the functioning of other consciousness. This functioning was determined, he saw, not so much by fact and logic as by mood, accident, prejudice, ambition.[17]

Before moving on to an examination of African American Christian consciousness, we need to review the nature of the concepts of the Apollonian and the Dionysian as Nietzsche employs them. There is little direct historical connection between Nietzsche's and the actual Greek usage. Direct historical connections, however, should not be the primary criterion for determining the usefulness of these concepts for illuminating the tragic vision and our experience of it. Since the work of Kuhn and others in the philosophy of science, we have discovered that most, if not all, of even our most helpful theoretical scientific constructs owe far more than heretofore realized to imagination, language, and metaphor for their capacity to illuminate reality in helpful and productive ways.[18]

The concept of the Dionysian, even in this early text, is an ontological category. It expresses one of Nietzsche's basic assumptions about the nature of reality. It discloses the primordial contradiction at the heart of reality. Nietzsche ontologizes both contradiction and pain. Writing of Raphael's "Transfiguration," he observes,

> The lower half of the picture, with the possessed boy, the despairing bearers, the bewildered, terrified disciples, shows us the reflection of suffering, primal and eternal, the sole ground of the world: the "mere appearance" here is the reflection of eternal contradiction, the father of things.[19]

This theme recurs throughout the text. Here it is again, but this time with reference to its singular relationship to music as the medium of its expression.

> Language can never adequately render the cosmic symbolism of music, because music stands in symbolic relation to the primordial contradiction and primordial pain in the heart of the primordial unity, and therefore symbolizes a sphere which is beyond and prior to all phenomena.[20]

It is at least theologically and philosophically important for me to point out here that Nietzsche's assertion of an ontological contradiction still occurs within a "primal" unity. It is difficult for me to imagine both a fundamental contradiction and a fundamental unity at the heart of reality unless it occurs in and is maintained through something roughly analogous to personal experience.

Primal suffering engenders Apollonian illusion. Nietzsche compares it to the experience of dreaming. It is the blissful beauty captured in the art of the sculptor, its most exemplary expression. The Apollonian is appearance and a second-order experience in the sense that it is an ontological derivative. This level of experience, where most of us live most of the time, is like the mist that rises from the turbulent Dionysian sea.

The Apollonian is also the principle of individuation and distinction. It is the principle of separation. As such it fragments reality into diversified forms. It individuates the Dionysian "Sturm und Drang" of surging life force into the diverse forms of existence much in the same way a prism divides or individuates light into a spectrum of colors. While it is the principle of division, it is not, however, the empty lifeless dissection of Socratic analysis or rationalism. At both the ontological and the human levels of existence, the Apollonian vision is a response to the longing engendered by the primal suffering at the heart of the primal unity. Note also that sparagmous, division, and fragmentation permeate the experience of the tragic. It is characteristic of both the Apollonian and the Dionysian.

> That he appears at all with such epic precision and clarity is the work of the dream-interpreter, Apollo, who through this symbolic appearance interprets to the chorus its Dionysian state. In truth, however, the hero is the suffering Dionysus of the Mysteries, the god experiencing in himself the agonies of individuation, of whom wonderful myths tell that as a boy he was torn to pieces by the Titans and now is worshiped in this state as Zagreus. Thus it is intimated that this *dismemberment* [italics mine], the properly Dionysian *suffering*, is like a transformation into air, water, earth, and fire, that we are therefore to regard the state of individuation as the origin and primal cause of all suffering, as something objectionable in itself. From the smile of Dionysus sprang the Olympian gods, from his tears sprang man. In this existence as a dismembered god, Dionysus possesses the dual nature of a cruel, barbarized demon and a mild, gentle ruler.[21]

Hence, even in the early Nietzsche we can see that there are philosophical insights that transcend this initial binary framework for expressing the tragic vision. In his later works, they will all be subsumed primarily under the rubric of the Dionysian. "In his later philosophy, the two deities are no longer separated and the concept of Dionysus represents a synthesis in which negation and affirmation, suffering and joy, are reconciled in terms of a Dionysian faith that includes both gods and achieves true tragic greatness."[22]

> For the more clearly I perceive in nature those omnipotent art impulses, and in them an ardent longing for illusion, the more I feel myself impelled to the metaphysical assumption that the truly existent primal unity, eternally suffering and contradictory, also needs the rapturous vision, the pleasurable illusion, for its continuous redemption.[23]

This primordial suffering, whether perceived philosophically at the heart of reality or encountered and mediated through human experience, engenders, indeed commands, Apollonian illusion. Longing as the motive force emerging from the Dionysian turbulence and pain is implicit in this formulation. The primal suffering necessitates the emergence of its complement. In fact, without the Apollonian illusion, the vision of the Dionysian, the primal terror of existence, would render life unbearable. We would not be able to look upon the naked truth and go on with life.

There is a longing, a deep desire, a craving or lack at the center of reality, the internal dynamics of which dialectically engenders the complement of the Dionysian—the Apollonian. Life—existence—is redeemed through the Apollonian illusion, which refracts the Dionysian through individuation into artistic form. This is the process by which tragedy or the tragic (as an always already aesthetic form) is produced. The emergence of the tragic vision is the consequence of a primordial *conjure* of Dionysian truth in the "holding environment" of Apollonian form. Nietzsche believes that tragedy is the most authentic form of this redemption. Its authenticity lies in the fact that it preserves the terrible truth of existence, while so transforming our experience of it that it transvalues the truth itself. The transvaluation of the truth is not the transformation of it. The truth, itself, is preserved. Tragedy so transvalues the experience that the reprehensible becomes the desirable; that which shocks and saddens yields joy; and that which crushes and ruins yields consolation. It is important to note that Nietzsche believes this Apollonian redemption to be necessitated at both the cosmic and human dimensions of existence, making tragedy, or the tragic, a fundamental aspect of reality. Within the philosophical framework that Nietzsche lays out, the production of tragedy (i.e., dramatic form) in human experience and the human experience of the tragic, where persons come to terms with their suffering through aesthetic sublation, is directly linked to the cosmic process of redemption. In fact, one can safely say that in the dynamic emergence of the tragic, persons approach in their experience something analogous to divine experience.

One might ask at this point, just what, exactly, constitutes redemption in Nietzsche's scheme? Redemption is directly linked to the idea of rendering existence bearable and maintaining its meaningfulness in the face of the absurd. Art rescues life from the clutches of the absurd. The meaningfulness of life is restored without distorting the terrible truth that once held it firmly in its grasp. Redemption takes place when one encounters the terrible truth of existence, the terrible wisdom of Silenus, in such a way that persons continue to affirm life as meaningful and worthwhile. The longing for redemption becomes poignantly conscious only after an encounter with the painful truth of existence. This encounter occurs at the limits, so to speak, when to our horror we see "how logic coils up at these boundaries and finally bites its own tail—suddenly the new form of insight breaks though, *tragic insight,* which, merely to be endured, needs art as a protection and remedy."[24] Given the centrality of subjectivity, it is not so much "life" but "living" that becomes threatened and must be endured.

A word more about this longing and what it implies about the structure of existence itself. Out of the encounter with the absurd, a profound sense of longing and loss emerges. The longing betrays the need for the restoration of the existential equilibrium disturbed by the shock of the horror. A question is raised about the meaning of existence, or, better still, the meaning of existence is "put into question." Once the question emerges, the sheer fact that there can be a question is a fundamental disturbance. It is the proverbial Pandora's Box. An interrogative "state of being" emerges with its unique psychic tone and quality. It is the not-knowingness of human being. It is the direct apprehension of life's essential ambiguity and openness; the "un-answering-ness" and unresponsiveness of the abyss to the query of being. This is essential to the matrix that constitutes the experience of the tragic. The interrogative state need not and more often is not captured or expressed conceptually or linguistically. One may witness this longing, in which the interrogative state is always implicit in the midst of a "linguistically" explicit affirmation of the meaning of existence. There is an always alreadyness to the entire quality of the experience that must be unpacked to appreciate and understand. Often, our moods and even our behavior put to the lie some of our strongest convictions. What one believes at one level may not hold true at other levels of our being. So much of life goes on in the depths, and what becomes conscious and clear is often a just derivative of more fundamental struggles—again, like that Apollonian mist that rises from the Dionysian surge beneath. What we see in no wise completely defines or exhausts what is there. In fact, I have discovered that when it comes to human experience, the lion's share and so much of the truth with it remain buried in the depths and are seldom made conscious except with great pain, turmoil, and resistance. It is important to note as well that too much attention paid to the language of a particular avowal may obscure the determinate reality of the pathos of that avowal. This is one reason why I believe there can be a legitimate tragic experience and expression of the Christian faith.

The traditional way of posing the problem of Christianity and tragedy, "Can there be a Christian tragedy?" is misleading at best. The issue should be posed differently. The question should be, "Can there be a legitimate tragic experience and expression of the Christian faith?" Although one may be inclined to answer in the negative to the former given the determinate perimeters established by the shape of the question, I would most certainly answer in the affirmative to the latter. In fact, I would argue that such an expression is the most authentic form of the Christian faith.

My considered position is that we see just such an expression in the flowering of African American religions, primarily, Christian experience and culture. It could be reasonably argued that there is a distinctly tragic strain that predominates in the whole of African American culture. Nietzsche asserts that there are three stages of illusion, which

> are actually designed only for the more nobly formed natures, who actually feel profoundly the weight and burden of existence, and must be deluded by exquisite stimulants into forgetfulness of their displeasure. All that we call culture is made up of these stimulants; and, according to the proportions of ingredients, we have either a dominantly Socratic or artistic or tragic culture.[25]

That the African American from the time of his capture, transportation, and enslavement up until this present time has felt "profoundly the weight and burden of existence" can scarcely be denied. Now, of course, it is true that throughout the history of Western culture there have always been existential virtuosi who have felt this weight as well. Alas, we are not alone in this experience. Yet in the African American, the sense of the "terrible wisdom" and the dynamic and dialectical transformation of it into a mode of aesthetic and religio-aesthetic expression became the loom on which this subculture was woven. In other words, it became the experience and expression not of a few intellectual and existential virtuosi, but rather, the experience of the "many" mediated through popular cultural forms in both the religious and the secular realms—two realms, we must remember, that have been hard to demarcate with hard-and-fast lines in the experience and the life world of the African American.

Finally, before moving to a more detailed layer of analysis there is one more concept of note that will thicken my theoretical contextualization of the subject matter. It is the idea, as Nietzsche identifies it, of the "forgetfulness of the displeasure" facilitated by the illusion. It is important to observe that Nietzsche's forgetfulness is not the same thing as, nor should it carry the pejorative implication of, the modern notion of "escape." The forgetfulness is not the forgetting, the forgoing, or the evasion of the reality of life's terrible wisdom, but more like a cessation of the displeasure that accompanies the encounter with it in its particularity under the actual conditions of life. There is an instructive family resemblance between the significance of this "forgetfulness" and Paul Tillich's notion of dreaming innocence. "Dreaming innocence" is "dreaming" innocence precisely because the reality of wakefulness is despair. Nietzsche's forgetfulness of the displeasure entailed by the profound experience of the weight and burden of existence resembles a dialectical sublation of Tillich's dreaming innocence on the one hand and the terrible wisdom of Silenus or, if one prefers, the terrible reality of "fallenness" on the other. His notion of a forgetfulness of the displeasure (while maintaining the truth of the insight) as I understand it begins to sound like the kind of redemption that human beings can hope to experience after the experience of such a life as humans have. Authentic redemption comes only through crucifixion, in full knowledge of the cross. "Tragedy begins with the 'going under' of the hero; but this going under is heroic, and bears within it the means of overcoming."[26]

This forgetfulness is the "forgetting unforgotten" of those whose response to trauma and great sorrow sweetens life's rivers instead of turning them to wormwood; a sweetening that in no small part is carried out through the power of aesthetic exaltation and transvaluation; a response so noble that it bears a striking resemblance to all things divine. This is the heart of African American religious experience, its beauty, its exaltation, its depth, its glory and its pain. Read African America for ancient Greece in the following quote. "But to Nietzsche, true gaiety and serenity can be achieved only after a baptism of fire. The beauty of ancient Greece was an outcome of suffering and pain; the greatness of its spirit was the result of profound inner strife and opposition. 'What suffering must this race have endured in order to accomplish such beauty.'"[27] These lines may well have been written about African Americans.

Chapter 5

Life within the Veil: African American Christian Consciousness Pt. 2

The tragic mood of the African American emerges and crystallizes most clearly in her music and religious expressions. The deep substratum or Dionysian element was supplied by both the rich spirituality of the African heritage and the brutal encounter with the "peculiar institution" in the Americas. The suffering and pain of slavery, as well as the subsequent experience of oppression and marginalization, situated the African American firmly at his existential "limits." The cultural taxonomies that defined black being, mediated explicitly through language, law, and social status and reinforced implicitly through styles of interaction, intensified the experience of fragmentation that conspired with the basic human desire to be free to create a profound sense of longing (melancholy, conceived of as nonpathological) and the surging Dionysian "Sturm," kept just beneath the surface by fear and force. Using Du Bois's tripartite division of the salient features of the liturgical expression of African American consciousness, the music, the frenzy, and the preacher (preacher expanded in this instance to mean mainly "preaching," although the "person" of the preacher is by no means minimized), I hope to perform something of an excavation, laying bare its dynamic structure.

Du Bois writes of the African American's religious music,

> The music of Negro religion is that plaintive rhythmic melody, with its minor cadences, which, despite caricature and defilement, still remains the most original and beautiful expression of "human life and longing [quotation marks mine] yet born on American soil. Spring from the African forests, where its counterpart can still be heard, it was adapted, changed, and intensified by the tragic soul-life of the slave,

until under the stress of law and whip, it became the one true expression of a people's sorrow, despair and hope.[1]

According to Nietzsche, tragedy bears a close relationship to music. Music has a metaphysical significance. It is the ontologically privileged art form. It most adequately expresses the nature and the pathos, the mood, if you will, of ultimate reality. Reality has a suffering center. It is tragic at its core, and music is the most effective medium of this truth.

> Language can never adequately render the cosmic symbolism of music, because music stands in symbolic relation to the primordial contradiction and primordial pain in the heart of the primordial unity, and therefore symbolizes a sphere which is beyond and prior to all phenomena.[2]

The encounter, experience, or perception of this painful contradiction at the center of reality, through its replication in human experience, created in the African American subject a mood that lends itself most readily to expression in and through music. Music is the language of the soul. The moan from which their music emerges is expressive of a pain and suffering so deep that words cannot express them. The mournful and musical moan of the African American expressed her existential condition when her words failed her. This is a significant point because it demonstrates a connection between music and trauma. What cannot be expressed in words because it cannot be recalled due to its complex and painful nature may, however, find expression through music. It might be that the mirroring of African American suffering through the expression of their mood in music helped to facilitate coping with experiences too painful to deal with through recall and direct cognitive processing.

Melody is the medium through which song can signify beyond the conceptual framing of its lyrics. The meanings of words are deepened by the sound of music and firmly fixed in experience through the creation and expression of mood. The plaintive dimension of the moan expressed both the African's/African American's excruciating contemporary reality and, at one and the same time, a longing for an unembodied future free of the pain of the present. Lament is inherently transcendent and prophetic. It is eschatological as well. It indicts prevailing worldly reality such that a better world than a world in which such pain exists as a matter of course through nature or man's inhumanity to man cannot only be conceived, but is in fact desired, even "called" for.

Music poeticizes expressive lyrics and qualifies poetic lyrics, vouchsafing the depth and tone of the experience they intend to convey. That the African American is a singularly musical, even lyrical, being can hardly be questioned. Levine gives a litany of reports documenting this proclivity toward musical expression far back into the period of slavery.

> White southerners, no matter how much they might denigrate the culture and capacities of their black bondsmen, paid tribute to their musical abilities, from Thomas Jefferson's observation that musically the slaves "are more generally gifted than the whites with accurate ears for tune and time," to the northern Mississippi planter who told Frederick Law Olmsted more than half a century later that "niggers is allers good singers nat'rally. I reckon they got better lungs than white folks, that they hev such powerful voices." "Compared with our taciturn race, the African nature is full of poetry and song," an anonymous correspondent in Dwight's Journal of Music wrote in 1856. "The Negro is a natural musician..." The slaves seemed to have agreed. "That's one thing that colored folks is blessed," an ex-slave exclaimed. "They certainly got the harp in their mouths."[3]

Levine goes on to note at the end of the paragraph in which this quote appeared, and not insignificantly for our purposes, "An examination of the shape and content of slave songs reveals much about slave culture and consciousness."[4]

That the music of the African American was (and is) often expressive of deep sorrow, and was everywhere colored by distinctly mournful qualities is equally incontestable.

> Of nearly all the songs, however, the music is distinctly sorrowful. The ten master songs I have mentioned tell in word and music of trouble and exile, of strife and hiding: they grope toward some unseen power and sign for rest in the end.[5]

Again, Du Bois writes of the sorrow songs, "They are the music of an unhappy people, of children of disappointment; they tell of death and suffering and unvoiced longing toward a truer world, of misty wanderings and hidden ways."[6] In addition to noting the deeply sorrowful nature of the music of the African American, Blassingame also intimates its often disclosive and dialectical character. "The sentiments of the slave often appear in the spirituals. Songs of sorrow and hope, of agony and joy, of resignation and rebellion, the spirituals were the unique creation of the black slaves."[7] I should also note that there is a tendency in some quarters to see in the sorrow songs merely the expression of sadness. This magisterial expression of the soul is viewed by some as nothing more than the expression of the slave's forlornness. To see these songs in this way is to fall prey to a fundamental racist assumption—that the mind and soul of the slave were childlike and simplistic, rather than the marvel of the human spirit and spiritual adaptation that they actually were. The tendency of the African American to express herself, particularly her sorrow and deepest aspirations, musically and lyrically signals the overwhelming and determinative presence of the Dionysian current in her life and culture. This Dionysian surge was that indestructible presence of "spirit" that rails against the darkness and hammers at the gate of Heaven. It was music and a ubiquitous lyricism in the context of the African American ritual expression that facilitated what Du Bois has provocatively labeled the "frenzy."[8]

> The mass of slaves, of course, played no instrument. Their solace came from singing. Robert Anderson asserted that the "steady rhythm of the marching songs carried many a slave across the tobacco and hemp fields ahead of a slave driving overseer, when their tired muscles refused to budge for any other stimulant other than that of the rhythm of song, while the weird and mysterious music of the religious ceremonies moved old and young alike in a frenzy of religious fervor."[9]

The frenzy frequently accompanies the preaching as well. The rhythmic patterns of plaintive preaching often yield a cadence that builds toward a crescendo, evoking the frenzied expression of life affirmation commonly called "getting happy." Here again, the preaching was and is, in its traditional form, and of course to varying degrees, no less shaped and colored by the ubiquitous lyricism mentioned above.

We see in the sorrow songs and the gospel of later times, as well as in the lyrical reproduction and narrative contextualization of key biblical symbols, paradigms, and themes in sermons, that the African American was able to face and accept the difficult realities of his circumstances, while at the same time drawing from them what Nietzsche called "metaphysical comfort." The aestheticized representation of her circumstances dialectically transformed the experience so that she could live with the bitter and terrible truth without "giving in" to it and hence "giving up" her humanity. Note the similarity here between this process of aesthetic transformation and what many scholars have argued is the distinctive trait and genius of Greek tragedy.

> The special characteristics of the Greeks were their power to see the world clearly and at the same time as beautiful. Because they were able to do this, they produced art distinguished from all other art by an absence of struggle, marked by a calm and serenity which is theirs alone. There is, it seems to assure us, a region where beauty is truth, truth beauty. To it their artists would lead us, illuminating life's dark confusions by gleams fitful indeed and wavering compared with the fixed light of religious faith, but by some magic of their own, satisfying, affording a vision of something inconclusive and yet of incalculable significance. Of all the great poets this was true but truest of the tragic poets, for the reason that in them the power of poetry confronts the inexplicable.[10]

If one were to replace the "power of poetry" with the "power of the aesthetic" in the passage above, which, as I have argued, is the real transformative element even in poetry, I think it fairly simple to see the connection that I am driving at. A number of different modes of expression may contribute to the overall aesthetic effect (i.e., poetry, metaphor, meter, voice, music, song, and perhaps even dance), but the transformation takes place in the achievement of the aesthetic effect. The transvaluation of the truth in and through the aesthetic alters the existential posture of the subject. I hesitate to call it a rebirth, but it is a "rebirthing." At the point at which the meaningfulness of one's existence is apprehended (affirmed), the subject assumes a posture of resistance toward everything that threatens the survival of the psychic self. To put it positively, there is, I am arguing, an ontological coincidence in the "re-cognition" of the meaningfulness of one's existence as the result of the affirmation through the impact of the aesthetic transvaluation; the apprehension of that meaningfulness always already in the face of threat to the same whether the threat is mediated through dramatic art or actual life experiences, and the aspiration toward freedom or in the very least an impulse to resist. It is at this rudimentary level that the elusive reality of human dignity takes shape and asserts its presence. We may not be able to empirically identify soul or a soul in the human subject, but like an electron in a vacuum chamber, its signature can be clearly identified in the vacuous chamber of traumatic oppression. The process effectuates a kind of second naiveté in the meaningfulness of existence.[11] The object of this aspiration may be given a utopian configuration, or it may remain formless and only vaguely apprehended. This "recognition" does, however, become a motive force in behavior at a most rudimentary level by securing the necessary conditions for personal and collective action.

What makes this scenario so fascinating is that here is a motive to act, an impulse to respond, that circumvents the aporias of existence, precisely at the point they are most likely to paralyze the will. When life comes under the shadow of the horror, and the Terrible Truth of Silenus rises from a sea of troubles to devour man—tossed about on the frail craft of his mortality—the worm rises, as if he himself were a god, and like Lear on the heath he curses the elements that flog him, though they lie far beyond his reach. This is why so many find the effect, affect, and general shape of tragic drama so perplexing. Art has its own reasons that even reason cannot comprehend. Not only history, but art, too, has its cunning.

> Nor is the tragic vision for those who, though admitting unresolved questions and the reality of guilt, anxiety, and suffering, would become quietest and do nothing. Mere sensitivity is not enough. The tragic vision impels the man of action to fight against his destiny, kick against the pricks, and state his case before God and his fellows.[12]

It may, perhaps, be argued that in the experience of the African American this impulse to act gets refracted through the identification with biblical characters and groups who themselves, in fact, provide a vicarious satisfaction of this impulse, thereby defusing a potentially explosive and revolutionary impulse. My initial response to such an argument would be that the religious imagination, rather than refracting the impulse to act, provides something of a last line of defense for the beleaguered humanity of the slave from whom effective material resistance appeared to be, by and large, hopeless. This act of religious imagination is no less of an act of resistance than actual material rebellion. The African American religious imagination possessed a psychic value and reality that helped maintain spiritual, emotional, and psychological equilibrium in the face of forces that fostered fragmentation as well as psychic and spiritual disintegration. The African American appropriation of Christian symbolism, the production of a religious ritual using all available resources, was a creative response to the "loss" endured during and sustained after transplantation.[13] It was a response to the structured marginalization and the chronic melancholia that ensued.

The mythopoetic structure of the Bible provided the symbolic matrix that gave Apollonian form to the African American's experience, providing, in large part, the other prerequisite for the emergence of an authentically tragic experience and an authentic spiritual expression of the tragic vision. The African American "appropriated" these symbols, narratives, and metaphors in a climate that provided for the crystallization of a tragic vision and the formulation of a distinctly tragic mood. The milieu in which the biblical text and the predominant themes, styles, and symbols of the faith were encountered determined the hermeneutical slant of the appropriation. The African American mood or "geist" was fundamentally tragic, and the peculiar expression of the African American's faith still bears the marks of the original matrix in which it was formed, as do so many other dimensions of her cultural experience, and for very good reasons. The marginalization and the cultural taxonomies have survived and continue to cast a long and determinate shadow over the African American community, whereas most, if not all, of the legal restrictions and reinforcements have been removed. Systemic marginalization continues through economic and cultural expressions of asymmetrical relations of power. The marginalization continues to be chronic in significant populations as it is readily identifiable in the growth, impoverishment, and profound alienation of the African American underclass and the urban abandoned.

There are those who argue that tragedy is fundamentally non-Christian, and that the tragic vision of life is fundamentally irreconcilable with that of the faith. Although I believe that such notions rest on fundamental misunderstandings of both tragedy and the Christian faith,[14] let us take a closer look at the broader outlines of the argument. The initial assertion is simply that an experience cannot be both tragic and Christian at the same time. Tragedy, by its very nature, they argue, is pessimistic, and the Christian vision is fundamentally one of hope and triumph. Although I think that the triumphalism characteristic of so many readings of the faith through a theological emphasis on the Resurrection is misleading at best and dangerously in error at worst, I will resist the temptation to engage the theological point here, leaving that aside for now. I should point out that the suggestion that shallow American optimism is somehow a constituent element of the Christian faith inadvertently cheapens the religion and reduces it to little more than a self-deceiving system of pious platitudes and positive thinking wrapped in the sanctimonious language of spirituality. Suffice it to say that such arguments, were they theologically correct, would not apply here. I am arguing that the African American expression of the faith is singularly tragic. The tragic conflict does not lie in the theoretical formulation of doctrine, but rather inheres in the existential predicament of the African American devotee.

The tragic *expression* or *mode of experiencing* the faith, then, can be said to be no more at odds with the essence of the faith than are the rationalistic expressions of modern Protestantism, the intellectualistic expression of academic theologians, the aestheticized, sacramental expression of Catholicism, or the ecstatic expression of mysticism. Each one of these modalities of expressing the faith must be situated in a sociocultural context to be fully appreciated, and this fact relativizes it in a significant sense. This is to say that one cannot take any one of these expressions of the faith as a priori the "real" one.

If you will allow me this generalization, the standard approach seems to rest on the presupposition that the faith is a seamless garment; that it is somehow completely and authentically contained within the straightjacket of the theological virtuosi's harmonized categories of systematic explication. Yet Sigmund Freud and others have more than amply demonstrated that humans can and do entertain contradictory ideas and feelings. Human beings are not the rationalistic automatons they would have to be to find merely the systematic conceptual presentation of the faith satisfying. Life as lived day to day does not conform to our highest demands for rational consistency, however attractive the prospect of such a life may be to some. That someone is a Christian does not rule out the possibility of a tragic consciousness. The tragic consciousness does not inhere mainly in ideas that in turn may or may not be deemed consistent with the faith. Rather, the tragic consciousness consists of a mood or disposition or, as the Germans would call it, a *geist*.

There is, of course, a dialectical relationship between mood and idea, but as Nietzsche has argued, the mood is primary or determinative in the last instance. The mood determines how the ideas, images, and symbols with which the person comes into contact are appropriated and, in turn, given expression. Some argue that the theme of hope is too prevalent in the faith for there to be any affinity with the tragic vision. There are several problems with this approach, not the least of which is the erroneous identification of tragedy with pessimism. It has been shown in more recent scholarship that the pessimistic posture not only does not define tragedy, but is, in a sense, antithetical to the authentic tragic vision.[15] We reviewed the philosophical difference between weak and strong pessimism in the last chapter. The association of the tragic with pessimism involves what Nietzsche would call weak pessimism. Moreover, the "hope" of the Christian is the collective yield of particular doctrines or beliefs. The consolation that the Christian experiences is given conceptual formulation in doctrinal assertions concerning, for instance, the afterlife, and the continued presence of God amid earthly crisis; but the fact that tragic drama does not allow for formulation of this type does not render an authentically tragic expression of the faith a perversion or refraction of authentic Christian faith.

The key word here is consolation. There are few who would argue that the experience of the tragic does not yield something easily designated as a feeling of consolation, which registers strongly in the overall impact of a tragedy.

> This metaphysical comfort—with which, I am suggesting even now, every true tragedy leaves us—that life is at the bottom of things, despite all the changes of appearances, indestructibly powerful and pleasurable...[16]

The idea (though this proposition, too, is by no means unassailable) that the primary source of consolation in the Christian faith comes in the form of doctrinal formulations of particular things hoped for, does not mean that the consolation the Christian faith yields is thereby exhausted. There is something deeper than the particularized hopes provided by any faith when it is practiced that cannot be reduced to the effect of the sum total of the propositions believed in; something deeper that shines light throughout the whole, illuminating each particular belief with its unique power to inspire. The assumption behind the approach under consideration is that one first believes in a proposition, then derives hope from assent. I am arguing that assent itself would not transpire; it would be meaningless without something, for want of a better term, spiritually prior. This primordial passion issues forth in an existential affirmation of life's worthwhileness or meaningfulness. This is the necessary condition for the formation of the "will to believe." Without it there would be no capacity to "believe in" anything. This is not to be confused with a discursive consciousness of the same. It is an existential predisposition, a "being for," an orientation to the world of intersubjectively available meanings. In this mode of being, one is predisposed, in the words of my African American ancestors, to "go on." We can also note here a "family resemblance" to Nietzsche's Dionysian substratum and the Apollonian vision.[17] It's something beyond the human being's brute instinct to survive, or its mere sublimation. It is perhaps another indication of that dimension of human being long associated with the term *spirit* or *soul*.

It is the ritual context of religion, the nonrational*ized* components, and the impact of myth taken as a whole that best mediates this deeper, more existentially primordial, experience. As I indicated in the first chapter, the aesthetic dimension is inseparable from these elements. They would not be what they are, nor would they have the power in experience that they have, without it.

The African American experience in religion is essentially Dionysian. The African American religious ritual richly displays those characteristics of the Dionysian as described by Nietzsche and others.[18] When I refer to the African American ritual, I am not simply referring to a set of gestures or postures undertaken by a priest, preacher, or worship leader on behalf of worshippers. The ritual component of African American worship was profoundly communal in terms of implementation and expression. It tends as it moves through its paces to become progressively decentralized in the expression of power and pathos. Nowhere is the range of elements outlined above more apparent than in the experience Du Bois aptly designated, the frenzy, more commonly referred to as shouting, the shout, or getting happy. Please note Du Bois's classic description of the experience in the two following quotations, one of which deals more exclusively with the "frenzy."

> And so most striking to me, as I approached the village and the little plain church perched aloft, was the air of intense excitement that possessed that mass of black folk. A sort of suppressed terror hung in the air and seemed to seize us—a pythian madness, a demoniac possession, that lent terrible reality to song and word. The black massive form of the preacher swayed and quivered as the words crowded to his lips and flew at us in singular eloquence. The people moaned and fluttered, and then the gaunt cheeked brown woman beside me suddenly leaped straight into the air and shrieked like a lost soul, while round about came wail and groan and outcry, and a scene of human passion such as I had never conceived before.[19]

A little further he writes,

> Finally the frenzy or "Shouting," when the spirit of the Lord passed by, and, seizing the devotee, made him mad with supernatural joy, was the last essential of Negro religion and the more devoutly believed in than all the rest. It varied in expression from the silent rapt countenance or the low murmur and moan to the mad abandon of physical fervor—the stamping, shrieking and shouting, the rushing to and fro and wild waving of arms, the weeping and laughing, the vision and the trance. All this is nothing new in the world, but old as religion, as Delphi and Endor.[20]

This experience, as Du Bois accurately describes it, betrays the presence of those elemental forces locked up in the human spirit that are released only in and through religion. In fact, Rudolf Otto argues that they are, indeed, the hallmark of an authentic encounter with the sacred. Describing the "mysterium tremendum," the primary expression of the apprehension of the numinous, he writes,

> It may burst in sudden eruption up from the depths of the soul with spasms and convulsions, or lead to the strangest excitements, to intoxicating frenzy, to transport, and to ecstasy. It has its wild and demonic forms and can sink to an almost grisly horror and shuddering.[21]

Unlike the sorrow songs and other forms of African American religious music, such as traditional gospel, the frenzy cannot be experienced, understood, or even observed outside of the ritual context. Nor is it something that can be simply conjured up. It must be more or less "worked up," whether by sermon, song, or both, and it remains until this day a vital part of traditional African American spirituality and religious experience. The frenzy, however, is not to be confused with merely yelling praise loudly or one of those pointlessly noisy pep rallies that characterize some of the "black" or would-be "black like" worship services that have devolved into little more than a carnivalesque caricature of traditional African American spirituality in the wave of cross-cultural, megachurch Pentecostalization that has recently swept through some quarters of North American Protestantism.

Now, let us examine the entire experience more closely, bringing our disparate reflections together in a summary of the ritual context or worship experience in an effort to understand the tragic structure of African American Christian consciousness. The African

American Christian worship experience is primarily oral, and thoroughly aesthetic. Art plays a truly central role, but unlike other traditions, there is little reliance on the visual, except for imaginative art. African American religious experience, while profoundly sensual, is no less cerebral and imaginatively nuanced. The problem in making this assessment in the past was that most analysts had bought into the bifurcation of reason and emotion, concluding that to the extent that emotion was present, reason was absent. Hence they reasoned, by implication, that since emotion was powerfully present, reason, was not. This, unfortunately, is a debilitating handicap of the Western mind. Even many African American thinkers remain intellectually crippled by this simplistic binary view of the human subject. It is also a very narrow view of the affective life of human beings, assuming in a serious sense that all emotions are the same and bear the same relationship to reason. Yet the aesthetic experience is a powerful affect. The imagination is an indispensable tool in the greatest works of genius from art to science and religion. All great scientists and scientific theorists are visionaries, from the experimental physicist who conceives of technically sophisticated experiments to test the far-reaching implications of the most counterfactual conjecture to the theoretician, who, through thought experiment, manages to revolutionize our very notions of time and space. Conversely, all great artists express the depth and power of the human mind at its best. Who would doubt or deny that some of our greatest poets and poetry have been expressions of the most exceptional genius?

African American preaching is usually packed with poetic recitations of and extrapolations on the biblical narratives, the scriptural texts serving as the medium of the spiritual virtuosi.[22] In the African American religious experience, art clearly serves something of a political purpose in that it preserves alive the hope for earthly liberation while at the same time providing for a path of survival in the place of bondage and oppression. This is made possible at a rudimentary level by the metaphorical structure of biblical narratives. Biblical narratives, as extended metaphor or myth capturing the movement from oppression to liberation and from captivity and servitude to deliverance in a highly symbolizing discourse, have, in themselves, a liberating structure. They send a message that resonates at multiple levels of meaning, particularly in a situation where meaning was potentially threatened from an overwhelming number of directions, portending, as we have shown, psychic and social death at every hand.

The message, "Life is yet alive!" discloses existence as yet alive with potential and possibility. Paul Ricoeur writes, "Lively expression is that which expresses existence as alive."[23] To the oppressed, the melancholic, ensnared in a web of vulnerability and pain, and locked in an absurd situation, to know that life is yet alive with possibility is "gospel." Ricoeur writes,

> To present men "as-acting" and all things "as in act"—such could well be the ontological function of metaphoric discourse, in which every potentiality of existence appears blossoming forth, every latent capacity for action as actualized.[24]

The biblical narratives, given their liberating structure (the liberating structure of the Bible itself for that matter), paradigmatic personages, and situations lend themselves to identification on the part of the devotee and provide a discursive/symbolic route to the "outside" of one's self and into a shared ritual space. The style of delivery has a deeply musical quality to it and consists of rhythm, which allows for direct verbal and enhanced personal participation, and almost systematic communal punctuation by the congregation. All this is well known. The sorrow songs and traditional gospel are, of course, music and therefore aesthetic by definition. What, however, adds an essential element to the unique and distinctive character of the experience is the concentration on communal as well as individual suffering, struggle, hardship, and pain combined with this pervasive aesthetic moment, which raises it in experiential terms to another level. This is, of course, precisely what the tragic poets did.

They raised profound suffering and hardship to a certain level of beauty, transforming an element of life so profoundly negative and devastating that it could potentially render life meaningless, absurd, and unworthy of being lived to something not only bearable, but beautiful, existentially gripping, and paradoxically invigorating. The very structure of African American religious experience functions, like tragic poetry, to produce a fundamental affirmation of life at its depths in the individual subject, facilitating life amid uncertainty and, in spite of the ever-present challenges, enabling the "will" to go on. It is the "cunning of art" that the most potentially devastating elements in human experience, such as undeserved suffering, inevitable conflict, moral ambiguity and paradox, the disintegration of cherished beliefs, family and group relations, the ambiguity of justice in the universe or lack thereof, and so on, can be "re-presented" in all their stark and threatening reality in such a way that they can be entertained without fostering the breakdown that accompanies the unabated experience of the "horror." In tragic theater, these experiences are brought up much in the same way threatening ideas are conjured from the unconscious in the controlled and therapeutic environment of classical analysis. They are unearthed from the sedimented experiences of our collective humanity, brought into awareness, and reworked. Instead of being overwhelmed and distraught as we feared, we experience a distinct feeling of empowerment and liberation.

These experiences are deprived of most of their existentially destructive potency. Although much of the tension remains, due to their certain reality, these experiences are, in a very real sense, "overcome." Art renders them existentially manageable, and life receives something like a vote of confidence. Howard Thurman captures this dimension of African American religious experience in his characterization of the spirituals as a transformed expression of a common experience. He writes, "In many ways they are the voice, sometimes strident, sometimes muted and weary of people for whom the cup of suffering overflowed in haunting overtones of majesty, beauty, and power."[25]

The structure of the actual worship experience unfolds in a socio-aesthetic logic that ignites when the religious subject makes contact with itself in the form and content of African American worship and when by the "logos" of the experience and the symbolic mediation, it gets transformed into a liberating experience of liminality. The assertion that the devotee has a liberating experience is no simple reference to the fact that there is an element of emotional release or catharsis, though this factor is obviously present. There are some deeper processes at work that I will discuss more directly in a moment.

One can observe or detect in the "hyperliminal"[26] experience of the frenzy or the shout (as it is more commonly called), particularly in the invigorated physical gyrations, the desire to throw off a yoke or heavy burden—or more to the point, an "acting out" of the same. There is an interesting family resemblance between what transpires in the ritual expression of African American Christian consciousness and what went on in the studies of hysteria and hypnosis in early psychoanalysis. In early psychoanalysis, a painful idea, desire, or reminiscence would be summoned forward into consciousness in a way that allowed for its invigorated expression and, hence, discharge of the affect attached to the desire, reminiscence, or idea (really always already a combination of all three), thereby achieving a catharsis and at least a momentary respite from the pain caused by the problematic emotional matrix. This will provide, I think, an interesting point of analysis in my future attempts to give a richer account of what appears to be the "healing effect" of the African American worship experience, as well as its restrictions, limitations, and possible areas of development.[27]

Chapter 6

From Strength to Strength: Toward a Theology of African American Christian Consciousness

The seminal dividend of the unique encounter of the African American with the Christian faith is unquestionably the yield of *strength*. Strength then, is the pivotal concept in the appreciation, evaluation, and characterization of African American Christian consciousness. It is, as well, the axis at which the religious experience (spirituality) and the theology of African American Christian consciousness intersect. At the theological level, the notion of strength heavily impacts the shape and selection of the root metaphors and the formation of dominant themes.[1] By replacing the notion of power with the notion of strength in key places, we are able to draw much closer to the existential epicenter of African American Christian consciousness. We can better understand, for instance, why the theodicy issue hasn't provided more of a disturbance than it has in the formation of an allegiance of the African American to the Christian God. In fact, I want to argue that the notion of "Christian God" could be misleading when applied to African Americans, if by that one is referring to the stale notion employed by many academic theologians, both black and white or otherwise. The experience of African Americans is best understood through the notion of the divine and communion with the divine.

The divine is a more "experience near"[2] way of understanding the African American's encounter with God. The divine conceptualizes God in terms of Her relation to the spiritually engaged subject. God cannot be conceived of outside of relations to the engaged subject. While speculative conceptions of God may be intellectually stimulating, the proper orientation to thinking God is always already in relation to the engaged subject. In other words we do not have access to a noumenal God to whom we can attribute attributes. We don't experience God's attributes. We experience communion with the divine. This communion is primordial and lends credence to other assumptions we make about God or attribute to Her based on revelation, but the experience is primary. The divine is always relational, and God and the engaged community always already linked intersubjectively, and the engaged individual subject is implicated in the notion of the divine. The divine signifies a relational context. The divine was and is a source of strength to the spiritually engaged African American subject. The reality of God, therefore, is tangible, material, and identifiable to the believer who "feels like going on." Hence, atheism or any kind of humanism that would deny the reality of God is abstract, experience distant and alien to the core African American community. The issue of theodicy is, in a sense, short-circuited. It is the experience, not the intellectual coherence, of an abstract theological ideal that is central in African American religion and culture.

The theodicy question sharpens on the interdependent issues of God's goodness and omnipotence. It is here that one would think that the oppressed African American would be severed from the God of her oppressors. These twin issues provide the clashing rocks that all-too-often crush and consequently ruin the Christian voyage of many sensitive, thoughtful, and spiritually courageous individuals. At the existential level, however, in spite of the Western conceptualization of God as all-powerful, the primary existential reality for the African American is *strength* and, more to the point, God's *strength*. This plays itself out in God's ability to share their burden and *His* strength, and, as a direct result, their capacity to successfully undergo frightening, potentially ruinous experiences. God's goodness is conceived of in terms of His "willingness" to do the same. Strength then, providing the root metaphor governing the formation of the African American's theological vision, robs something of the edge and the urgency of the theodicy question classically conceived. While the question remains to be sure, particularly given the firm belief in what God *can do,* existentially, it is *defanged.* This is of course not unrelated to the nature of the experience in so much as it is tragic. The strength to go on remains and flourishes in the face of unanswered questions and in the presence of deep and abiding suffering. Closure need not be imposed by providing a foolproof theological rationale to cope with the contradiction implied in the classical formulation of the theodicy issue.

There are other serious implications that result from the displacement of the key significance of power by the emergence of the centrality of strength in the theology of African American Christian consciousness. It shifts the theological spectrum and provides for a meaningfully different take on some other key issues. It militates against the apotheosis of power, its identification with the being of God, its pernicious impact on the formation of Christian consciousness in general, and the dangerous triumphalism at the heart of so much of the Western Christian tradition. The Western formulation and appropriation of the notion of the all-powerful God has led, far too often, to a psychologically disturbing and potentially sociopathic identification with the God and *His* power. While the Christian faith encourages an identification with Christ, that identification becomes socially pernicious when it encourages an image of the self refracted through the image of the "Christian nation" that makes one, as an integral part of the whole, the chosen vessel of an absolutely right and all-powerful deity. It is this refraction through the social and collective self that allows for the fundamental challenges of the Gospel to all human pretensions (particularly to those dangerously smug pretensions that vaunt themselves in European American chauvinism) to be circumvented. By virtue of the intensely individualistic nature of American Christian experience, particularly the version practiced by the fundamentalist and other conservative sects, some of the most dangerous and potentially psychotic of all pretensions remain safe and secure, refracted through a realm insulated from the direct scrutiny or critical reflection otherwise inspired by some of the essential challenges of the Gospel. To the extent that one participates in, say, the Christian America and inasmuch as one reflects in one's being the written and unwritten, conscious and unconscious values that constitute the essential core identity, particularly "whiteness," one shares in the invulnerability, superiority, and omnipotence of God almighty.

Why must power be conceived of as unlimited or eternal? Power is not God, nor is God tantamount to power. Power is not coeternal with God. It may very well be that power, understood as the ability to determine the shape of reality by imposition of will and uninhibited manipulation of forces and objects is a limited phenomenon. It is a characteristic of the finite world and hence, must of necessity be finite itself. What is it in the Western religiocultural imagination that insists on an all-powerful attribution of God, in the classical theistic sense, for him to be worthy of worship? Although I do not believe that you can determine the truth status of an idea simply or even primarily by its social or ethical utility, I do think that it is significant to note that the apotheosis of *power* has some very dangerous consequences and implications for modern cultural consciousness. Moreover, it only makes sense to say that God is all-powerful in so much as he has all the power that can be exercised over the created order, but power, itself, need not, and in fact is not, an unlimited phenomenon as such. Western theology, to the extent that power has been made coeternal with the being of God, has practiced a pernicious form of spiritual idolatry.

The fact that the notions of power and strength are closely related accounts for one being capable of replacing or at least displacing the other. In fact, they are often used interchangeably. This may be why the notion of strength has never risen to its proper place in the characterization of both God and Christian spirituality. It was always overshadowed by the attractive and often intoxicating seduction of the notion of power. After all, the idea of power is equally attractive to so deeply dichotomize a pair as the oppressor and oppressed, albeit for different reasons. But there are differences in the two ideas that are philosophically and theologically decisive.

In the theology of African American Christian consciousness strength is best understood as an always already dynamic or kinetic attribute of God. It is an emergent attribute, dialectically engendered; the by-product of telos, will, power, and personality meeting resistance. It is the morally, spiritually, and existentially superior attribute because it emerges from living. Unlike power, which evokes a vulgar sense of control and detachment, strength commands in its wake the traits of endurance, commitment, and perseverance, as well as the images of toil, labor, and lifting. It is the yield of the dynamic engagement of life at its fullest. Strength is the *complement* of the depth affirmation of being, of life. In a word, strength is the result of living; it is the substance of life, it is the measure of being.

The central significance of power has also shaped the way key events in the Christian narratives have been hierarchically arranged and configured to determine the shape of Christian theology. There is a deep, even euphoric, triumphalism radiating heavily from the common understanding of the Resurrection as the most significant event of the Christian faith. This triumphalism, and even the nature of the focus on the Resurrection itself, has a lot to do with the obsession with power and the victory of the now all-powerful Christ over his enemies and the resultant guarantee of the same to his followers (taken to mean, of course, at both the ultimate and the penultimate levels), in the case of which the idea of enemies is all-too-often too loosely defined. It is a guarantee of triumph that has been called upon to bolster the fading hopes of the faithful throughout the ages. It has been a refuge for the beleaguered dreams and aspirations of the oppressed, the ground and source of the vicarious conquests of the impotent.

I have always been suspicious of the shallow triumphalism that characterizes so much of the popular piety in the church. As both my research and my direct experiences of the faith in the church have continued, my suspicions have strengthened and perhaps been confirmed. There is a false sense of finality in the wake of the Resurrection, seen as the climactic moment of the Christian story. Salvation having been wrought and guaranteed, all after the Resurrection is of only secondary significance; God's tidying up of loose ends, so to speak. The triumphalism and the finality are read into Jesus' acts, words, and deeds. This is the result of theological refraction through the conceptual lens of power. The Gospel has been read unfortunately from the Resurrection back in order to determine the meaning and significance of Jesus' words and deeds. The Gospel, as understood by most, climbs to the climactic Resurrection, its auspicious peak, where we witness the *true greatness* and *glory* of God in His *power,* and then trails off into everything else. This is, I think, a fundamental theological error, one that has gravely handicapped the spirituality and the development of the church.

The Gospels should be read from the *unfulfilled* promise of the second coming backward. We should see in the acts of the Christ the strength motivated by his tragic love to bring about the fulfillment of the promised Kingdom, taking heart from the manifestation of God's powerful presence, but understand the deep sense in which the whole process is left unfinished and unfulfilled. The traditional triumphalism is, in spirit, heretical. Jesus himself shuns the temptations to triumphalism and renounces the premature joys of any preliminary or penultimate victories short of the complete consummation of God's will in the full reconciliation of humanity, and with a profoundly, even essentially, tragic vision and sense relates this to his disciples at the last supper. "Verily I say unto you, I will drink no more of the fruit of the vine, *until* the day that I drink it new in the kingdom of God." (*KJV* Mark 14:25)

In African American Christian consciousness, this theological sense is grounded in its deep structure, in the experience of longing and the instantiated state of the interrogative that implies a fundamental openness to the future and an equally fundamental dissatisfaction with the present. As such it is prophetic in its structure, but nevertheless deeply priestly in spirit and content as well, as the experience of consolation is fostered by the forms, mode, and mood of religious experiencing. The theology of African American Christian consciousness shuns the simplistic classification of "radical" (often identified with black theologies of liberation) and "conservative" for a wider reading of the always already interdependent priestly and prophetic strains of the experience. This approach also seeks to understand these themes in terms of the deep structures of the experience itself.

Religious Experience and the Theology of African American Consciousness

The religious experience of African Americans was and is shaped by their sociocultural context. The matrix of social relations always already imbued with relations of power and force provided the context in which the Christian faith was encountered and appropriated. The process was, however, dialectical, with the appropriated symbols, narratives, paradigmatic stories, and so on acting back on the African American's interpretation of reality and the way he perceived and evaluated the matrix of social relations in which he found himself. The matrix of forces, however, that constituted African American Christian consciousness as such was, however, more than simply the Christian faith and the matrix of social relations. This process took place in the uniquely African soul, in the process of its reconstitution on American soil, with all that the African could manage to bring to bear upon the process, consciously and unconsciously. The factors involved in this process have been examined earlier in this text.

The black theologian James Cone has said that black theology (to which I am referring here broadly as theology done in, and of, the African American Christian community) should be grounded in black experience. He states,

> For theology to be black, it must reflect upon what it means to be black. Black Theology must uncover the structures and forms of black experience, because the categories of interpretation must arise out of the thought forms of the black experience.[3]

Black is being used here obviously as a criterion for authenticity. For theological reflection to be authentically black or true to the black experience, the categories and the forms must be taken from the experience itself. With this point I am in agreement. Yet while I believe that the categories of interpretation by which theological reflection should proceed ought to be derived from the religious experience of African Americans, I think that the examination of that experience should proceed by methods appropriate to the experience itself. In other words, if one is going to do theology based on the experience of a people, particularly their religious experience (where I think it ought to be based), one needs to first examine the structure of the experience itself, with methods appropriate to that task. I don't think that African American theology should restrict itself to a kind of journalistic reporting on what African Americans may have said and thought in the past, or present for that matter. I am not even sure at this point that the verbal articulation of beliefs by the African American can be trusted at face value to disclose what is really going on theologically in the African American Church or in the religious experience of her devotees. No people's consciousness is ipso facto transparent to itself.

I think that the relationship between theology and the African American experience is far more complicated than Cone and others want it to be and far more ambiguous. The criterion of authenticity and, I assume, validity for any theology claiming to be black theology is that it must be truly or at least meaningfully black. So then the question becomes, "How does one determine that?" Cone has an answer.

> The real test of whether any given articulation of Black Theology is black does not depend on what Wilmore, Cone, or any other theologian says; rather, it depends upon whether the particular theology is consistent with what black people believe to be the basis of their struggle. Therefore we will have to wait and see how black people respond to what we say. Their response is the only test.[4]

Based strictly on these criteria, Cone's theology was not, nor is it now, authentically black. By and large it was never grasped or even entertained seriously by a wide audience of the African American Church. More to the point here, however, are the anthropological assumptions he seems to be making in the establishment of this criteria for black theology. Cone wants to argue that the theology must be "consistent with what black people believe to be the basis of their struggle." To say the least, I think this whole approach is fundamentally flawed (although Cones's actual theology is brilliantly insightful) and would present an almost interminable set of logical difficulties to anyone who wanted to spend the time plodding through the argument, analyzing its implications and checking for serious disturbances of internal coherence.

Consciousness is not transparent to itself. There are many things that go on at an unconscious level that actually shape our behavior and betray what we really believe, in spite of our consciously held and stated convictions. Our deepest convictions about the nature of reality and what we really believe must often be inferred from the broader text of life and practice; disclosed by methods that are able to unearth our axial assumptions. The theology of African American Christian consciousness is under no romantic illusions about the people's ability or interest in lifting to systematic self-consciousness their convictions concerning their religious faith. Moreover, it might be that African Americans' reactions to black theology are refracted through the distorted experience of oppression, and this can only be attenuated through a serious pedagogy or process of consciencism.

One of the serious difficulties of black theology has been its methodological shortcomings. In developing its understanding of the black church and working with a method and methodological presuppositions that preclude the development of a sophisticated philosophical anthropology, it failed to take into serious consideration the extent to which the black church reflects the deep pathology generated in the African American community by the structures of oppression and the impact that this might have on African Americans even recognizing themselves in an accurate theological articulation of "black being." A theology that is not immediately recognized by black people, and one would assume that by black people Cone means of course the "real" black people, is not necessarily invalidated thereby. This assumes, of course, that you would be able to identify who the real black people are.[5] Out of a more nuanced analysis of the inherent ambiguity of the African American Christian Church, with more emphasis placed on understanding and explanation rather than the ubiquitous moralistic preoccupations that characterize so much of the work to date, we may be able to forge ahead into more diversified theological approaches and develop a more effective practical theology. This approach would be more fruitful and provide those who want to do theology in the African American experience with a much broader range of options than is currently available. The theology of African American Christian consciousness resists the innate proclivity of the black theology movement to dissolve itself into a kind of historical religious journalism on the one hand and social ethics on the other.

While there is a great deal to be learned from the study of certain, in many ways, paradigmatic personages and historical African American figures, this should not be the primary focal point for developing a theology of the African American Christian experience. The method must not be primarily historical or even textual for that matter. In other words, the focus should not be on particularly historic events or the words of individuals when forced to attempt a discursive articulation of the faith. Theology is not religious journalism to the second power. The rich-textured experience of the unsung heroes that bore their burden in the heat of the day and persevered that we might have a chance at the tree of life is the primary focus of the theology of African American Christian consciousness.

Nathan Irvin Huggins gives eloquent articulation to this position when referring to the experience of the slave and the orientation of his study of the peculiar institution.

> It is not that we would give less respect to Gabriel Prosser, Denmark Vesey, and Nat Turner; nor can we say enough of the importance of Harriet Tubman and the many thousands who "voted with their feet" for freedom. Rather, it is my intent to reach for the heart of a people whose courage was in their refusal to be brutes, in their insistence on holding themselves together, on acting, speaking, and singing as men and women. For the majority of African Americans did that. Their lives were not marked by extraordinary acts of defiance. They lived and they died as captives within a system of slave labor....
>
> Within that tyranny, looking beyond the acts of defiance, rebellion, and escape, we will find a *quality of courage* [italics mine] still unsung. It is in the triumph of the human spirit over unmitigated *power* [italics mine]. It raised no banners. It gained no vengeance. It was only the pervasive and persistent will among Afro-Americans to hold together through deep trauma and adversity.[6]

In the quotation above, in the second paragraph, Huggins makes reference to "a quality of courage" that remains unsung. This quality of courage is in fact a manifestation of the phenomenon of *strength* we have been referring to throughout. It is also significant he points out that one sees it, that it can be observed in the triumph of the human spirit over *"unmitigated power," absolute power,* if you will. Here, Huggins testifies to the existential, moral, and spiritual superiority of *strength* over power, marking its concrete manifestation the in the *souls of black folk*. Strength won out over unmitigated power, as slaves became "*more* than conquerors." In strength we see the true glory and greatness of the human and of the divine. Jesus of Nazareth exercised such strength and dramatically epitomized the ontological tension of these clashing titanic deities when, standing before Pilot, he proclaimed, "My kingdom is not of this world: if my kingdom were of this world, then would my servants fight, that I should not be delivered to the Jews: but now is my kingdom not from hence" (John 18:36 *KJV*). Power, the unmitigated control exercised over Jesus by his captors provided the occasion and the foil for the revelation of God's *strength* through the passion and in the cross.

We were able to uncover the deeper phenomena, of which Huggins's "unsung courage" is but a manifestation, and raise it to a level of theological self-consciousness because of the nature of the method we employed to get at the deep structure of the experience. To really develop a theology of African American Christian consciousness with intellectual integrity, one that is credible, recognizable, and existentially available, one would have to give articulation to the structure, mood, religious sentiments, and concerns that are constitutive of the religious subjectivity of the "unsung," those people who held "together through deep trauma and adversity." I have tried, in some small way, to contribute to this project in this text. It has been my intention to analyze and characterize African American Christian consciousness. I have found the religious experience and consciousness of the "unsung" to be tragic in structure, mood, color, and tone. Any theology based on that experience must in fact be a tragic theology or rather a theology of the tragic.

The Theological Unconscious of the African American Church and the Theology of African American Christian Consciousness

If you were to canvas African Americans and ask them what they believe about God or what the Christian faith is or what it means to them, you are likely to get as many different responses as the number of people asked. You will find common agreement on some things of course, such as Jesus Christ being the center of their faith; but then, find them more often than not using Jesus as center or "God as the center" interchangeably with absolutely no qualms about the myriad theological implications. Currently, you will often find them expressing their faith in fundamentalist terms. This relatively recent development is the result of the rise of the charismatic movement, the vulgar commercialization of black gospel music and the religious confusion introduced into the African American community by the many thoughtless individuals heading congregations now; some who will justify the use of any "the-ideology" or method designed primarily to exploit the Christian "market" as long as Jesus is mentioned and it leads (or as long as they *believe* it leads) to personal wealth and fame. In light of the changing climate in the church today, if the black theology movement were to remain committed to Cone's original methodological assumptions, criterion of authenticity, and judgment, Black Theology would amount to nothing more than "an articulation of the intellectual interests of black professors."[7] But of course we know the contribution of Cone and the subsequent developments in black theology to be of more significance than that.

Unlike Cone's brand of black theology, the legitimacy of the theology of African American Christian consciousness does not rest, in the final analysis, on mass acceptance. Anyone who places the legitimacy of anything like truth on mass acceptance comes dangerously close to ruling out all truth as inadmissible evidence in the trial of life. It has often been the case throughout history that even widely erroneous views have lived on at the expense of human advancement when contrary but more correct views have been presented. What would have come of science and the subsequent transformations of our views of the universe and notions such as the nature of the solar system, matter, gravity, space, and time had it been left to the court of public opinion. While theology is not an exact science, by any stretch of the imagination, it does make truth claims. The validity of these claims must rest on more than the instant recognition of their immediate audience for their epistemological status. Moreover, we are on particularly unstable ground when dealing with truths about ourselves and our inner life, which depth psychology has more than adequately demonstrated, to be most often the hardest to accept or gain wide acceptance. An examination of the theological unconscious and, more pointedly, unconscious dynamics in the formation of African American subjectivity as it plays itself out in the religious sphere, which is always already fraught with ambiguity, will reveal both pleasant and unpleasant truths, and almost never truths with an impact that is easy to accept. But if we are going to have clear theological vision and effective praxis, this road less traveled is the route that must be taken.

By the term "theological unconscious," I merely wish to indicate, rather broadly, those dimensions of the faith of a community that are implicated in their vision of reality, their mood or geist and its structure; in key dynamics in the worship experience or at the point of its most intense and passionate articulation, and the implications of these elements for theological reflection. By the use of the term *unconscious*, I do not mean simply *convictions* of which persons remain unaware or dynamics that lie below the discursive level of articulation, but also the *implications* of what is actually experienced in their faith, lives, and worship process. The implications of some of the elements in the theological unconscious may at points stand in stark contrast to some of the doctrinal positions held consciously by the community in question. They may also be in contradiction to some of the doctrinal positions held consciously by the community in question. They may be in contradiction to each other as well. Human beings often hold contradictory ideas concerning their religious faith that I have found to actually function in tandem in the process of what we have referred to earlier as *spiritual adaptation*. Like the *ordinary* unconscious of the human subject, the theological unconscious of the African American Christian Church contains contradictions or contradictory notions that do not necessarily cause conflict or create conscious tension. They remain there, for the most part without difficulty, unless summoned or aggravated by a combination of individual or intersubjective predicaments and the circumstantial matrix. The ethical issue of homosexuality is a case in point.

The African American Church is a scripturalist tradition. African American Christian consciousness is not as literalistic as is the fundamentalist tradition, having been given to the task of demythologization from the beginning. Demythologization was not provoked, however, by the intellectual conflict produced by the awareness of critical academic methods in the study of scripture or the need to adjust intellectually to the growth in the authority and prestige of science, as was the case with Rudolf Bultman. It was prior to that movement and linked closer to the exigencies of psychic and spiritual survival and the part that the myths, symbols, paradigmatic personages, and situations in the Bible have played in that effort. At any rate, if pressed to formulate a position on the issue of homosexuality, the African American scripturalist would present a position sounding much like that of the fundamentalist. Yet there is a strong tradition of tolerance for homosexuality in the church. Granted, there are differing degrees of this tolerance and different thresholds drawn on it, but most impartial observers would admit that the tolerance is relatively ubiquitous. Knowledge of someone's alleged homosexuality does not provoke the same heated furor as it would in a fundamentalist community in spite of the almost identical scriptural position assumed. This can be most easily observed in the case of church musicians, where the issue has been traditionally most notably present, albeit not exclusively so. This is not due to an ethical lapse of any kind, or an ethical surrender to practicality, which would be no more than hypocrisy, but to the particular shape of African American Christian consciousness. There is a deep abiding *strength* that permeates African American Christian consciousness, directly attributable to its tragic nature as defined earlier in the text that grounds an unusual breadth of acceptance, and sympathy for the wounds and difficulties of others, enabling the devotee to absorb community-destroying tensions without recourse to bad faith or self-deceptive defensive strategies, such as denial and rationalization. This can be witnessed even in those cases where other scripture-centered traditions yield more often to the council of spiritualized cruelty for those who are different. Because of the conflict, of course, tensions persist and are not always resolved in the church in constructive ways. It is the task of the theologian to provide direction through reflection so as to ensure the best possible outcome in as many cases as possible. For the theology of African American Christian consciousness, the phenomenon of homosexuality in the church becomes another cipher in the attempt to give theological articulation to African American Christian consciousness as such.

The characteristic capacity of this *strength* to absorb community-destroying tensions is also an extremely significant cipher in the understanding of God. This experience points to the pre-oedipal nature of the African American transmoral self, about which I will say a little more below. It also indicates the centrality of the maternal dimension of the experience of God and its importance for a full appreciation of the divine in African American Christian consciousness. This maternal dimension is an essential element of the experience of God in African American Christian consciousness. Inasmuch as we believe African American religious experience to be a distinct experience, though not insulated or isolated in any fundamental way from common human experience as such, it is a contribution to the broader view of the nature and the relationship of the divine and the human and it has serious implications for the entire church's theological vision.

The theological unconscious as I am using it here has strong connections to Christopher Bollas's notion of the "unthought known." Just like the tragic and its expression in African American religious and cultural spirituality, the "unthought known" is prior to language. It is pre-linguistic. If we think of this priority to language less as chronological and more as ontological, the deeper connections begin to come into focus. In Bollas's view, the "shadow of the object" is cast over the child in terms of how it is oriented to the world rather than merely the internalization of objects or introjects in a self with an established or preset structure.

> Not yet fully identified as an other, the mother is experienced as a process of transformation and this feature of early existence lives on in certain forms of object-seeking in adult life, when the object is sought for its function as a signifier of transformation. Thus, in adult life, the quest is not to possess the object; rather the object is pursued in order to surrender to it as a medium that alters the self, where the subject-as-supplicant now feels himself to be the recipient of enviro-somatic caring, identified with metamorphoses of the self. Since it is an identification that begins before the mother is mentally represented as an other, it is an object relation that emerges not from desire, but from a perceptual identification of the object with its function: the object as enviro-somatic transformer of the subject. The memory of this early object relation manifests itself in the person's search for an object (a person, place, event, ideology) that promises to transform the self.[8]

The penetration to this level of structure in the human subject precipitated by crisis activates a primordial mode of experiencing and perceiving the world. By primordial, I mean fundamental, not "primitive." We must avoid the evaluative judgment usually associated with what are perceived to be "earlier" or more fundamental levels of existence that make of them "lesser," or "immature," so therefore something merely to be superseded as we become more sophisticated.

At this primordial level, Bollas helps us to see that there is a relation to the object grounded in those experiences that are transformative and healing. The healing and transformational relation to the object at a prelinguistic level is precisely where African Americans found themselves in the moan that became music; the longing that became a pain and imperiled hope; the relation that became religion; and the mother that became God. This is the spirituality that emerges from human subjectivity prior to its elaboration in symbol systems and in the case of Christianity and Western monotheism, a repressive, oedipal, "imposition-al" patriarchalism. Elaborating on this relevance to thinking about religion, James W. Jones writes,

> So potent is this primary transformational tie to the mother that it casts a long shadow extending throughout a person's life. In times of crisis, the person longs for a transformational object that can facilitate the integration of new experience. In moments of ecstasy, like that described in much religious literature, a new transformational object has been discovered in another person or overpowering piece of music, an evocative text, or the awesomeness of nature.[9]

African Americans lost the "mother" land, culture, religion, and relationships and continued in a state of loss, so that loss and longing became the orientation to the world. The shadow of the object stretched through the length and breadth of our culture and manifested its dark tonality in our mournful song. This primordial experience in the African American subject, which was at the same time a longing and an affirmation, was grounded in her aesthetic performance, and when in contact with the ground of her being erupted in the frenzy. "In the aesthetic moment the subject briefly reexperiences, through ego fusion with the aesthetic object, a sense of the subjective attitude towards the transformational object."[10]

In a similar and related vein, Fairbairn, distinguishing the "good" and "bad" early objects (mother) that, unlike Bollas's shadow object are internalized, thought that "the 'bad' maternal object derives from and represents her inaccessibility, her untouchability, and the frustration, rage, and anxiety that this engenders."[11] Let us suspend for a moment the potentially obfuscating evaluative language. This orientation of the human subject to relate to loved objects that are lost or, as he says, are "unavailable" or "untouchable" has implications for the deep structure of the human subject that orients us to ultimate reality in a trauma and certainly a chronic crisis. It is the ultimate frame of reference and basic trust systems that are disturbed in traumatic loss. This, I have shown, was particularly poignant for the African Americans. So the gods, the soothing comfort of resting in a familiar matrix of meaning, were unavailable. There was a profound sense of abandonment or forlornness. This, I have argued, is one of the constituent dynamics in the generative dialectic of hope/affirmation and resignation that is part and parcel of the tragic vision. It yields the longing and the plaintive pain. The point to note here is the identical subset of affective states in African American religious subjectivity, unconscious and preconscious orientations, and their connection to the maternal foundation of our most primordial and formative experiences.

> The "bad" object (internalized and repressed) is then experienced in two ways (also split). On the one hand, it is felt to withhold contact (the rejecting object), and on the other, to hold out a never-to-be-fulfilled promise of contact (the exciting object). The dual "bad" internal object elicits terror and rage in response to its withholding quality and longing in response to its promise. (This second splitting is of the bad internal object.)[12]

I believe God was decisively reflected in Christ; but it seems no less compelling that she appeared on the face of Mary as well. It is the empathic connection between mother and child that establishes the initial connection long before access to language and leaves the shadow of the object for which we long and sometimes pine under pressure. We see the face peering down at us from the cross, but the one peering up at it is hidden. The empathic connection between the two insured that the suffering was meaningfully shared, as we have come to believe that God shares our own.

> Sometimes I feel like a motherless child
> Sometimes I feel like a motherless child
> Oh Lord, Sometimes I feel like a motherless child
> Den I get down on my knees and pray
>
> Sometimes I feel like a motherless child
> Sometimes I feel like a motherless child
> Sometimes I feel like a motherless child
> A long ways from home

The theological unconscious is significant because despite its remaining, for the most part unconscious or preconscious, it is nevertheless highly influential in the overall shape of the experience and manifests its effectual presence in what is self-consciously experienced as religious, particularly the affective states. Certain processes may indicate, as I believe they do in African American Christian consciousness and religious experience, the *signature* of the divine, yielding information about the divine nature and the nature of its interaction with humanity. By exploring these levels of the experience with the appropriate methods, we are able to achieve a higher level of theological understanding. We enrich the meaning and the meaningfulness of the faith experience of the individual subject and the group in question. We can also deepen our analysis and evaluation of the inherently ambiguous phenomena of religious experience and hence, enhance the creative, enabling, and empowering elements, while minimizing or transforming the countercreative, life-inhibiting, pathogenic, and constraining dynamics. The exploration of these latter issues would be the particular focus of and of particular interest to practical theology proper, with its emphasis on the "arts of ministry." While a complete analysis such as the one I indicated above is beyond the ambitions of the present text, I do believe it both safe and beneficial to sound the depths on some relevant issues.

The Divine Immanence

The first issue I would like to consider is the notion of the divine immanence as it relates to the theological unconscious, given what we have learned of it from our analysis of the tragic structure of African American Christian consciousness. There was and still remains a powerful poetic component in African American Christian consciousness involving a deep and abiding relationship with nature that Africans brought with them to the Americas. Its survival rested on a number of things, but the most significant was the fact that it was intangible, embedded in the African's soul.[13] Moreover, the same moon, stars, sun, and water were still visible. While the flora may have changed, it was still green. Flowers still bloomed, and beasts still roamed the edges of the "village." That endless sky stretched until its straining arms enfolded the perimeter of the Earth, making of all water and dry land one in the end. Earth, sky, and sea all kissed, touched and everywhere mingled until their intimate relations bled them together into a cosmic whole. African Americans lived their daily lives in a spiritual milieu that brought them into close and intimate relations with their natural surroundings. Hence all of life was always already imbued with that same power that pulsated in the gurgling stream; rose and fell with the jostling wind, that shocked and summoned with the rippling lightening and rolling thunder that soothed with the falling rain.

> *Steal away, steal away, steal away to Jesus!*
> *Steal away, steal away home,*
> *I ain't got long to stay here.*

> My Lord, He calls me,
> He calls me by the thunder;
> The trumpet sounds within my soul,
> I ain't got long to stay here
>
> Green trees are bending,
> Poor sinners stand a-trembling;
> The trumpet sounds within my soul,
> I ain't got long to stay here.
>
> My Lord, He calls me,
> He calls me by the lightning;
> The trumpet sounds within my soul,
> I ain't got long to stay here.

This pulsating, mysterious power, like the wilds on the edge of the village, lay always on the fringe of daily life and although it must always be approached reverently and with care, it remained intimately accessible to the African and her progeny. It was this power that flowed and surged at the molten center of African American spiritual life that erupted in worship and poured through individual vents, spilling itself in a Dionysian flow of shout and song, of the frenzy and the dance, the prayer and the spoken word.

The ritual process in which all these elements manifest themselves peaks in a dialectical negation of the existing self and its reconstitution or rememberment in a ritual space free of the debilitating cultural taxonomy, by which the original "sparagmous," the inner crucifixion of the African American self, fractured along a thousand lines of fissure. It was inevitable that much of this debilitating cultural "stuff" was internalized and equally inevitable then, that strong intrapsychic tensions were established. These strong intrapsychic tensions, along with the lack of the reinforced boundaries provided by a coherent cultural framework into which the African American was thoroughly and *meaningfully* integrated, conspired to tear the self apart, scattered in its several, severed pieces. Like ill-fated Dionysus torn asunder by titanic forces, the African American is as well; but again, like the eternally youthful chthonic god, he is reconstituted, and the self is recentered and adjusted in ritual space and time. Being is reaffirmed in and through the ritual process. He may not know exactly what it all means or know/accept exactly where his *place* is in the everyday framework of life processes, but he knows that life means and that there is a "place" of his own—somewhere. This healing that the devotee undergoes and experiences directly reaffirms the meaningfulness of life. It strengthens the self against the threat of fragmentation and yields a deep and abiding sense of strength and well-being. African American Christian consciousness and religious experience are a marvel of spiritual and cultural adaptation. It helped her to effectively cope with the potentially overwhelming immiserization of slavery and the continued oppression and marginalization that followed—and follows. It does so by infusing the subject with the existential life blood necessary to keep the spirit alive, quickened and actively engaged in the day-to-day struggle for psychic and spiritual survival. The religious consciousness provided the sinew that held the fractured self together in spite of the ever-present pressure of disintegration and breakdown.

A centered self is in some respect the necessary precondition for liberation or of a freedom that is truly free. A self that is not strong enough to effectively resist and hold at bay the overdetermination that forever threatens to impinge upon the self with forces, internal and external, imposing on the will, can never adequately ground the authentic exercise and experience of freedom. Liberation presupposes an *adequate* space in which the will can make meaningful and healthy choices. Ritual experience helps to contain and even quarantine the destructive forces that would ravage the will and destroy the capacity of the subject to envision alternative worlds. The ritual process itself provides the optimal conditions for the envisioning of alternative worlds, leaving in its wake the indelible imprint of the possibility of an altered state of being. Even though the self may not be truly free with respect to internal or external constraints when it returns to daily life, the ineradicable imprint of an alternative state of being is left upon the soul of the subject. It is branded there by a combination of biblical imagery signifying emancipation, and the heat of the hyperliminal state. The soul of the subject is marked *for life,* the fullness of life. Hence, even where overt action is not taken by the subject on behalf of its own emancipation, the possibility of liberation is instantiated in a dispositional intentionality that issues forth in an intense longing. The longing can only find complete rest and satisfaction in total reconciliation. In other words, it possesses an inherently eschatological and utopian dimension. This is the subversive element always already entailed in the ritual process which is constitutive of African American Christian consciousness. This consciousness continues to this day to be the greatest repository of the aspirations, hopes, and dreams of this oppressed people.

Paul Tillich and others have pointed to the fact that there are processes at work in nature that have certain functions, such as anxiety reduction and emotional healing. These reflections of his are recorded in a number of places but are most accessible in the text entitled *The Meaning of Health*.[14] With respect to his reflections on the issue of healing inherent in nature, or rather, intersubjective processes, they came mostly in relation to his explorations of psychoanalysis. It is my contention that there is a strengthening/healing dynamic at work in the African American Christian ritual process in a unique and unusually potent way. This dynamic healing process that leads to the centering and strengthening of the self, the healing telos of its fracture, and its work on behalf of African American emancipation in a penultimate sense (with the *promise* of complete reconciliation), is the signature of the divine immanence.[15] God is present in the ritual process deploying the divine strength on behalf of human health, wholeness, and emancipation. Emancipation is itself the necessary prerequisite for the ultimate aim of human health or salvation.[16] God has committed the divine being to the tasks broadly identified above. God is *personally invested* in the process.

The decision-making process for human beings is hardly an unambiguous one. For salvation to occur meaningfully on an individual basis, the decision must be made by a centered self free of the overdetermination that distorts human experience and refracts human choices. The same is true of authentic worship. I realize that this picture is something of an ideal construct; depicted in an existential purity of process along somewhat chronological lines and quite impossible given the dialectical, always already nature of human existence.[17] But from within the matrices of the life situation, God labors on behalf of freedom in the cause of freedom to bring about the fullness of life. His labors, as we have noted above, to optimize freedom at several levels from within the nature/culture matrix of humanity characterizes the divine immanence and attests to his caring, laboring, and lifting nature. It also bespeaks the necessity of labor within conditions that are at once enabling and constraining in nature. The decisive factor in this ambiguous atmosphere is the divine immanence that tips the scales in the human being's favor. This "tipping of the scales" demonstrates an imminent dimension of God's grace. This grace comes about by the exertion of God's strength in the labors of God on our behalf.

The Divine Transcendence

In spite of strong intimations of God's immanence in African American Christian consciousness, there is also a deep sense of the divine transcendence. The experience of the divine transcendence is implicated in the perception of the divine immanence. The African and African American maintained a strong sense of the presence of God in their daily experiences, in nature, and in the larger drift of history, but the meaning of the divine was never and could never be exhausted in or by those frames of reference. The divine immanence was both an indication of the divine in itself and also everywhere a cipher of the God beyond. There is a deeply mystical element in African American Christian consciousness that is indicated, of course, by the union that takes place with the invasion of the Holy Spirit, erupting during worship in the frenzy. But there is also a lingering sense outside of the immediate framework of the ritual itself that combines elements of the immanence and the transcendence of the divine in a profoundly mystical way. This sense of the beyond or God's transcendence allows the African American to both experience God within, or I should say in spite of, her oppressive circumstances while at the same time transcending or being *carried beyond* them by the God who is and goes beyond.

This sense of transcendence is reflected in the pervasive imagery of rivers and the vital part they play in the formation of African American Christian consciousness. Rivers roll. They flow. They glide over and around obstacles with a singleness of purpose that vaguely intimates the focus of a determined personal presence. Rivers can be seen as the essence of monotony, but then again, to the eye of deeper discerning, it is the essence of purposeful being. The African American must live each day on purpose. It requires the exertion of existential effort just to go on. This going on, however, must be properly understood. It is not the being driven on like blind cattle before the rod and the lash. It is the mode of the resolute with the gaze directed toward the remote. Life is not something that happens *for him* from day to day. The sheer rolling on of "it," is intentional activity. Rivers are here; but there as well. Even the *here* is always going *there*. Rivers come from an "I know not where," picking up my soul, as it collects so many other things in its path, and carries it on. They are an endless source of mystery; a world in and of themselves with their life *underground,* hidden, and away. Their flow indicates other places, obscure destinations, change;

and if change, then difference; if difference, then hope. Rivers are dividing lines. They mark the border line between "this," and "that." However formidable their loping currents and groaning tides, they are always in principle, navigable. Rivers are an indication that "life is yet alive."[18]

> In this way, the object of slaves' worship was realized: to re-establish the relationship of self with the life force of the universe; to achieve unity of the self with all life.
>
> Black religion was thus a celebration of life, of feeling, of both the tangible and the spiritual. The great joy was in the affirmation by the living spirit that the self was part of the living substance of all life, and that one had meaning, therefore, in the largeness of life, the bosom of God. This was a guarantee of support in this world as well as in the next.[19]

If there is something beyond, then we know that reality is never exhausted by what we see. If I am not exhausted by what is seen, then there is something of me that transcends my circumstances, a dimension of my being that cannot be quantified, labeled, forced to work, whipped, or spat upon. There is a part of me that cannot be owned or enslaved. My being cannot be exhaustively captured in the cultural taxonomy. A slave with a sense of God's transcendence need not submit physically to the implications of the present order as God's will because there is more to God's will than what can be perceived. We do not know that the present order means what it appears to mean or what the oppressor says it means. What we do know is that there is *something* more.

In the consciousness, there is a deep sense of *something* out there and an equally profound hesitation in many cases to name what that something is. This is significant. Even when the reference is obviously God, Jesus, or the Holy Spirit, African American Christians have preferred, in many cases, to use the ubiquitous "something." Even when completely conscious of the site for a biblical phrase, African American preachers have again and again opted to use "somewhere": "I read somewhere...," for instance. In the past there has been a failure to really understand the nature of the use and the function of this kind of language in African American Christian conscious. When one is preaching, for instance, communication is not a monolithic evocation of a one-to-one correspondence in sense and syntax. It functions in a way that besides the communication of *ideas,* it contributes to the creation of an experience. Preaching in the African American religious experience grows out of and participates in the engendering of the African American Christian consciousness. It is dialectical in the deepest sense and plays a key role in driving the ritual process to a cathartic crescendo.

Words operate in a variety of ways in creating the overall effect. Some words function like circuits or switches and can send the current of religious sentiment in other directions. For instance, when preaching speakers within the tradition commonly say, often in the form of an emotional refrain, "I read somewhere...," in most cases, the preacher is indicating to his audience that he read what he is referring to in the Bible. That is the direct sense. The switch word here, however, is "somewhere." That directs current to the sense of mystery and awe and activates it, adding to and thickening the entire psychic milieu of the experience, creating an overall effect far deeper than the communication of a shared proposition. The way in which the different dynamics come together in the creation of the overall effect or in the creation of the ritual milieu is similar to the way different instruments, sections, movements, and melodies are brought together, in the process actualizing a musical composition. There are things going on in every dimension of the process that add to the overall shape and effect of the piece. Preaching, as well as other elements in African American religious experience, is laced with switch words, trap doors, and hidden passages that presuppose an entire tradition and a great deal of nondiscursive knowledge[20] or the "unthought known" on the part of the devotee before they can participate fully in the richness and wealth of the experience. Add to that, of course, the sociocultural context of marginalization and multilayered oppression. All African American Christians are not equally religiously musical, hence a great deal is left to the distinctive sensitivities of individuals within the framework itself. The sense of transcendence is a fundamental element of the theological unconscious of the African American Church.

Moral Theology and the Theology of African American Christian Consciousness

While the primary or axial dynamic in the experience of European American Christians was and remains the notion of guilt, it was otherwise for the African American, who came to the Christian faith from a different sociocultural matrix and whose subjectivity was constituted by a different configuration of forces. This observation has been made by many others. Nathan Huggins observes, "Afro-American Christianity was less guilt-burdened than white Christianity. Evil and sin existed, but they were forces of the universe, not of man's natural condition.... [The African American] Man was weak but not corrupt."[21] He did not have to be first convinced of his guiltiness and then after, convinced of his need to be forgiven for it and then given Jesus as a cure-all. The experience of the Christ in the African American frame of reference suffered much less from this vulgar, utilitarian, commoditization it underwent generally in New World Protestantism, particularly Southern evangelicalism. While the guilt of sin and the *worthlessness of all humanity* served as the primary progenitors of the psychic milieu in which Christianity was engaged by European Americans; the existential predicament of the enslaved, culturally marginalized, economically commoditized, and generally oppressed African American provided the matrix from which Christ was doing the delivering. The tragic field provided the context within which the African Americans experienced Christ's saving and salving work.

The encounter of the African American Christian who seriously engaged the faith tended by virtue of circumstance to be, by and large, more existentially thoroughgoing than her European American counterpart. It tended to be far less the typical "head trip" from the proposition of human guiltiness; to the proposition of you need forgiveness (driven home of course on the notion of eternal damnation versus heavenly bliss), to the proposition Jesus is savior, dipping only occasionally into the surface of the depths by the psychological exacerbation of guilt feelings; feelings, again based on greater or lesser clarity and intensity of conceptual perception. This is not to say that guilt and all the thorny issues of the Christian morality did not enter the picture for African Americans early on; indeed they did, but at a vastly different social location, and far more ambiguously. The psychic, cultural, and spiritual milieu was and remains different for the African American. This is why some African Americans' attempt to approach the Christian faith today from fundamentalist phenomenal and experiential frames of reference are producing interesting disturbances, existential disjunction, a great deal of bad faith, and forced expressions that smack right off as false, pretentious, defensive, and self-deceptive. There is a fundamental disingenuousness about the whole phenomenon of "cross-over" African American Christians even today as they attempt to integrate religions *concepts* within frames of experience that cannot adequately facilitate penetration to the depths.

The appropriation of the Christian faith by African Americans was a successful, albeit not unambiguous, exercise in cultural, spiritual, and psychic adaption. The development of African American Christian consciousness displays the marks of its origin in its dominant themes, its structure, and in its existential issue. An important dimension of the existential issue is, of course, the ethical—that which is made manifest in life through practice. Here again, remaining faithful to our methodological assumption that our theological investigations should take African American Christian consciousness as its primary source, let us turn for a moment to sketch, in a broad and most preliminary fashion, some key considerations in the formation of a theological ethics.

First of all, I must say that no detailed or programmatic ethics of African American Christian consciousness can be completely worked out without paying some very serious attention to the particular configuration of forces that is at work in and on the African American community today as well as in the larger American framework. Too little attention has been paid to the sociocultural and psychological realities operative in the community and the church itself. For instance, too little attention has been paid to the idea that far from insulating or absolving African Americans from evil, oppression, in the full measure of its diabolical character, may make African Americans far more vulnerable to it, and not simply as victims. And given the identifiable pattern of oppression involving issues such as marginalization, disparagement of self-image, and the stubborn persistence and even evolution of debilitating cultural taxonomies, there ought to be some typological consistencies in the emergent social pathologies. Close and extensive attention needs to be given to the characteristic pathologies emerging from this unique sociocultural matrix and how they are playing themselves out in the church and the broader phenomena of Christianity among African Americans. How one evaluates the operation of evil, or more consistently with the view being developed here, *spiritual pathology* among African Americans is another issue; but failure to take the pervasive presence of certain symptomatic realities seriously has caused a deep crisis at the level of practical theology or theological praxis in the African American Church.

With this qualification stated, however, I do think that there are some things, on the more positive side, that can be pointed to as constituent elements of the ethical dimension of any theology of African

American Christian consciousness. These dimensions are the result of the miracle of spiritual adaptation that the emergence of African American Christian consciousness actually was. As indicated earlier, strength is at the center of the consciousness, indeed at the center of African American being, and must play a central role in the formation of a positive moral theology. The Christian life, as indicated by an exploration of African American consciousness, is first and foremost a life of strength. It is, by nature, life affirming and therefore always constructive and given to endurance and long suffering in pursuit of the abundant life, the emancipated life. While *ought* does not necessarily imply *can* in this approach, because of the proximity of moral mandate and experience itself that issue does not hold the same urgency for this type of reflection that it may have held for classical ethical systems. Indeed, it is in the exertion of this strength for the coming Kingdom that the moral life finds its purpose and meaning and reaches its fulfillment. We witness the manifestation of this strength in a variety of ways; but, for the purposes of this brief discussion, we will consider it and its ethical import as we reflect on it in relation to the forms of resistance characteristic of African American Christian consciousness as they are cataloged by Nathan Huggins.

Let me say initially that while I appreciate Huggins's cursory and preliminary attempt to give articulation to the existential/ethical dimension of African American Christian consciousness, I do not submit to the generally refractory, moralistic tenor of his account. Due again, as in the case of James Cone, to serious methodological shortcomings, he fails to take seriously the ambiguity of the experience, replacing an assessment of the genuinely complex nature of the experience and its colossal challenge to anything like conventional morality with a somewhat romanticized moralistic account. The "soul's great challenges" to the oppressed, the primary focus of her resistance, were three in number—fear, deception, and hatred. What does he mean by "soul's great challenge?" We get a hint in the sentence at the end of the chapter dealing with these issues.

> Indeed it was these qualities among slaves that enabled them *to survive with integrity;* and it was these qualities that caused whites, looking on as agents of oppression, to remark at the strength and natural dignity of Black people.[22]

The great challenge for Huggins appears to be survival; but not just survival for the sake of survival. It was not just survival at any cost but survival with integrity. On the surface this seems to be a solid statement. However, I am concerned with the equivocal use of the term *integrity*. In as much as integrity means to act with a measure of psychic unity, centeredness, and self-integration; to have the capacity to process information and determine one's responses, justifying them with a rationale that at least demonstrates a basic grasp of reality and the basic capacity to process that reality; as well as to form relationships where possible and have hopes and dreams—in other words, all the things that make life worthwhile—I am in total agreement. It is the moralistic undertones of the term *integrity* that marks the other side of the coin of equivocation in this instance. If integrity and the challenge to the soul mean that the slave stood in danger of losing his soul or of sacrificing her integrity for being fearful of or deceiving and hating the appropriate European Americans, then I disagree with Huggins For one reason I am not sure from the structure of the argument whether he is arguing on the grounds that these forces are immoral in and of themselves or because they are forces that destroy the fabric of the soul, however he may be construing the notion of soul. He seems to want to say both. In the case of "loss of integrity" being a danger to the fabric of the soul, he needs to establish that by some other, appropriate discipline and by the use of some other mode of argumentation besides moralization. If we take the other dimension, that it is in and of itself immoral to fear, to deceive, or to hate *anyone*, including a person who stole you, owns you, whips you at will, sells your children and sorely oppresses you, then I want to ask by whose morality is he making these claims. By what claims can a slave master legitimately make moral demands on a slave? He is involved and stymied by the barrier of self-contradiction as soon as he makes claims on property only appropriately placed on human beings. These kinds of confusions and difficulties run throughout his spiritually and intellectually seductive but, in the end, methodologically muddled discussion of religious experience.

There is a lot of truth in Huggins's discussion of African American Christian consciousness. In fact, his work brims with insight and flashes of brilliance throughout. Yet it must be read with an appreciation for its shortcomings when it comes to his ranging and highly generalized examination of religion. It is true, I think, that by and large the slave was able to avoid succumbing to these three elements that were a part of their daily experience; moving in and out of the individual and collective life of the slave and later African Americans for that matter with the tide of daily events, traumas, and the offences of the slave masters and other European Americans. But these elements were there to be overcome and to come to terms with. They were not magically exorcized like demons, by the *naturalized* version of religious superstition—the power of purity—or the naturalized version of the magical talisman—the possession of one's soul.

The tragic self is at one and the same time the transmoral self, whose primary attribute is its strength. It finds in religion and, more specifically, in the Christian faith something far more basic and necessary to life than a moral code and the inspiration to live by it, something far more necessary in the logical sense of being presupposed in all meaningfully moral behavior.

> A conscience may be called "transmoral" which judges not in obedience to a moral law but according to the participation in a reality which transcends the sphere of moral commands. A transmoral conscience does not deny the moral realm, but it is driven beyond it by the unbearable tensions of the sphere of law.[23]

In the truly tragic expression of the ritual experience comes the rush of life's response to the philosopher's query, "Why be moral at all?" It may be said of the transmoral conscience that its answer is not in intellectual or conceptual terms but in the basic affirmation of life and its meaningfulness. This is beyond morality as such and deeper than conceptual language. It succeeds where all forms of discourse are subject to fail. It effectively bypasses the inoperative values of the human being's broken heartedness, restoring the flow of the existential life blood to the incapacitated body, making it flush again with the boldness of life's surging current. It restores the vitality to the spiritual body's several members—relationships, morality, hopes, dreams, and even mind—so that it is once again meaningful to raise questions such as, "Why be moral at all?"

The ethical dimension of the tragic religious experience lies in its strength and its related capacity to see the truth, accept the truth, and absorb the truth. In identifying the transmoral self of African American Christian consciousness as tragic, we intend to imply at the outset the facilitation of life or living amid ambiguity. This suggests an ethically enabling power in cases such as choosing amid conflicting "goods" in full view of the consequences, when these consequences themselves may be harbingers of great suffering. You are able to face difficult choices by the strength imparted by this tragic breadth of spirit and its capacity to absorb tensions because of the fallout of choices and their often unintended consequences. Your decision-making capacity is enhanced by the tragic religious experience, strengthening your grasp of reality, securing a basis for the best possible decisions, because as such it does not require delusion or falsehood to enable the devotee to live on. No, on the contrary, the tragic religious experience encourages the devotee to face the truth, even court it. The devotee is able to face the truth through the religious rearticulation of the situation in the tragic mode because it transvalues by lifting and transforming without in any way essentially altering the truth. Ambiguous choices need not paralyze the will. Moreover, life is ambiguous by its nature, hence this mode of experience facilitates life. It encourages and provides the necessary condition for the authentic life; a life lived in view of its truth. For these and any other reasons, I believe African American Christian consciousness marks potentially the most spiritually mature and authentic expression of the Christian faith in the modern world. Its full theological articulation promises to be a blessing to the church.

Epilogue

The Fate of Dionysius or Everything Is Going to Be Alright

Nobody knows the trouble I've seen
Nobody knows my sorrow.
Nobody knows the trouble I've seen,
But Glory, Hallelujah!

African American Spiritual

How will I do or
How will I make it
How will I make it?
I won't that's how!
Everything's going to be alright boy.

Naughty By Nature

The two songs above, one being traditional African American Gospel and the other some would consider Gangsta' Rap, have their origin and ground in the African American cultural consciousness. What seems like a wide gulf separating the two forms of aesthetic expression at first is considerably narrowed, almost to the point of being obliterated when viewed through the articulation of the deep structure of African American cultural consciousness and subjectivity. There is a union of opposites that constitutes the fundamental dialectic in which the ranges of experiences play themselves out. The dialectic has been referred to as that of hope/affirmation and resignation (despair, fatalism, etc....). In an attempt to deepen our appreciation of the dynamics involved, we applied at one-point, a semantic grid provided by psychoanalysis and made use of the manic-depressive polarity, with qualifications. The rap piece quoted in the epigraph above is of interest because it demonstrates the continuity and persistence of this dynamic structure of African American cultural consciousness and demonstrates the fact that modern art forms arising indigenously in the African American urban context still remain faithful expressions of African American being and retain at a fundamental level an undeniable continuity with the more widely "accepted" and, for some, "acceptable" forms of African American cultural production. I will try to elaborate.

It is clear from the structure of the text quoted above that there is a creative tension between the attitude expressed in the lead rapper's words and articulation of his reality and the refrain. In spite of the hopeless and angry tenor of his wording the refrain returns with the phrase, "Everything is going to be alright." To really understand and appreciate what is going on in the piece, this observation must be borne in mind. Many people, particularly those in the larger European American community, simply focus on the aggressive lyrics and rhythms. Yet anyone in the least bit familiar with the African American Church knows that this is a common refrain ("everything is going to be alright") and ubiquitous theme in the preaching tradition of the church. It is used to console the troubled and encourage the faint hearted, even in situations of tragic or catastrophic proportions. When it is used, it is seldom taken by the person to be consoled as an indication that the person using it has failed to grasp the gravity of the circumstances or is trivializing the subject's pain. On the contrary, it usually signals a note of camaraderie in suffering that goes far past sympathy and on to empathy at a depth where there is a mutual recognition of a contiguous fabric of shared pain. It is the intersubjective grounding of this mutually shared reality that allows for the comfortable acceptance of consolation in the often-repeated phrase.

An interesting, subtle, but not insignificant shift takes place in the rap piece as opposed to the more traditional and self-consciously religious expression of the experience in the spiritual quoted above concerning "trouble." And that is that the manic shifts to the expression of the more fatalistic dimension of the song and the consoling dimension or function is taken up in the refrain. For instance, in the spiritual quoted above, the manic affirmation is in the "Glory Hallelujah." This is obviously the affirmative dimension. In the lament that marks the first part of the spiritual you get a distinctively consoling element. There is consolation in the musical texture of the supplicant's *statement of the case*. This is the unique and distinctly transformative and essentially tragic dimension of African American Christian consciousness and another dimension of its creative genius. Even the suffering itself is transformed and robbed of its sting in the "statement of the case." This is also an indication of how thoroughgoing the tragic transformation of latter experience was and is at the distinctly, self-conscious Christian level. Not so in the rap piece. The emotional content is present and agitated but not reworked on the side of stating the case. It remains raw. It remains untransformed; or, shall we say, that the broader experience itself, in the inner or structural world of the piece taken as a whole, and, by implication in the subjectivity of those who engage it, remains less thoroughly transvalued; which is to say that the dialectic is more thoroughgoing in the spiritual but nevertheless clearly present in the rap. The total dialectic remains unequivocally present in the overall structure of the piece. Moreover, the rap piece more thoroughly states the case so to speak and is far more discursively self-conscious than the spiritual. This has its advantages.

There is a somewhat different variation in Tupac Shakur's, "My Block." There are several tracks in Tupac Shakur's CD "Better Dayz" that are illustrative of my point. In fact his art deserves a lot more attention than I can give to it here as a resource for thinking theologically about African American spirituality in the deeper sense, but I do plan to return to it later in at least one other work. Tupac was brought to my attention by my daughter Selah in a conversation we were having about my vision of African American culture and spirituality while I was hard at work on an article titled "The Middle Passage, Trauma and the Tragic Re-Imagination of African American Theology."[1] I was describing the tragic vision, the sense of homelessness and their relationship to eschatology. I expected a look of incomprehension but instead I got a suggestion. "Daddy you should look at Tupac's 'Better Dayz.'" Had anyone else but my daughter said that I may have dismissed it. I didn't. After listening to "My Block," "Thug Mansion," and "Better Dayz," I was sold.

Shortly after I began to reflect on this material, my sister was killed in a car accident. I lost my brother a decade or two ago under questionable circumstances on 145th Street and St. Nicholas in New York City, and several first cousins over the years; not to mention friends, all to "street life"—the contemporary forum for so much of what continues to plague African America. The sorrow of my sister's death seemed to churn up a host of memories from my home town of Hackensack, New Jersey, all the pain we've witnessed over the years, and what it may or may not mean. Unfortunately, black suffering is not restricted to our historic past. It continues. Under the circumstances, I found, for instance, only cold comfort in contemporary Gospel, which is so often characterized by a cheap sentimentality borrowed from some secular and Christian traditions not our own, music simply not equipped to do the "heavy lifting" expected from the African American church tradition. So much of it seemed soulless, when soul was precisely what was called for. I turned to Tupac and his CD "Better Dayz." It helped get me through. I was able to draw from Tupac what I could not find in so much contemporary "church" music. I could also find some comfort in traditional gospel tunes. That is when I really detected the deep structural similarity of reworking our experience of pain into tragic art that reflects our geist and feeds our souls in a much broader range of hip-hop material than I initially expected.

If you look at the structure of "My Block" here again you get the dialectic much like Naughty by Nature's "Ghetto Bastard." Tupac states the harsh realities of his block, even wondering at one point "if the Lord still cares, for us niggaz on welfare,"capturing the essential ambiguity of the tragic. Yet in spite of his questions, pining, and at points despair, the refrain returns to the fundamental "in spite of" that is so fundamental to traditional African American spirituality.

> Living life is but a dream
> Hard times is all we've seen
> Every block is kinda mean
> But on our block we still play.

The affirmation of life contained in the phrase "*But* on our block we still play," contextualized amid the dangers, the loss, and suffering is a quintessential reflection of the tragic vision characteristic of African American religion and culture at its "best," as I have tried to lay it out in this text. The beat goes on. I think it also speaks to the possibility that God may be immanent and perhaps actively working to heal in places one might least expect, if you know how to look and what you are looking for, if you are attuned to her voice.

I don't know all those who helped put these pieces together. Rap is not my forte. I am no uncritical or diehard fan of the art in all its guises, to be sure. But I think it safe to say, however, that Naughty by Nature, Tupac, and those that worked with him were "feeling *it*." They were "there," there where their ancestors had been hundreds of years before. They locked into something fundamental. They were what the Africans were in the smoldering cauldron of resentment that boiled beneath the surface of every unbroken spirit, with the sting of its apprehension poised and aimed directly at its target. They were, in the moment of creating the piece, what we became and remained under the pain of oppression and the sting of the lash. They were not *there* through any historical consciousness or because of any intense consciencizing, although a sense of that awareness is apparent. It was not diachronicity, but synchronicity. They were *there* by virtue of their participation in the deep structure that remains until this day the defining constituent element of African American cultural consciousness and indeed Christian consciousness. They did not go back into history during the creative act, but down into their present. Time is not always horizontal, but sometimes vertical when you live out of the depths.

One distinct difference between these young men and their slave and sorely oppressed forbears is, however, that these men have taken their drums back and they worked out the rhythm of our condition at several different levels, with a complex of form and content approaching in these two cases and some others, nothing short of genius. Nobody knew the troubles the slave had seen because in so many ways the slave was silenced, muted, or unable to tell them. The traumatic nature of much of what African Americans suffered prevented recantation. On the other hand the slave African Americans during the Jim Crow era and even now could be seen, but never *heard*, no not even when allowed to speak. The African American was not so much the invisible man as he was and remains the inaudible man; the man who dare not speak *lest* he be heard or dare not be heard *"lest I see myself"* (italics mine). I am aware, of course, of the polysemy of meaning experienced through symbols and how they were often used to refer to the oppressors and so forth. They *signified* then and so many of us still do. These young men, however, are talking *straight up*. They are telling you precisely what troubles they are dealing with and undergoing, daily. Although I am sure in their cases, among many young African American women as well as their mothers and fathers, there remains a host of troubles that no one can know.

Another element in these particularly disclosive instances of the rap art form is the distinctly feminine or maternal dimension of the consolation. In the case of Tupac's piece it comes through the voice of children much like Jay Z's brilliant track "Hard Knock Life." In Naughty by Nature's "Ghetto Bastard," it comes through in the phrase "everything is going to be alright boy," sung, of course, by a female chorus. The power of the phrase or, I should say, part of the power in this piece is that it draws on the uniquely maternal or feminine genius of consolation as it is experienced in African American culture and consciousness and its characteristic modes of experiencing. Whatever psychological ground you choose to give it, or grid you wish to subject the experience to, the fact of the matter is that we do not live in a world constructed of theories but of experiences. Consolation to the grieving and grieved spirit, whether one happens to think this manifestation of it is due to some form or forms of regression (indicating, of course, emotional immaturity or phase retardation, etc....), makes life better. It heals. It lifts. It transvalues and never destroys. It is the signature of the divine through the cipher of the feminine, particularly in the maternal manifestations of African American cultural consciousness. It is clearly present in the piece.

In other rap pieces, I have also noticed that it is the manic side of the dialectic that has come to dominate its expression. In rap, by and large, what we witness is a wide swing of the pendulum toward an extreme end of the dialectical binary with the nature of the expression of the depth affirmation being influenced thereby. It has mingled with the pathological narcissism of our age, compounded by an already-exacerbated need for recognition in the African American community that manifests itself in the focus of the rapper's lyrics on a grossly inflated image of himself or herself. This, in turn, invites identification from others, mostly young African Americans, starving for a legitimate recognition, so long denied, that it has become exorbitant in its demands and finding fulfillment in the *affirmation rush* of the identification itself, begins to act out some of the preposterous boasts of the fantasy-filled world of the artists and self-destructive behavior. In many cases, "fans" end up drawing on the self-images provided by the artists for and as their primary source of strength, main source of meaning, and self-definition or identification. This effectual symbolic connection replaces the legitimate religious content (and by that I mean sources of symbols and meanings with references to, and their primary origin in, *ultimate* reality) with corrupt cultural formations, becoming, thereby, demonic in form, effect, and affect. However, one still can witness paradigmatic fulminations of *the consciousness* with all its essentials present in pieces of particular and marked genius such as the ones identified above and Coolio's "Gangsta's Paradise," placing these pieces, and those like them, as well as the artists who created them in a class by themselves.

Dionysius was the mysterious god on the fringes of the Greek pantheon. He was the god of Greek tragedy. Out of his mythos and ritual, Greek tragedy sprung with its profundity and power. Yet he was the god most marginalized, of disputed origin, of dubious moral worth and texture. He was Janus, the two-faced god, the god divided within himself. He was the crucified god, dismembered and ripped asunder, torn in a thousand pieces by the Titans and assumed to be thoroughly despoiled of life. He was the crucified god. He nevertheless was resurrected through rememberment. In his capacity as the crucified and resurrected god of the mystery cults he became for so many an indication of the eternal life and indestructible nature of the soul. He came to grasp and symbolize the fullness of life and its presence amid its equally fundamental ambiguity. He was torn asunder, but reconstituted, resurrected. In his return, he came up from the depths with strength; in fact his return was the manifestation of the *strength to be* in the fullness of life. Through his death by dismemberment and his return, the young god became at one and the same time the god of suffering and the god of joy—Lord of the Crucified. This is not incidental. Only the god of one could truly be the god of the other. In the depths, the two in their most authentic and meaningful expressions are fundamentally linked and always constituent elements of the field that constitutes the experience of one or the other. This is the fate of Dionysius. This is also, as we have shown, the essential nature of African American Christian consciousness.

The invasion of the African American Church by right-wing religious ideology and ideologues brings in its wake an attempt to bleach religious language and the subsequent restriction of the African American Church's self-interpretation to categories managed and controlled by mainly fundamentalists and prosperity religious ideologues who oversee the "mass production" and "distribution" of popular sources of religious *legitimization*. We can see it in the scuttling of certain legitimating terms endemic to the religious consciousness of the African American community, such as "having religion" for the more static and inherently individualistic terminology of "being saved." The marginalization and the despoilment continue to exacerbate the condition of the African American community. The divided, complicated, and morally ambivalent American psyche has encouraged a continued fascination and a fundamental ambivalence toward the cultural presence and reality of the African American community.

For reasons deeply embedded in the American psyche itself, including the impact that the overall cultural taxonomies have had on the formation of the identity of its European American component, there is an attraction and a repulsion at one and the same time, directed toward the cultural products of African America, the "dark side" of America.[2] The fascination with and influence of the power of darkness on the American psyche has been attested to in the analysis of American literature and popular culture.[3] In the case of the African American community, there are some areas that touch on our concerns here that I wish to mention only briefly.

The African American community and its cultural production are approached in ways strikingly similar to the modes of relating to the numinous or the holy identified by Rudolph Otto in his classic text, *The Idea of the Holy*. One dimension of the encounter with the holy is the mysterium, the sense in which the person approaches the phenomena before them as "wholly other." Otto writes,

> The truly "mysterious" object is beyond our apprehension and comprehension, not only because our knowledge has certain irremovable limits, but because in it we come upon something inherently "wholly other," whose kind and character are incommensurable with our own, and before which we therefore recoil in wonder that strikes us chill and numb.[4]

The profound sense of the otherness of African Americans is rooted in the deep structure of the American psyche. It is so fundamental that it operates in something of the same ontological mode as the encounter Otto is discussing. There is in this otherness, with which the African American community and its cultural yield are approached, a profound repulsion and/or dread that is exacerbated by the specificity of the cultural taxonomy defining "black being." At the same time, there is a fascination in America with almost everything African American. With this dimension of fascination and a certain hunger there is a constant effort on the part of much of European America and culture to possess and own African American culture while shunning the African American himself and refusing him a dignified status, not to mention a status in accord with the power of his presence as manifested in and through his culture. There is a profound resistance to acknowledging the power and sway the African American community holds over the American imagination. This leads to an exploitative relationship, given the particularities of the asymmetrical relations of power extant in the American situation, resulting in the expropriation of African American cultural production and the consequent despoliation and frustration of the African American community as a whole.

> The daemonic-divine object may appear to the mind an object of horror and dread, but at the same time it is no less something that allures with a potent charm, and the creature who trembles before it, utterly cowed and cast down, has always at the same time the impulse to turn to it, *nay even to make it somehow his own*. The "mystery" is for him not merely something to be wondered at but something that entrances him; and besides that in it which bewilders and confounds, he feels a something that captivates and transports him with a strange ravishment, rising often enough to the pitch of dizzy intoxication; it is the dionysiac-element in the numen.[5]

To add another dimension to an appreciation for the complex and troubling status of the African American Christian consciousness in its religious form and its broader derivatives, there is a craving for its forms as American society meets, head on, the vacuous nature of late modern or postmodern Western civilization with its extremely commercialized cultural production. The commercialization is creating conditions for the distortion of the meaning of the experience as it is absorbed and repackaged like fast food. This can be seen in so much of the modern and contemporary gospel movement, the attempted appropriation and crass commercialization of its form by European American fundamentalists of various ilk, as well as the use of African American forms of expression, particularly the musical, to advertise, more often than not, withwhite voices being used to replace the original African American ones. One of the reasons the African American cultural aesthetic can be used to market and sell products that have nothing to do with it in content or spirit, and add life to otherwise insipid, overly rationalized modes of Christian experience is because it makes people feel good or better. This, however, is not to be trivialized. Its capacity to make one *feel better* is indicative of its therapeutic or healing dynamic referred to earlier in this text. With a particular added dimension for European Americans because of the reasons I have identified above, and for another of equal and related significance.

Because of the emptiness of so much of modern personal experience, the African American cultural aesthetic has a strong appeal. The threat of meaninglessness in the encounter of the absurd, the consequent spiritual emptiness, and the devaluation of life and relationships were the conditions it evolved to respond to. Hence, it has antidotal powers and appeal in a culture increasingly threatened by a poisonous compound of identity diffusion, superficiality, emptiness, meaninglessness, frustration and fragmentation. The unique cultural residue of the tragic experience that emerged in African American Christian consciousness and spilled over into popular culture has antidotal powers and meets a fundamental need in modern American culture. African American Christian consciousness and popular African American culture have the dubious distinction in the larger American cultural context of both satisfying the jealousy and filling the void created by the stressed white identity of the popular American psyche. All of this aggravates and deepens the complexity of the increasingly untenable position of the African American in America.

The marginalization persists. The stress and strain of titanic forces continue to threaten the African American community and the African American self with dismemberment and diffusion. African American Christian consciousness itself is everywhere threatened with its own disintegration and in many cases with the temptation to become a caricature of itself—the superficial joyous romp, in an ever-expanding ring of denial that many of its less intelligent and superficial students and critics have made it out to be. Gospel has become the new route to fame and fortune to so many second-rate, failed, and *want to be* entertainment stars that the tradition itself has fallen victim to a kind of strip mining by its own. It is enough to frustrate and indeed frighten any conscious and conscientious "Church Person." It is said that the owl of Minerva flies only at dusk. Some believe we are at the end of an era and a new one of unknown shape or kind is swift approaching.

> And what rough beast, its hour come round at last
> Slouches toward Bethlehem to be born?[6]

Notes

Introduction

1. For a balanced assessment of the current state of black theology, see Matthew V. Johnson Sr., "Black Theology," *Encyclopedia of Religion*, 2nd ed., Volume 2 (New York: Macmillan Reference, 2005), 963–967.
2. Cornel West, *Prophesy Deliverance! An Afro-Revolutionary Christianity* (Louisville, KY: Westminster Press, 1982).
3. For an interesting and succinct exploration of the issue of retentions and the emergence of African American culture, see Sidney W. Minz and Richard Price, *The Birth of African American Culture: An Anthropological Perspective* (Boston, MA: Beacon Press, 1976). See also the insightful article and rich bibliographical information on the issues surrounding African retentions and their relation to African American religion by Tracy E. Hucks and Dianne Stewart, "African American Religions: History of Study," *Encyclopedia of Religion*, 2nd ed., Volume 1 (New York: Macmillan Reference, 2005), 73–83.
4. For a thorough, cogent rehabilitation and challenging reexamination of the scholarship on Du Bois's conflicted relationship to American Christianity and reassessment of his views on Christianity see, Edward J. Blum, *W. E. B. Du Bois: American Prophet* (Philadelphia: University of Pennsylvania Press, 2007). Mindful of Edward J. Blum's significant qualifications, see also Phil Zukerman, ed., *Dubois on Religion* (New York: Altamira Press, 2000).
5. Experience near" means closer and truer to the experience, than theological abstractions that are formulated then imposed on the experience. The phrase is self psychoanalytic in origin. See Charles B. Strozier and Heinz Kohut, *The Making of a Psychoanalyst* (New York: Other Press, 2001), 238–239. Heinz Kohut, *How Does Analysis Cure*, eds Arnold Goldberg and Paul E Stepansky (Chicago: University of Chicago Press 1984), 187–190. The use of the term here also implies the centrality of affect and personal meaning in determining both the nature of religious experience and its theological implications and usages. For instance the experience near approach to religious experience and any subsequent theological reflections claiming to give articulation to the same would suggest that affect is more significant than ethic in determining the meaning and value of that experience for a believer or believing

community. See Robert D. Stolorow, "Integrating Self Psychology and Classical Psychoanalysis: An Experience-Near Approach," in Arnold Golberg, ed., *Learning from Kohut: Progress in Self Psychology,* Volume 4 (Hillsdale, NJ: The Analytic Press, 1993), 63–70. The experience near method renders and purifies theological concepts through the religious experience of the group rather than rendering the experience of the group through presupposed formulations of theological categories. It definitively privileges religious experience in determining theological meanings and a phenomenological approach for elucidating religious experience.

Chapter 1

1. See Irene Smith Landsman, "Crisis of Meaning in Trauma and Loss," in *Loss of the Assumptive World: A Theory of Traumatic Loss,* ed. Jeffrey Kaufman (New York: Brunner-Routledge, 2002), 13, 20–21.
2. Paul Tillich, "Anxiety-Reducing Agencies in Our Culture," in *The Meaning of Health: Essays in Existentialism, Psychoanalysis, and Religion* (Chicago: Exploration Press, 1984), 58.
3. Albert Camus, "An Absurd Reasoning," in *The Myth of Sisyphus & Other Essays* (New York: Vintage Books, 1955), 5.
4. Anthony Giddens, *The Constitution of Society* (Berkeley: University of California Press, 1984), 50.
5. Landsman, "Crisis of Meaning," 14.
6. Peter Berger and Thomas Luckman, *The Social Construction of Reality: A Treatise in the Sociology of Knowledge* (Garden City, NY: Anchor Books, 1967), 101–102. The implicit distinction in Berger and Luckman's formulation between the institutional order and the symbolic universe complements the more recent and self-consciously psychological approach of Irene Smith Landsman to give articulation to the same basic experience. She draws the distinction between "ordinary" and "extra-ordinary" or "existential meaning" (see Landsman, "Crisis of Meaning: 14–15).
7. Berger and Luckman, *Social Construction of Reality,* 103.
8. Mircea Eliade, *Myth of the Eternal Return, or Cosmos and History* (Princeton, NJ: 1974, 96–98.
9. William Storm, *After Dionysus: A Theory of the Tragic* (Ithaca, NY: Cornell University Press, 1998), 75.
10. Ibid., 81.
11. Ibid., 72–73.
12. Ibid., 86.
13. Murray Krieger, *Visions of Extremity in Modern Literature,* vol. 1, *The Tragic Vision: The Confrontation of Extremity* (Baltimore: Johns Hopkins University Press, 1960), 2–3.
14. Storm, *After Dionysus,* 80.
15. See Paul Tillich, "The Relation of Religion and Health," in *The Meaning of Health,* especially the section "The Unity of Salvation and Healing as Presented in Religious Myth," 16.

16. Terry Heller, *The Delights of Terror: An Aesthetics of the Tale of Terror* (Chicago: University of Illinois Press, 1987), 3. I am following Heller's usage of Edward Bullough's concept. Aesthetic distance "is the utmost decrease of distance without its disappearance."
17. John G. Jackson, "Egypt and Christianity," *Egypt Revisited, Journal of African Civilizations* 4, no. 2 (Reprint of November 1982): 65–80.
18. Krieger, *Visions of Extremity*, 3.
19. Friedrich Nietzsche, *The Birth of Tragedy*, trans. Walter Kaufman (New York: Vintage Books, 1967), 49.
20. M. S. Silk and J. P. Stern, *Nietzsche on Tragedy* (New York: Cambridge University Press, 1984).
21. Richard B. Sewall, *The Vision of Tragedy* (New Haven, CT: Yale University Press), 103.
22. Kitty Ferguson, *The Music of Pythagoras: How an Ancient Brotherhood Cracked the Code of the Universe and Lit the Path from Antiquity to Outer Space* (New York: Walker and Company, 2008).
23. Krieger, *Visions of Extremity*, 4.
24. Lucien Goldmann, *The Hidden God: A Study of Tragic Vision in The Pensées of Pascal and the Tragedies of Racine*, trans. Philip Thody (New York: The Humanities Press, 1976), 52.
25. Ibid., 56.
26. Ibid., 57.
27. Theophus H. Smith, *Conjuring Culture: Biblical Formations of Black America* (New York: Oxford University Press, 1994), 143.
28. Joseph Conrad, *Heart of Darkness* (New York: Alfred A. Knopf, 1967), 100.
29. Ibid, 94.
30. Ibid.
31. Joseph Conrad, *Heart of Darkness,* (New York: Alfred A. Knopf, 1967), 98.
32. Sewall, 100.
33. Herman Melville, *Moby Dick,* in *Melville: Redburn, White Jacket, Moby Dick* (New York: The Library of Americas, 1983), 973–974.
34. Ibid., 990–991.
35. Krieger, *Visions of Extremity*, 3.
36. Max Scheler, "On the Tragic," trans. B. Stambler, in *Tragedy: Vision and Form*, ed. R.M. Corrigan (San Francisco: Chandler, 1965) 10 (Get Book site).
37. See also Melvin J. Lerner, *The Belief in a Just World: A Fundamental Delusion* (New York: Plenum Press, 1980), 18.
38. Heller, *Delights of Terror*, 1–2.
39. J.-P. Vernant and Pierre Vidal-Naquet, *Myth and Tragedy in Ancient Greek,* trans. Janet Lloyd (New York: Zone Books, 1988), 33.
40. Recall here Bullough's principle of aesthetic distance as opposed to Abram's, "the utmost decrease of distance without its disappearance." This state would naturally optimize psychic tension and sharpen the perception and experience of conflict.
41. Conrad, *Heart of Darkness*, 100.
42. Ibid., 100–101.

43. Michelle Gellrich, *Tragedy and Theory: The Problem of Conflict since Aristotle* (Princeton, NJ: Princeton University Press, 1988), 14.
44. See also J-P Vernant. Figures such as Max Scheler, William Storm, and Paul Tillich can also be read this way.
45. Anthony Giddens, *The Constitution of Society* (Berkeley: University of California Press, 1984), 14–15.
46. Scheler, "On the Tragic," 13.
47. Ibid., 14.
48. Sewall, 13.
49. See Storm, *After Dionysus*, 92–117. When I use the term *tragic field*, I am using it in a form more historical or, I should say, historicized than that implied in Storm's more literary approach. I use it to refer to the socially and historically constituted converging lines of force that insinuate the rending at the sight of the self and selves of a group. In the case of African Americans the group takes on added significance in the shape of the tragic field in that the same forces that constitute group existence manifest themselves in and as the sparagmous of (the) group *consciousness*.
50. Sewall, 174.
51. George Lukács, *Soul and Form*, trans. Anna Bostock (Cambridge: The MIT Press, 1974), 103.
52. I use "mirror" here not in its pure sense but rather in the more oblique sense that characterizes, say, Lacan's or Heinz Kohut's usage of the concept in self-psychology, where a child is or is not *mirrored* in the mother's responses.
53. Lukács, *Soul and Form*, 92.
54. "The deepest longing of human existence is the metaphysical root of tragedy." Ibid., 162.
55. Ibid., 93–94.
56. It is here in the projective experience driven by desire, where it assumes specific forms, that the African American quest for liberation takes shape in its particularity at the ultimate level, in the ultimate frame of meaning—spiritual experience.
57. Nietzsche, *Birth of Tragedy*, 60.
58. Silke-Maria Weineck, *The Abyss Above: Philosophy and Poetic Madness in Plato, Holderlin and Nietzsche* (Albany: State University of New York Press, 2002), 1–2. This is particularly relevant to eschatological visions, which, particularly in Christianity, always imply the present endurance of an ordeal.
59. Jeremiah 31:15.
60. Camus, "The Myth of Sisyphus," *The Myth of Sisyphus & Other Essays*, 89.
61. Ibid.
62. Ibid., 90.
63. Quoted in Sewall, 127.
64. Classic positions, such as those that rely too heavily on Aristotle, collapse the analysis of the effect of tragedy on an audience with the articulation of the tragic affect as such or the affective state of the tragic experience. The analysis of the effect of tragedy should be carried out on its own terms and more in conversation with the tragic vision. Aristotle's approach is

somewhat reductive in this respect. In my perspective, the mechanics or technology of the affect-yielding tragic effect is a different issue from articulating the quality of the tragic affect itself. Nietzsche's position (of which we will see a great deal more in the chapters to come) is a response to similar concerns. "For instance, we find him protesting against Aristotle's emphasis on tragedy as action (*praxis*) and—repeatedly—against the Aristotelian concept of *katharsis*. The precise terms of his objections to *katharsis* vary, but there is one fundamental ground of complaint: the notion fails to do justice to tragedy's life-enhancing force—on which point the Nietzsche is more or less at one with the Author of BT [*Birth of Tragedy*]. His alternative to *praxis* is the Greek loan-word *pathos*. In the *Poetics* this word refers to a 'scene of suffering'; in ordinary Greek it means 'misfortune' or 'experience' or 'emotion'; and emotion, especially intensity of emotion, is what it signifies in German. Nietzsche's implicit alternative to action, it would seem, is something approaching *Stimmung*, 'mood' or 'impression,' and in such an elevation of mood above action we have a very German propensity." "Very German propensity" or not, I think it to be quite to the point and on the mark. Silk and Stern then go on to emphasize parenthetically but importantly, especially for the standpoint assumed in this text, that "'tragedy'—Trauerspiel, 'mourning play'—emphasizes mood" (Silk and Stern, 226).
65. Camus, "The Myth of Sisyphus," 90.
66. Sewall, 174.
67. W. E. B. Du Bois, "Of The Faith of the Fathers," *The Souls of Black Folk* (New York: New American Library, 1969), 212.

Chapter 2

1. Betty Wood, *The Origins of American Slavery: Freedom and Bondage in the English Colonies* (New York: Hill and Wang, 1997), 92.
2. Ibid., 25.
3. See Joseph E. Holloway, *Africanisms in American Culture* (Indianapolis: Indiana University Press, 1990) and Michael Gomez, *Exchanging Our Country Marks: The Transformation of African Identities in the Colonial and Antebellum South* (Chapel Hill: University of North Carolina Press, 1998).
4. Saidiya V. Hartman, *Scenes of Subjection: Terror, Slavery, and Self-Making in Nineteenth-Century America* (New York: Oxford University Press, 1997), 95.
5. See, Richard L. Rubenstein, *The Cunning of History: The Holocaust and the American Future* (New York: Harper Perennial, 1987). Professor Rubenstein makes a persuasive and powerful argument in this short but disturbingly potent text that the Holocaust and slavery were fundamentally connected through a virus that infects Western culture. In spite of the broad generalizations, the depth and the passion of his argument frightens and convinces, leaving one with a sense that while certain portions of his argument rests on

family resemblances and perhaps informed intuition at best, it nevertheless rings profoundly true!
6. Edward J. Blum, *W. E. B. Du Bois: American Prophet* (Philadelphia: University of Pennsylvania Press, 2997), 122.
7. Albert J. Raboteau, *Slave Religion: The "Invisible Institution" in the Antebellum South*, Updated Edition (New York: Oxford University Press, 2004), 168–169.
8. Ibid.
9. Ibid., 169–170.
10. Matthew V. Johnson Sr., "The Middle Passage, Trauma and the Tragic Re-Imagination of African American Theology," *Journal of Pastoral Psychology*. 53, no.6 (July 2005): 547–548.
11. Vincent Harding, *There is a River: The Black Struggle for Freedom in America* (New York: Vintage Books, 1983), 27.
12. Ibid., 27.
13. Walter Johnson, *Soul by Soul: Life inside the Antebellum Slave Market* (Cambridge: Harvard University Press, 1999), 22.
14. Ibid, 19.
15. Jeffery Kauffman, "Introduction," *Loss of the Assumptive World: A Theory of Traumatic Loss*, ed. Jeffery Kauffman (New York: Brunner-Routledge), 4.
16. Ronnie Janoff-Bulman, *Shattered Assumptions: Towards a New Psychology of Trauma* (New York: The Free Press, 1992), 71.
17. A contemporary manifestation of this in political affairs is the "eruption" of the Barack Obama political phenomenon in the African American community. Historically disenfranchised and resigned, particularly in the wake of the neoconservative rendering of racism as respectable, African Americans existentially divested from the culture of American politics. They could ill afford to risk much on its contemporary possibilities. Pessimism about the possibilities of effectively if not absolutely overcoming racism became the deeply embedded norm of the "black person on the streets." The inaccessibility of the presidency was the ultimate measure of the strength and persistence of presumed white supremacy, normativity, and African American alienation. The hopes, indeed the needs and drives, of African Americans would, of course under these conditions retreat to the remote location. Onlookers would think that the hopes were absent, even some African Americans and expressed as much when Barack set out on his journey. As if out of nowhere, however, the community energized and rallied and became the driving spiritual force behind his ascendancy. Barack Obama as symbol opened up the psychic space and facilitated the retrieval of hopes, incubating and perhaps recovering in the remote location of the African American communal psyche. Not all dreams deferred fester or explode; some have a much longer shelf life.
18. Roy F. Baumeister, Jon E. Faber, and Harry M. Wallace, "Coping and Ego Depletion: Recovery after the Coping Process," In *Coping: The Psychology of What Works*, ed. C. R. Snyder (New York: Oxford University Press, 1999), 50.
19. Ibid., 55.

20. Ibid., 59–60.
21. Robin Horton, "African Traditional Thought and Western Science," in *Rationality*, ed. Bryan R. Wilson (Oxford: Basil Blackwell 1973), 147.
22. Cisco Lassiter, "Relocation and Illness: The Plight of the Navajo," *Pathologies of the Modern Self: Postmodern Studies on Narcissism, Schizophrenia, and Depression*, ed. David Michael Levin (New York: New York University Press, 1987), 228.
23. Ibid., 229.
24. Michelle Sobel, *Trabelin' On: The Slave Journey to an Afro-Baptist Faith* (Princeton, NJ: Princeton University Press, 1988), xxii.
25. Ibid., 205.
26. Lerone Bennett, Jr., *The Black Mood* (New York: Barnes and Noble, 1971), 63.
27. Alex Bontemps, *The Punished Self: Surviving Slavery in the Colonial South* (Ithaca, NY: Cornell University Press, 2001), 142–143.
28. W. E. B. Du Bois, *The Souls of Black Folk* (New York: New American Library, 1982), 8–9.
29. Ibid, 8.

Chapter 3

1. Herbert Marcuse, *The Aesthetic Dimension: Toward a Critique of Marxist Aesthetics* (Boston: Beacon Press, 1978), xii.
2. Lerone Bennett, Jr., *The Black Mood* (New York: Barnes and Noble, 1971).
3. Oliver Taplin, "Emotion and Meaning in Greek Tragedy," in *Oxford Readings in Greek Tragedy*, ed. Erich Segal (New York: Oxford University Press, 1983), 9–10.
4. Bernard M. W. Knox, *The Heroic Temper: Studies in Sophoclean Tragedy* (Los Angeles: University of California Press, 1983), 6.
5. Christopher Lane, "The Psychology of Race: An Introduction," In *The Psychoanalysis of Race*, ed. Christopher Lane (New York: Columbia University Press, 1998), 5.
6. Edward J. Blum, *W. E. B. Du Bois: American Prophet* (Philadelphia: University of Pennsylvania Press, 2007).
7. Richard B. Sewall, *The Vision of Tragedy* (New Haven, CT: Yale University Press, 1980), 42.
8. W. E. B. Du Bois, *The Souls of Black Folk* (New York: NAL Penguin, 1982), 98–99.
9. Ibid., 107.
10. Walter Kaufman, *Tragedy and Philosophy* (Princeton, NJ: Princeton University Press), 364.
11. Knox, *Heroic Temper*, 6.
12. Du Bois, *Souls of Black Folk*, 98.
13. Ibid., 104.
14. Ibid., 108.
15. Ibid.

16. Heinz Kohut, *The Restoration of the Self* (New York: International Universities Press, 1977), 286. For a deeper discussion of this whole relationship between tragedy and self psychology, see Peter F. Donaldson's "Conflict and Coherence: Narcissism and Tragic Structure in Marlowe," in *Narcissism and the Text: Studies in Literature and the Psychology of Self*, ed. Lynne Layton and Barbara Ann Schapiro (New York: New York University Press, 1986). I should say here that I find the discussion of the relationship between tragedy and the psychology of the self very helpful. I think, however, Donaldson's position suffers from a lack of a deeper understanding of what tragedy is. If he had a deeper appreciation of the subtle and complex ways that all tragedy leads to or involves the experience of emptiness, he would see that the relationship between the self psychology of Kohut and tragedy extends beyond merely "the distinctively post-Renaissance sense of what tragedy is" that he accuses Kohut of being limited to. I think that his basic problem lies in the essence of tragedy as inhering in the intratextual structure of the plot and message rather than in the overall tragic effect on the audience as it was discussed above.
17. Kohut, *Restoration of the Self*, 102.
18. Ibid., 103.
19. Gary F. Greif, *The Tragedy of the Self: Individual and Social Disintegration Viewed through the Self Psychology of Heinz Kohut* (New York: University Press of America, 2000), 68.
20. Vincent Harding, *There is a River: The Black Struggle for Freedom in America* (New York: Vintage Books, 1983), 16.
21. Ibid.
22. Peter Homans, "Introduction," *Symbolic Loss: The Ambiguity of Mourning and Memory at Century's End*, ed. Peter Homans (Charlottesville: University Press of Virginia, 2000), 16.
23. Du Bois, *Souls of Black Folk*, 103.
24. Sigmund Freud, *Mourning and Melancholia*, Collected Papers, Vol. iv, 1917 (London: The Hogarth Press, 1953), 167.
25. Ibid., 165.
26. Ibid., 174.
27. Ibid., 166.
28. Ibid.
29. Langdon Gilkey, *Shantung Compound* (New York: Harper & Row, 1966), 80.

Chapter 4

1. Rose Pfeffer, *Nietzsche: Disciple of Dionysus* (Lewisburg, PA: Bucknell University Press, 1972). I am in complete agreement with Rose Pfeffer when she writes, "Nietzsche's philosophy is based on the conviction that the greatness of man and the development of culture can be realized only within a spirit that he calls tragic. I contend that it is the central aim and purpose of his philosophical writings to clarify the meaning of the "tragic disposition"

and to help initiate the coming of a tragic age, which he sees as the only hope for the future of mankind." (29)
2. Ibid., 38–39
3. Ibid.
4. Lawrence Levine, *Black Culture and Black Consciousness: Afro-American Thought from Slavery to Freedom* (New York: Oxford University Press, 1977), 39.
5. Ibid., 53–54.
6. W. E. B. Du Bois, *The Souls of Black Folk* (New York: NAL Penguin, 1982), 212.
7. Friedrich Nietzsche, *The Birth of Tragedy and the Case of Wagner*, trans. Walter Kaufman (New York: Random House, 1967), 60.
8. See, for instance, Edgar S. Brightman in *A Philosophy of Religion* (New York: Prentice Hall, 1940), 246.
9. Edith Hamilton, *Mythology: Timeless Tales of Gods and Heroes* (Boston, MA: New American Library, 1942), 104.
10. Nietzsche, *Birth of Tragedy*, 140.
11. M. S. Silk and J. P. Stern, *Nietzsche on Tragedy* (New York: Cambridge University Press, 1981).
12. Nietzsche, *Birth of Tragedy*, 33.
13. Silk and Stern, *Nietzsche on Tragedy*, 204–295.
14. Nietzsche, *Birth of Tragedy*, 33.
15. Michelle Gellrich, *Tragedy and Theory: The Problem of Conflict since Aristotle* (Princeton, NJ: Princeton University Press, 1988), 266.
16. See Nietzsche, *Birth of Tragedy*, 33.
17. Ronald Hayman, *Nietzsche: A Critical Life* (England: Penguin Books, 1982), 1–2.
18. See Thomas S. Kuhn, *The Structure of Scientific Revolutions* (Chicago: University of Chicago Press, 1971). Ian Barbour, *Myths, Models and Paradigms* (New York: Harper & Row, 1974).
19. Nietzsche, *Birth of Tragedy*, 45.
20. Ibid.
21. Ibid.
22. Pfeffer, *Disciple of Dionysus*, 31.
23. Nietzsche, *Birth of Tragedy*, 44–45.
24. Ibid., 98.
25. Ibid., 110.
26. Pfeffer, *Disciple of Dionysus*, 184.
27. Toni Morrison, *Playing in the Dark: Whiteness and the Literary Imagination* (New York: Vintage Books, 1993).

Chapter 5

1. W. E. B. Du Bois, *The Souls of Black Folk* (New York: NAL Penguin, 1982), 212.
2. Nietzsche, *Birth of Tragedy*, 55.

3. Lawrence W. Levine, *Black Culture and Black Consciousness: Afro-American Folk Thought from Slavery to Freedom* (New York: Oxford, 1977), 5–6.
4. Ibid.
5. Du Bois, 270.
6. Ibid., 267.
7. John W. Blassingame, *The Slave Community: Plantation Life in the Antebellum South* (New York: Oxford University Press, 1972, 1979), 137.
8. For more information on the relationship between music and "possession," see Gilbert Rouget, *Music and Trance: A Theory of the Relations between Music and Possession* (Chicago: University of Chicago Press, 1985).
9. Blassingame, *Slave Community*, 127.
10. Edith Hamilton, *Mythology: Timeless Tales of Gods and Heroes* (Boston, MA: New American Library, 1942), 165.
11. Paul Ricoeur, *The Symbolism of Evil* (Boston, MA: Boston Press, 1967), 351. Kierkegaard also has a notion similar to this.
12. Richard B. Sewall, *The Vision of Tragedy* (New Haven, CT: Yale University Press), 6.
13. See Peter Homans, *The Ability to Mourn: Disillusionment and the Social Origins of Psychanalysis* (Chicago: University of Chicago Press, 1989), 37. He demonstrates, through an examination of the thought of Sigmund Freud and the development of the psychoanalytic movement in a sociocultural context, how persons respond creatively to the loss of significant cultural products and symbol systems.
14. For an interesting if not compelling statement of this misreading, see Louis A. Ruprecht, Jr., *Tragic Posture and Tragic Vision: Against the Modern Failure of Nerve* (New York: The Continuum Publishing Company, 1994).
15. Ibid.
16. Nietzsche, *Birth of Tragedy*, 59.
17. Ibid., 46–47, 49.
18. Ibid., 36–37, 40. See also Rudolph Otto, *The Idea of the Holy* (New York: Oxford University Press, 1923; reprint, 1981), 34.
19. Du Bois, 211; see also Otto, *Idea of the Holy*, 33.
20. Du Bois, 212.
21. Otto, *Idea of the Holy*, 12–13.
22. Blassingame, *Slave Community*, 131.
23. Paul Ricoeur, *The Role of Metaphor: Multi-Disciplinary Studies in the Creation of Meaning in Language* (Buffalo and Toronto: University of Toronto Press, 1981). 43.
24. Ibid.
25. Howard Thurman, *Deep River and the Negro Spiritual Speaks of Life and Death* (Richmond: Friends United Press, 1975), 111.
26. Victor Turner, "Religion in Current Cultural Anthropology," in *Concilium: What is Religion: An Enquiry for Christian Theology*, ed. Mircea Eliade and David Tracy (New York: Seabury Press, 1981), 70.
27. Joseph Breuer and Sigmund Freud, *Studies on Hysteria* (Basic Books/Harper New York), 6.

Chapter 6

1. David Tracy, "Metaphor and Religion: The Test Case of Christian Texts," in *On Metaphor*, ed. Sheldon Sacks (Chicago: University of Chicago Press, 1979).
2. For a basic understanding of how I am using the phrase "experience near," see Charles B. Strozier, *Heinz Kohut: The Making of A Psychoanalyst* (New York: Other Press, 2001), 338–339. "What is 'near' in this case for Kohut is present, observable, palpable, and self-psychological. What would be "distant" would be an explanation from the outside, and in Freudian drive terms. A theory of self, one might say, inevitably keeps one experience-near."
3. James H. Cone, *God of the Oppressed* (New York: Seabury Press, 1975), 18.
4. Ibid., 252–253.
5. I have a suspicion, however, that lurking behind this poorly defined, homogenized, potentially romanticized notion of black people, a more explicit definition is assumed, i.e., those who accept Cones's theological reading of African American religions experience.
6. Nathan Huggins, *Black Odyssey: The African-American Ordeal in Slavery* (New York: Vintage Books, 1977), xxiv–xxv.
7. Cone, *God of the Oppressed*, 253.
8. Christopher Bollas, *The Shadow of the Object* (New York: Columbia University Press, 1987), 14.
9. James W. Jones, *Terror and Transformation: The Ambiguity of Religion in Psychoanalytic Perspective* (Routledge, 2002),87. See also James W. Jones, *Religion and Psychology: Psychoanalysis, Feminism and Theology* (New Haven, CT: Yale University Press, 1996), 87.
10. Bollas, *Shadow of the Object*, 17.
11. Harriet Lutzky, "The Sacred and the Maternal Object: An Application of Fairbairn's Theory to Religion," in *Psychoanalytic Reflections on Current Issues*, ed. Howard B. Siegel (New York: New York University Press, 1991), 29.
12. Lutzky, "The Sacred," 29.
13. Huggins, *Black Odyssey*, 77.
14. Paul Tillich, *Meaning of Health: Essays in Existentialism, Psychoanalysis, and Religion* (Chicago: Exploration Press 1984).
15. I am using the term *signature* here to indicate the detection of God's presence in the ritual process and in African American Christian consciousness in general much in the same way, albeit in an analogous sense, physicists use it when referring to experimental evidence of subatomic phenomena in the physical universe. Note also that the term *physical* in reference to the universe, usually interpreted as referring to matter understood in terms of classical physics has undergone a significant transition, a paradigm shift, as a result of advances in quantum theory. I believe that the transformation of the term expands the *semantic kernel* (Paul Ricoeur), making the analogical usage even more meaningful.
16. For an interesting and provocative meditation on the relation of the meaning of health and salvation in the Gospel, see Paul Tillich's "The Relation of

Religion and Health: Historical Considerations and Theoretical Questions, in *The Meaning of Health*, 17. I am basically employing his conceptualization of the relationship between the two concepts.
17. This discussion has been influenced in very broad but I think significant outlines by the thought of Jürgen Habermas. See Jürgen Habermas, *The Theory of Communicative Action, Volume 1: Reason and the Rationalization of Society* (Boston, MA: Beacon Press, 1985) and *The Theory of Communicative Action, Volume 2: Lifeworld and System: A Critique of Functionalist Reason* (Boston, MA: Beacon Press, 1985). Translated by Thomas McCarthy.
18. Paul Ricoeur, *The Role of Metaphor: Multi-Disciplinary Studies in the Creation of Meaning in Language* (Buffalo and Toronto: University of Toronto Press, 1981). 43,
19. Huggins, *Black Odyssey*, 178.
20. My usage of the term *nondiscursive* is heavily influenced by the work of Anthony Giddens and his theory of structuration. While I would like to indicate that influence I am not sure that I am following him closely enough or systematically enough for him to bare any of the responsibility for any misreading I might be accused of. See Anthony Giddens, *The Constitution of Society* (Berkeley: University of California Press, 1984).
21. Huggins, *Black Odyssey*, 74.
22. Ibid., 182.
23. Paul Tillich, *The Protestant Era* (Chicago: University of Chicago Press, 1957), 145.

Epilogue

1. Matthew V. Johnson, "The Middle Passage, Trauma and the Tragic Re-Imagination of African American Theology," *Pastoral Psychology* 54, no. 6 (July 2005).
2. For an excellent illustration of this point, see the treatment of Ardelia Mapp and African American heritage and culture in the work of Thomas Harris; particularly his treatment in the third installment of the Hannibal Lecter trilogy. Thomas Harris, *Hannibal* (New York: Delacorte Press, 1999).
3. See, for instance, Toni Morrison, *Playing in the Dark: Whiteness and the Literary Imagination* (New York: Vintage Books, 1993) and Harry Levin, *Power of Darkness: Hawthorne, Poe, Melville* (Athens: Ohio University Press, 1958).
4. Rudolph Otto, *The Idea of Holy* (New York: Oxford University Press, 1950), 28.
5. Ibid., 32.
6. William Butler Yeats, "The Second Coming," *Immortal Poems of the English Language: An Anthology*, Oscar Williams, ed. (New York: Pocket Books, 1952), 489.

Bibliography

Barbour, I. (1974) *Myths, Models and Paradigms*. New York: Harper & Row.
Berger, P., and T. Luckman. (1967) *The Social Construction of Reality: A Treatise in the Sociology of Knowledge*. Garden City, NY: Anchor Books.
Blassingame, J. (1972) *The Slave Community: Plantation Life in the Antebellum South*. New York: Oxford University Press.
Blum, Edward J. (2007) *W. E. B. Dubois: American Prophet*. Philadelphia: University of Pennsylvania Press.
Breuer, J., and S. Freud. *Studies on Hysteria*. Translated by J. Strachey. New York: Basic Books /Harper.
Brightman, E. (1940) *A Philosophy of Religion*. New York: Prentice Hall.
Camus, A. (1955) *The Myth of Sisyphus and Other Essays*. New York: Vintage Books.
Cone, J. (1975) *God of the Oppressed*. New York: Seabury Press.
———. (1972) *The Spirituals and the Blues: An Interpretation*. New York: Harper & Row.
Du Bois, W. (1982) *The Souls of Black Folk*. New York: New American Library.
Eliade M. (1974) *The Myth of the Eternal Return, or Cosmos and History*. Princeton, NJ: Princeton University Press.
Eliade, M., and D. Tracy, eds. (1980) *Concilium: What is Religion? An Enquiry for Christian Theology*. New York: Seabury Press.
Freud, S. (1953) *Collected Papers*. Vol. IV. London: The Hogarth Press.
Gellrich, M. (1988) *Tragedy and Theory: The Problem of Conflict since Aristotle*. Princeton, NJ: Princeton University Press.
Gilkey, L. (1977) *Reaping the Whirlwind: A Christian Interpretation of History*. San Francisco: Harper San Francisco.
———. (1966) *Shantung Compound*. New York: Harper & Row.
Giddens, A. (1984) *The Constitution of Society*. Berkeley: University of California Press.
Hamilton, E. (1942) *Mythology: Timeless Tales of Gods and Heroes*. Boston, MA: New American Library.
Harding, V. (1983) *There Is a River: The Black Struggle for Freedom in America*. New York: Vintage Books.
Hayman, R. (1982) *Nietzsche: A Critical Life*. London: Quartet Books.

Homans, P. (1990) *The Ability to Mourn: Disillusionment and the Social Origins of Psychoanalysts*. Chicago: University of Chicago Press.

Huggins, N. (1977) *Black Odyssey: The African American Ordeal in Slavery*. New York: Vintage Books.

Jones, Lindsey (2005) *Encyclopedia of Religion*. Vols. 1 and 2. 2nd ed. New York: Macmillan Reference.

Kaufman, W. (1968) *Tragedy and Philosophy*. Princeton, NJ: Princeton University Press.

Knox, B. (1983) *The Heroic Temper: Studies in Sophoclean Tragedy*. Berkeley: University of California Press.

Kohut, H. (1977) *The Restoration of the Self*. New York: International Universities Press.

Krieger, M. (1973) *The Tragic Vision*. Baltimore: Johns Hopkins University Press.

Kuhn, T. (1970) *The Structure of Scientific Revolutions*. Chicago: University of Chicago Press.

Levin, D., ed. (1987) *Pathologies of the Modern Self: Postmodern Studies on Narcissism, Schizophrenia, and Depression*. New York: New York University Press.

Levine, L. (1977) *Black Culture and Black Consciousness: Afro-American Thought from Slavery to Freedom*. New York: Oxford University Press.

Long, Charles H. (1995) *Significations: Signs, Symbols, and Images in the Interpretation of Religion*. Aurora, CO: The Davies Group.

Mintz, Sidney W., and Richard Price (1992) *The Birth of African American Culture: An Anthropological Perspective*. Boston, MA: Beacon Press.

Nietzsche, F. (1967) *The Birth of Tragedy and the Case of Wagner*. Translated by Walter Kaufman. New York: Vintage Books.

Noel, Lames A., and Matthew V. Johnson, eds. (2005) *The Passion of the Lord: African American Reflections*. Minneapolis, MN: Fortress Press.

Otto, R. (1923) *The Idea of the Holy*. Reprint 1981. New York: Oxford University Press.

Reprecht, L. (1994) *Tragic Posture and Tragic Vision: Against the Modern Failure of Nerve*. New York: The Continuum Publishing Company.

Ricoeur, P. (1977) *The Rule of Metaphor: Multi-Disciplinary Studies in the Creation of Meaning in Language*. Translated by Robert Czerny; with Kathleen McLaughlin and John Costello. Buffalo and Toronto: University of Toronto Press.

Rouget, G. (1985) *Music and Trance: A Theory of the Relations between Music and Possession*. Chicago: University of Chicago Press.

Sacks, S., ed. (1979) *On Metaphor*. Chicago: University of Chicago Press.

Segal, E., ed. (1983) *Oxford Readings in Greek Tragedy*. New York: Oxford University Press.

Sewall, R. (1980) *The Vision of Tragedy*. New Haven, CT: Yale University Press.

Siegel, H. B. *Psychoanalytic Reflections on Current Issues*. New York: New York University Press, 1991.

Silk, M., and Stern, J. (1981) *Nietzsche on Tragedy*. New York: Cambridge University Press.
Sobel, M. (1988) *Trabelin' On: The Slave Journey to an Afro-Baptist Faith*. Princeton, NJ: Princeton University Press.
Thurman, H. (1975) *Deep River and the Negro Spiritual Speaks of Life and Death*. Richmond, VA: Friends United Press.
Tillich, P. (1984) *The Meaning of Health: Essays in Existentialism, Psychoanalysis, and Religion*. Chicago, IL: Exploration Press.
Tracy, David (1998) *The Analogical Imagination: Christian Theology and the Culture of Pluralism*. New York: Crossroad Publishing Company.
———. (1979) *Blessed Rage for Order: The New Pluralism in Theology*. New York: Seabury Press.
———. (1994) *Plurality and Ambiguity: Hermeneutics, Religion, Hope*. Chicago: University of Chicago Press.
Vernant, J. (1988) *Myth and Tragedy in Ancient Greece*. New York: Zone Books.
West, Cornel (1982) *Prophesy Deliverance! An Afro-Revolutionary Christianity*. Louisville, KY: The Westminster Press.
Wilson, Bryan, ed. (1985) *Rationality*. Oxford: Basil Blackwell.
Zukerman, P., ed. (2000) *Dubois on Religion*. New York: Altamira Press.

Index

abyss 17, 19, 21, 24–6, 28, 35, 37–8, 52, 88, 103, 166
acculturation 57, 92–3
adaptation 9, 49, 51, 85
adversity 56, 131–2
aesthetic 6, 10, 20–6, 29–31, 36–8, 49, 66, 93–5, 97–8, 102, 104–5, 111, 118–20, 137, 161, 165
aesthetic element 23, 95
aesthetic form 23, 26, 29–30, 66, 98, 102
aesthetic transformation 60, 111
affect 23, 26, 37–8, 49, 112, 118, 120, 158, 163, 166–7
affective life 118
affirmation 8, 34, 39, 50, 64–6, 82, 88–91, 101, 111, 137, 144, 156
Africa 23, 44, 52, 83
African/African American 47, 49–50, 52, 59–61
African America 87, 105, 160
African American 1–11, 40–3, 63–6, 73–4, 79–83, 85–8, 90–1, 104–5, 107–10, 112–14, 116–20, 123–4, 128–31, 133–7, 143–9, 153–63
 oppressed 124, 146
 shallow emotionalism 88
 the tragic vision of 10–11
African American alienation 168
African American Christian 5, 9, 21, 37, 39, 61, 73, 80, 85–6, 89, 123, 125–8, 130–5, 138–9, 141–51, 161–2
African American Christian Church 130, 134
African American Christian Consciousness 10, 40, 123, 132, 145
African American Christian Consciousness Pt 9, 85, 107
African American Christians 144–5
African American Church 4, 10, 79, 129, 132, 134, 145, 147, 154, 159
African American Church's self-interpretation 159
African American Consciousness 128
African American culture 10–11, 56, 64, 74, 104, 155, 158, 160, 163
African American emancipation 142
African American expression 114
African American forms of expression 161
African American mood 113
African American Ordeal in Slavery 176

African American Religion   2, 4, 6,
    8, 10, 12, 14, 16, 18, 20, 22,
    24, 26, 28, 30, 162–3
African American Theology   129
African American worship   116, 120
African American worship
    experience   121
African culture   42–3, 55
African cultures, traditional   52, 55
African slaves   58, 83
Africans   4, 41–6, 53–4, 58–60,
    77, 87, 117, 139, 147, 157
Africans/African Americans   45–6,
    52, 55, 78
Ahab   25, 28–9
alienation   13–14, 49, 54–5, 69, 113
ambiguity   7, 25, 28, 33–4, 86, 91,
    93, 95, 98, 103, 119, 130, 133,
    148, 156, 177
  facilitated life amid   9
  moral   32–4, 119
America   41–5, 56, 74, 83, 86, 91,
    107, 139, 160
American culture   11, 41, 46–7, 74
American psyche   160
ancestors   54, 157
anxiety   14, 34, 53–4, 75–6,
    112, 137
Apollonian   97, 99–102
Apollonian illusion   100, 102
Aristotle   29, 32, 98, 166–7,
    171, 175
art   22, 24, 27, 34, 61, 63–4, 66–7,
    78, 95, 100, 103, 111–12, 118,
    120, 155–6
art rescues life   102
articulation   5, 7–10, 19, 36, 86,
    129, 132–4, 148, 153–4,
    163–4, 166
artistic   37, 64–7, 78, 94, 97,
    102, 104
artistic imagination   64
artists   111, 158–9
aspirations   20, 50, 64, 66, 70–1,
    90–1, 111–12, 127, 141

authentic encounter   26, 38, 117
authentic life   151
authenticity   10, 102, 128–9, 133

beauty   24, 105, 111, 119–20
being in question   34
Bennett, Lerone   169
Berger, Peter   15, 164, 175
Better Dayz   155–6
Bible   5, 57, 113, 119, 134, 145
biblical narratives   118–19
Birth of Tragedy   9–10, 85, 94,
    96–7, 165–7, 171–2, 176
Black Mood   56, 169
black people   47, 129–30, 148, 173
black theology   3, 50, 128–30,
    133, 163
blacks   45–6, 117, 128
Blassingame, John W.   82, 109,
    172, 175
Blum, Edward J.   163, 168–9
Bollas, Christopher   136, 173
breakdown   16, 25, 120, 141

Camus   37–9, 166–7, 175
caricature   40, 87–8, 93, 107, 162
cast, ego   51
catastrophe   17, 19, 33, 71
categories   4, 13, 16, 25, 59, 69,
    71, 91, 128–9, 159
catharsis   30–1, 120
celebration   87, 91, 144
chaos   15–16
  order experiential   18
Chicago   4, 57, 163–5, 171–4,
    176–7
children   16, 37, 44, 47–8, 109,
    149, 158
Christ   75, 89–90, 125, 127,
    138, 146
Christian   5, 85, 113–15, 133, 145
Christian experience   93, 104, 161
Christian faith   1–4, 6, 9–10, 80,
    86, 104, 113, 115, 123, 125–6,
    128, 132, 146–7, 150–1

Christian life 148
Christian Theology 126, 172, 175, 177
Christian tragedy 104
Christianity 6, 104, 146–7, 163, 166
chronicity 78–9
church 1–2, 4, 6, 11, 127, 133–5, 147, 151, 154
  black 130
claims 9, 12, 55–6, 58, 70, 86, 98, 133, 149
classical psychoanalysis 16, 75, 77, 164
closure 24–5, 30–1, 36, 95, 98, 124
coeternal 125–6
coherence 7, 18, 22, 46, 53, 56, 58, 170
color, kingdom of 63
community 3, 5, 24, 42, 48, 87–8, 134, 147, 164, 168
Cone, James 73, 128, 148
conflict 19–20, 30, 32–4, 66, 90, 93, 98, 134–5, 165–6, 170–1, 175
connection, empathic 138
Conrad, Joseph 38, 165
conscience, transmoral 150
consciousness 10–11, 21, 60, 87, 92, 99, 109, 120, 130, 132, 141, 144, 148, 158
  tragic 8, 31, 114
consolation 102, 115, 128, 154–5, 157–8
  tragedy's 27
context 4–5, 33, 58–9, 65, 69, 79, 88, 97, 110, 128, 146
  clinical 80
contradictions 31, 86, 89–90, 100, 124, 134
contribution 10, 57, 73–4, 133, 135
control 15, 19, 81–2, 126
convictions 5, 34, 95, 103, 130, 134, 170
cosmos 20, 56, 58, 164, 175

cosmosing 58
courage, quality of 131
creative tension 2, 65, 97, 154
crisis 16–17, 136–7, 164
crisis of meaning 164
the Crucified 41, 43, 45, 47, 49, 51, 53, 55, 57, 59, 61
cultural consciousness 90, 153–4, 157–8
cultural forms 3, 78
cultural production 154, 160–1
cultural taxonomies 41, 44–5, 59–60, 81, 83, 90, 107, 113, 140, 144, 147, 160
culture 13, 42, 46–7, 53, 55, 59, 64, 75–8, 81–2, 86, 92–3, 104, 109–10, 124, 137, 160
  popular 74, 160, 162

danger 8, 32, 36, 53, 94, 149, 156
dasein 34, 82
death 33, 36–8, 68, 70–1, 94, 109, 156, 159, 172, 177
demythologization 134
depths 8, 19, 21, 43, 50, 53, 56, 66, 68, 85–8, 103, 105, 109, 117–19, 146–7, 159
descendants 41, 54, 58, 60, 83
despair 36–7, 40, 50, 54–5, 65–6, 70–1, 75, 87, 93, 105, 108, 153, 156
devotee 117, 119–20, 129, 135, 140, 145, 151
dialectic 8, 11, 20, 28, 64–5, 67, 69–70, 72, 75, 77, 79, 90, 98, 153, 155–6, 158
  perpetual 64
dialectic of hope and resignation 8, 11, 75, 77
dimensions
  aesthetic 22, 63, 93, 116, 169
  maternal 135, 157
Dionysian 89, 96–7, 99–102, 110, 116
Dionysius 153, 159

Dionysus   11, 23, 70, 88, 96, 101, 164, 166, 170–1
Disciple of Dionysus   96, 170–1
disclosive   8, 65, 75, 109
dissolution   15, 45, 48, 51–2
distance, aesthetic   22, 31, 165
divine   1, 55, 105, 123–4, 132, 135, 138, 143, 158
divine immanence   139, 142–3
divine transcendence   143
doctrinal positions   134
dread   47, 160–1
dreaming innocence   105
dreams   31, 50, 71, 92, 141, 149–50, 156, 168
Du Bois, W. E. B.   8, 10, 40, 44, 59–60, 63–5, 67–8, 72, 79, 85, 107, 109–10, 116–17, 163, 167–72, 175

Eliade, Mircea   175
emancipation   141–2
emotions   26, 65, 74, 118, 167, 169
empathy   66–7, 69, 74, 154
empowerment   26, 120
emptiness   15, 35, 75, 82, 161–2, 170
energy   33, 50–1
enslavement   44, 104
epistemological   7, 73, 87, 99, 133
European Americans   43, 125, 146, 149–50, 154, 160–1
Europeanization   93
evil   2, 25, 33, 64, 69, 88, 146–7, 172
exile   14, 37, 68, 109
existence   2–3, 6, 8–9, 17, 19–20, 22, 25, 34–6, 41, 45, 53, 64, 94–6, 101–5, 111–12, 119
  absurdity of   36, 94
  pained   4, 43
  terrible truth of   102–3
experience
  aesthetic   95, 118
  assimilation of   18, 94
  black   128
  common   81, 120
  common selfobject   76
  historical   7, 91
  liberating   120
  lived   8, 19
  moral   34
  past selfobject   76
  second-order   100
  sedimented   120
  self object   76
  slave   92
  spiritual   166
  tragic religious   150–1
  traumatic   48
  unhealthy   80
experience near   11, 123, 173
expression
  aesthetic   93, 153
  cultural   74, 79, 113
  cultural forms of   76–7
  musical   93, 109
  religio-aesthetic   104
  tragic   114–15, 150
expression of melancholy   78

facilitation   26, 28, 150
faith   1, 3–6, 12, 25, 72, 91, 113–15, 127, 131–4, 146
  biblical   4
  religious   111, 130, 134
faith experience   139
fascination   159–60
fate   38–9, 49, 54, 70, 159
feminine   157–8
field   2, 4, 7, 15, 18, 34, 36, 38–9, 48–50, 59, 64, 67, 73, 81–2, 91, 166
forces   30, 82–3, 112, 125, 128, 141, 146–7, 149, 166
foreclosure   6–7, 24
forgetfulness   104–5
formation   8–9, 22, 47, 52, 55, 59, 77, 82, 115, 123–5, 133, 143, 147–8, 160

Index 183

fragmentation   1, 7, 9, 15, 49,
    53–4, 56, 59–60, 75, 82, 94,
    107, 141, 162
fragmentation anxiety   76–7, 94
Frazier, E. Franklin   73
freedom   51, 57, 67, 111, 131,
    141–2, 167–8, 170–2, 175–6
frenzy   10, 107, 110, 116–17, 120,
    137, 140, 143
Freud, Sigmund   77–81, 175
fulfillment   35, 127, 148, 158

geist   113–14, 134, 156
genre   6, 20, 22–4, 29, 37, 69
Giddens, Anthony   52, 164,
    166, 174
God   2, 5, 61, 112, 123–7, 132,
    135–6, 138, 142–4, 156,
    173, 175
  experience of   135
  reality of   124
God, Christian   123
God labors   142
gods   36, 38, 54, 71, 94, 101, 137,
    171–2, 175
God's transcendence   143–4
Gospel   5, 46, 125, 127, 162, 173
  traditional African
    American   153
Greek Tragedy   22, 97, 111,
    159, 169
Greeks   9, 23, 29, 39, 59,
    97, 111
ground   35–6, 64, 77, 82, 100,
    127, 137, 141, 153
group   5, 53, 57, 60, 64, 66–7, 79,
    81, 112, 139, 164, 166
group identity   53–4
guilt   14, 32, 112, 145–6
  tragic   32–3

Hamilton, Edith   171–2
Hard knock Life   158
hardship   119
Harris, Thomas   174

healing   36, 94, 136, 140, 142,
    161, 164
health   57, 99, 142, 164,
    173–4, 177
  human   12, 142
heart   17, 20, 23, 29, 40, 66, 87,
    100–1, 105, 108, 125, 127, 131
Heart of Darkness   28, 165
heaven   25, 50, 110
Hegel, Georg W. F.   30, 32, 98
Heidegger, Martin   34
hell   25, 57
Hero, young   78
history   43, 54–5, 60, 63, 66, 72,
    104, 112, 133, 143, 157, 164,
    167, 175
Holocaust   167
Holy   160, 172, 174, 176
Homans, Peter   170, 172
home   13–14, 25, 48, 52, 54, 56,
    60, 68–9, 72, 80, 82,
    138–9, 146
homosexuality   134–5
hope   8–9, 11–12, 34, 36–7, 40,
    50, 64–6, 68–73, 90–1, 96,
    98–9, 107–8, 112–15, 136–7,
    149–50, 168
hopefulness   91
hopes   91, 141, 149–50, 168
Hopkins, Dwight   73
horror   6, 15, 17, 19, 28–9, 36,
    43–4, 68, 87, 94–5, 103, 112,
    120, 161
Huggins, Nathan   131–2, 146,
    148–9, 173–4, 176
human existence   6, 26, 33–4, 48,
    52, 94, 142, 166
human experience   2–3, 6, 15,
    18–20, 30, 38, 82, 95, 99,
    102–3, 108, 119, 142
  common   64, 135
human life   27, 40, 93, 107
human soul   12, 25
human subject   6, 24, 32, 55, 111,
    118, 134, 136–7

identification 31, 69, 87, 112, 119, 125, 136, 158
identity 45, 48, 53, 58, 60, 82–3, 160
ideology 6, 50, 81, 92, 94–5, 136
illusions 14, 27, 58, 95, 101, 104–5
images 9, 28, 39, 60, 76–7, 96, 114, 125–6, 176
imagination, religious 55, 112
individuation 101–2
institution, peculiar 45, 58, 81–2, 91, 93, 107, 131
integrity 6, 26, 39, 66, 148–9
interrogative state 34–5, 103
introspection 99
Ishmael 25, 28–9
isolation 13–15

Jesus 99, 127, 132–3, 139, 144, 146
Jews 83, 132
Johnson, Matthew V. 174, 176
Johnson, Walter 48, 168
Johnson Sr, Matthew V. 163, 168
Jones, James W. 137, 173
Jose 70–2
joy 38–9, 64, 66, 75, 79, 87–91, 101–2, 110, 159
Jürgen Habermas 174
justice 4, 14–15, 119, 167

katharsis 167
Kauffman, Jeffery 168
Kaufman, Walter 165, 169, 171, 176
kingdom 70, 127, 132, 148
knowledge 27–9, 31, 54, 105, 135, 160, 164, 175
Knox, Bernard M. W. 71, 169, 176
Kohut, Heinz 75–6, 164, 170, 173, 176
Krieger, M. 21, 23, 26, 29–30, 165, 176
Kurtz 31

labor 1, 5, 43, 59, 82, 126, 142
lament 87, 108, 154
land 23, 53–4, 56, 58, 66, 81–3
Landsman, Irene 164
Lane, Christopher 169
language 10, 13, 19, 44, 92, 96, 100, 103, 107–8, 136, 138, 144, 172, 174, 176
laws 30, 41, 46–7, 107, 150
Levine, Lawrence 89–90, 109, 171, 176
liberation 12, 50, 118, 120, 128, 141, 166
life affirmation 110
life amid uncertainty 119
lifeworld, singular 8
limitations 27, 70–1, 121
limits 91, 94–5, 103, 107
  life's 95
Lincoln, C. Eric 73
location, remote 50, 168
Long, Charles 73
longing 4, 22, 34–7, 40, 50, 60, 65, 89, 91, 93–4, 101–3, 107–8, 127, 136–8, 141
  great 35–6
Lord 75, 117, 138, 140, 156, 159, 176
loss 4, 16–17, 19–20, 38, 48–9, 54, 59–60, 73, 76, 78–9, 81, 103, 113, 137, 156, 164
lyricism 110
lyrics 108–9

mad 28, 117
madness 28–9
mania 77, 79–80
manic 154, 158
Mapp, Ardelia 174
marginalization 4, 41, 52, 78, 83, 107, 113, 141, 145, 147, 159, 162
Marlow 28, 31
mask 29, 35
masters 28, 45–6

Meaning of Health 142, 164, 173–4, 177
meaningfulness 15, 18–19, 26, 48, 58, 82, 94, 102, 111–12, 115, 139, 141, 150
meaninglessness, threat of 6, 90, 161
melancholia 49, 77, 79–81, 170
melancholic mood 68, 81
memory 14, 31, 39, 54, 65–7, 78, 136, 156, 170
metaphor 172–4, 176
metaphors 76, 100, 111, 113
mimic African American forms 74
moan 108, 117, 136
Moby Dick 28, 165
modern Self 169, 176
mood structure 8–9, 39, 60
moral life 148
morality 14, 148–50
mother 72, 136–8, 157
motherless child 138
motive 29, 33, 102, 112
mourning 4, 49, 78, 170
music 9–10, 24, 74, 92–3, 100, 107–11, 119, 136–7, 156, 172, 176
  religious 89, 107, 117
music of negro religion 93, 107
My Block 155–6
myth 13–15, 22, 24, 38, 101, 116, 118, 134, 164–5, 171, 175, 177
  tragic 24, 95
Mythology 171–2, 175
mythopoetic 18, 22, 36
  contextualized 22

Naughty by Nature 153, 156, 158
New World 4, 43, 46–7, 54–5, 59
Nietzsche, Friedrich 9, 24, 36, 88, 95–100, 102, 104–5, 108, 110, 114–16, 165–7, 170–2, 175–7
Noel, JamesI 73
nonbeing 6, 14, 24, 36, 83, 90

Obama, Barack 168
object 31, 36, 112, 125, 136–8, 144, 161, 173
ontological security system 49
oppression 12, 50, 53, 58, 60, 67, 70, 107, 118, 130, 141, 147–8, 157
order 5, 15–16, 18, 22–3, 26, 29–30, 37, 43, 51–2, 61, 63, 69, 82, 98, 105, 126–7
  institutional 15–16, 164
  present 144
  universal 30
  universal moral 29
orientation 18, 54, 116, 123, 131, 137
Osiris 23
othering 42
otherness 25, 44, 160
Otto, R. 160, 172, 176

pain 2, 4, 9, 17, 19, 33–4, 37–8, 53, 64, 67–8, 87, 93–5, 105, 107–8, 119, 156–7
passion 38, 72, 132, 167, 176
pathetic 70–1
perception 6, 8, 10–11, 19, 99, 108, 143, 165
personal experience 98, 100
  modern 161
perspectives 38, 66, 70, 167
pessimism 49, 87–8, 114–15, 168
pessimistic foundation 88
Pfeffer, Rose 96, 170–1
philosophy 96, 100–1, 169, 176
philosophy of science 100
pity 25, 59
place 82–3, 86, 90, 93–4, 103, 111, 118, 126, 128, 136, 140, 143, 154
plantation life 55, 172, 175
poetry 64, 86, 109, 111, 118
  power of 111
polarities, life's 27

power   1, 14, 17, 26, 30, 50, 63, 67, 94–5, 111, 116, 125–7, 131–2, 139–40, 150, 158–60
  antidotal   162
  apotheosis of   125–6
  relations of   128, 161
  unmitigated   131–2
prayers   54, 140
preacher   10, 48, 107, 116, 145
preaching   4, 107, 110, 144–5
presuppositions   5, 7, 16, 67, 95, 114
primal unity   100–1
primordial contradiction   100, 108
process, generative   98
production   43–5, 98, 102, 112
psychic pain   26, 32, 34
psychic survival   9, 56, 85–6
psychoanalysis   2, 18, 38, 73, 142, 154, 164, 173, 177
  early   120
punishment, delusional expectation of   79–80

question, theodicy   124

race   8, 75, 105, 169
Rachel weeping   37
rage   1, 137–8
rap   153, 155–6, 158
rationalism   28, 57, 97–8, 101
rationality   18, 169, 177
Re-Imagination of African American Theology   174
reality   16, 53, 60, 96–7, 100, 102, 105, 108, 110–12, 120, 125, 128, 130, 134, 144, 149–51
  experience of   16, 53
  heart of   25, 100, 102
recognition   7, 20, 24, 38, 43, 88, 112, 158
reconciliation   22, 30–1, 98, 127
redemption   22, 102–3, 105
regularity   31, 52

relations   1–2, 17, 20, 45, 52–3, 55, 77, 82, 96–8, 123–4, 136, 142, 148, 163, 172–3, 176
religion   2, 5–6, 8, 11–12, 14, 16, 22, 34, 42, 63–4, 85–6, 116–18, 136–7, 149–50, 163–4, 171–7
religious experience   3–8, 10–11, 60–1, 73, 76, 86–8, 93, 105, 117–18, 120, 123, 128–9, 132, 138–9, 145, 163–4
religious experience functions   119
religious experience of African Americans   128–9
religious expression   9, 77, 86–7, 90, 107, 154
  aestheticized   89
  native   44
relocation   54, 169
reminiscence   120
remote, (the existentially)   50, 92, 99, 143, 168
rending   7, 20, 23–4, 33–4, 53, 166
resignation   8, 11, 39, 49–51, 61, 64–6, 68–9, 75, 77, 110, 137, 153
resistance   7, 36, 44–5, 74, 76, 81, 103, 111–12, 148, 160
resists   37, 69, 111, 113, 130, 141
resources   4, 8–9, 42, 50–1, 57, 85, 93, 155
  volitional   51
responses, second-order   22
restoration   30, 58, 75, 103, 170, 176
resurrection   113, 126–7
retentions   42–3, 55, 59–60, 82, 163
rhythms   74, 110, 119, 154, 157
Ricoeur, Paul   119, 172–4
ritual context   116–17
ritual experience   141, 150
ritual process   140–2, 145, 173
ritual space   140
rivers   143–4, 168, 170, 175

Index 187

salvation 127, 142, 164, 173
sanity 9, 23, 95
Scheler, Max 30, 165–6
science 2–3, 18–19, 52, 100, 118, 133–4, 150, 169
scientific 18, 73, 99–100, 118, 171, 176
security 19, 47, 81–2, 92
  ontological 15–17, 47, 58–9, 83
self 15–16, 19–20, 24, 34, 36, 47–9, 51, 53–5, 58–60, 75–6, 81–3, 119, 135–6, 140–2, 144, 170
  centered 53, 141–2
  transmoral 150
self-consciousness 59–60
self-images 147, 158
self-observation 99
self psychology 77, 164, 170
self-regarding feelings 79–80
self-revilings 79–80
self structures 76
selfhood 59, 81
separation 20, 39, 52, 81, 101
Sewall, Richard B. 25, 67, 165–7, 169, 172, 176
shadow 34, 68, 72, 92, 112, 137–8, 173
Shakur, Tupac 155–7
shattering 24, 48–9, 53
shock 24, 53, 102–3
shouting 3, 116–17
Sigmund Freud 8, 73, 75, 114, 170, 172
Silk, M. S. 96, 165, 167, 171, 177
sin 146
Sisyphus 37–8, 164, 166–7, 175
slave codes 47, 92
slave communities 42–3
Slave Community 172, 175
slave conversion 45–6
slave existence 43, 93
slave masters 45, 48–9, 149–50
slave songs 92, 109

slavery 7, 32, 38, 41, 46, 49–50, 57–8, 63–4, 77, 79, 81, 107, 109, 167, 171–3, 176
slaves 40, 42, 44–6, 48–50, 55–7, 59–60, 75, 77, 82–3, 89–90, 92–3, 109–10, 131–2, 144, 148–9, 157
  process of 43–4
Sobel, Mechal 56–8, 177
social relations, matrix of 128
society 7, 15–16, 45–6, 54, 74, 76–7, 164, 166, 174–5
songs 78, 86, 90, 108–11, 116–17, 140, 153–4
sorrow 38–9, 66, 72, 75, 78, 87–90, 110, 153, 155
sorrow songs 60, 77, 89, 109–10, 117, 119
soul 28, 36, 39–40, 55, 59, 63, 70, 75, 93, 110–11, 116–17, 140–1, 148–50, 156, 166, 168
soul life 9
  tragic 9, 86, 93
Souls 8, 10
Souls of Black Folk 8, 60, 63, 65, 85, 167, 169–71, 175
sparagmus 7–8, 11, 20, 24, 30, 32–5, 41, 43, 45, 47, 49, 51, 53, 55, 57, 59
spirit, human 1, 42, 110, 117, 131
spiritual life 140
  creative 7
spirituality, traditional African American 117, 156
spirituals 64, 89–90, 110, 120, 175
stability 15–16, 34, 58
state 15, 32, 34–5, 47, 49, 54, 76, 80–1, 91–2, 101, 112, 128, 137, 155, 163, 165
  affective 37, 137–8, 166
  interrogative 34–5, 103
state of being in question 34
Stern, J. P. 96, 165, 167, 171, 177
Storm, William 20, 22, 164, 166

188　Index

strength　1, 10, 19–20, 38, 48, 56, 123–7, 129, 131–3, 135, 137, 139, 141, 143, 147–51, 158–9
stress　51, 58, 162
structure　15, 19–20, 32, 61, 76, 85, 89, 98, 103, 120, 128–30, 132, 134, 136, 147, 154–6
　deep　11, 85, 98, 127–8, 132, 137, 153, 157, 160
　liberating　118–19
struggle　1, 3, 8, 35, 68, 111, 119, 129, 141
subject　7, 22, 24–5, 43, 45, 49, 51, 58, 67, 71, 76, 78, 95–6, 111, 136–7, 141
　engaged　123–4
subjectivity　3, 8, 47, 59, 77–8, 86, 103, 138, 146, 153, 155
survival　23, 49, 57, 111, 118, 139, 148–9
sustain　15, 17, 48, 67, 76
symbols　9, 35, 37, 113–14, 134, 157–8, 168, 176
symptomatology　79, 81
system　18–19, 24, 30, 32, 45, 58–60, 95, 131, 174

tension　2, 9, 13–14, 26–7, 31, 36, 38–9, 53–4, 59, 64–5, 97, 120, 132, 134, 154, 165
tensions　9, 14, 25–6, 31, 53–4, 59, 64, 90, 120, 135, 150
　community-destroying　135
　strong intrapsychic　140
terror　15, 25, 34, 165, 167, 173
theodicy　95, 123–4
theological reflection　3, 11, 128–9, 134
theological unconscious　132, 134
theology　5–6, 10–11, 90, 123, 125–6, 128–33, 135, 139, 145, 147, 173, 177
threat　14, 26, 38, 48, 51–2, 60, 82, 111, 141
Thurman, Howard　73, 120, 172

Tillich, Paul　142, 164, 166, 173–4
tolerance　134–5
Tracy, David　3, 172–3
traditional African American Christian consciousness　98
tragedy　6, 9–10, 20–7, 29–34, 37–9, 65, 69, 85, 88, 94–8, 102, 104–5, 113–15, 165–7, 169–72, 175–7
　authentic　64
　classic　32
　effect of　166
　experience of　37, 65, 97
tragic effect　23, 26, 37, 67, 98, 170
tragic experience　6–8, 32, 39, 60, 64, 95, 113, 162, 166
　legitimate　104
tragic field　34, 146, 166
tragic man　74–5
tragic nature　9–10, 37, 135
Tragic Re-Imagination of African American Theology　155, 168
tragic soul-life　40, 107
tragic vision　2, 4, 6–14, 16, 18, 20–30, 32, 34–40, 94–8, 100–2, 112–16, 126–8, 136–8, 154–6, 164–6, 176
tragic vision impels　112
tragic vision resists　38
transcendence　89, 95, 143, 145
transfiguration　100
transfigure　4, 6, 9, 38, 95–6
transformation　101–2, 111, 133, 136, 173
transformational object　137
transvaluation　5, 88, 102, 105, 111
transvalues　102, 151, 158
trauma　7, 16–17, 19, 53, 73, 105, 108, 137, 149, 155, 164, 168, 174
　deep　131–2
traumatic field　4, 48, 81–2
traumatic loss　48, 73, 78, 137, 164, 168

traumatic relocation   54–5
triumph   75, 113, 127, 131
triumphalism   126–7

unity   26, 29–30, 33, 144
universe, tragic   65, 69, 71
unsung   131–2
unthought known   136, 145

value systems   31, 33–4, 53, 69
values   12, 17–18, 20, 26–7, 30, 36, 42–5, 47–8, 53, 65–6, 71, 73–4, 88, 94–6, 129, 163
Vision of Tragedy   165, 169, 172, 176
Visions of Extremity   165
voice   37, 75, 109, 111, 120, 156–7
vulnerability   19, 25, 36, 119

Wagner, Richard   96, 99, 171, 176
water   13, 54, 101, 139

West
 Cornel   3, 163
 the   41, 52, 74, 86, 177
West Africans   42
Western expansion   41
whites   44–7, 53, 74, 80, 109, 148
wholeness   21–2, 35, 60, 142
wisdom, terrible   104–5
women   4, 20, 42, 44, 131
 young African American   157
world
 assumptive   17, 49, 164, 168
 cultural   13
 modern   6, 151
worldview   7, 55–6, 58, 92
 coherent   55–6, 58
 coherent religious   7
worship   3–4, 10, 125, 140, 143–4
worship experience   10, 117, 120, 134
worthlessness   90, 146
worthwhileness, life's   115

Lightning Source UK Ltd.
Milton Keynes UK
UKHW021846080421
381676UK00006B/229